D0599582

THE ART OF THE

KITCHEN GARDEN

THE ART OF THE

KITCHEN GARDEN

ETHNE CLARKE

with illustrations by Sharon Beeden

ALFRED A. KNOPF
NEW YORK

THIS IS A BORZOI BOOK
PUBLISHED BY ALFRED A. KNOPF, INC.

Copyright © 1987 by Ethne Clarke
Illustrations copyright © 1987 by Sharon Beeden

All rights reserved under International and Pan-American Copyright
Conventions. Published in the United States by Alfred A. Knopf, Inc.,
New York, and simultaneously in Canada by Random House of Canada
Limited, Toronto. Distributed by Random House, Inc., New York.
Originally published in Great Britain by Michael Joseph Ltd., London.

Owing to limitations of space, acknowledgments to use illustrations,
other than those by Sharon Beeden, appear on page 161.

Manufactured in Italy

First Edition

CONTENTS

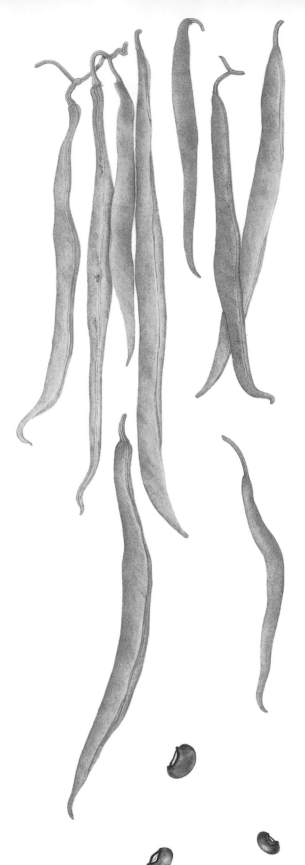

Left Runner beans
Opposite A kitchen garden paradise in East Anglia at the house of John Last, The Mill, Corpusty, Norfolk.

To the memory of my father, Elmer H. Reuss, who taught me
the value of patience – a gardener's most precious commodity.

INTRODUCTION

THIS BOOK is a look at the parallel development of the kitchen garden and the kitchen, for it seems that these two domestic offices walked hand in hand down history's highway; and when events overtook one, the other was never far behind. I begin with the medieval monastic period with the occasional backward glance to Rome, and end with the turn of the eighteenth century, by which time the style and methods of the kitchen garden and also of cookery were established and basically not that different from what we know today.

Throughout this period, external influences, chiefly Italian and later French, were playing in the field of English gardening, swinging the pendulum of fashion in garden and cookery style back and forth until we achieved the English landscape style and responded to Hannah Glasse's plea for good sensible home cooking.

Things developed along these lines for a time, but change was inevitable, and its course almost predictable. By the turn of the twentieth century we were looking again at Italian gardens and appreciating French cuisine. As if we ever needed reminding that the past is the greatest teacher.

The appearance of the garden has changed dramatically over the centuries but, on the whole, the way we garden – our tools and techniques – has experienced little change. With the exception of raised beds, which in the kitchen garden have been supplanted by 'flat earth'.

Originally, beds were 'raised' to improve upon the natural drainage of the land or to make better use of irrigation systems. 'Raised' simply refers to the elevation of the soil achieved by the fairly deep digging and thick layer of manure put into each trench as it is dug. However, raised beds have in the past been more sophisticated. In pre-Columbian Bolivia, the ancient culture of Tiwanaku turned the now barren Pampa Koani into an intensely productive farming region by creating massive raised fields. Deep layers of fertile topsoil were laid over a base of cobblestones and impermeable clay to prevent pollution by the slightly salty water of Lake Titicaca. The fields were up to 5 feet high, 50 feet wide and 600 feet long, and their remains can be detected today, making a corrugated pattern across the Pampa. Fascinating stuff – especially to the modern-day villagers who are reconstructing the system to improve levels of food production vastly.

Thus far the ornamental garden has benefited most from our interest in history's design. Now it is the turn of the kitchen garden, where the use of raised beds and mixed planting can lighten the workload and make more decorative use of a purely functional garden area.

It makes sense to save yourself trouble and effort in gardening whenever possible, especially in the kitchen garden. One of the most efficient ways of achieving this is to organise the plot into a system of individual raised beds separated by pathways, which is a much less labour-intensive way of cultivating vegetables.

^DE HISTORIA, NATV·
RA AC VIRIBVS ARBORVM ET FRVTICVM,
Et primo,

DE HORTO ET IIS QVAE IN EO
nafcuntur, plantis, & arboribus.

B

DE SOLI, FVNDI, AC TERRAE
adparatione, paftinatione, ftercoratione,
atque cultu.

 RINCIPIO igitur, quando de arboribus & cultu hortorum tradere propofitum nobis eft, etiam de foli conditione & qualitate aliquid præmittendum uidetur. Terra igitur ea, quæ in locis fqualidis & ficcis uafta incultaq; iacet, folis ardore plerunq; ita tor retur & induratur, ut humorem tranfmittere facilè non pofsit, neque imbribus aut rore reficiatur. Deinde ut plurimum ita quoque confolidatur, ut neq; frumenta, neq; quicquid aliud in ea feritur aut plantatur, protuberare facilè, aut ad fru gem peruenire pofsit. Quare fi qua eiufmodi fuerit, ea principiò fodiendo, paftinando, aut etiam arando diligenter ac multum fubigi præpariq; debet, ut hoc pacto duritiem ac feritatem illam priftinam exuat, cultuq; uelut manfuefacta mitefcat.

Quod fi qua autem in tantum folida ac fpiffa erit, ut fubinde in glebas maiores ac duriores concrefcat, ea omnino furculis aut fuftibus

a

This engraving, from the 1542 original by Hans Weiditz, and taken from the *Botanico* of Adam Lonicer, 1565, shows a gardener hard at work, setting out young plants into a raised bed, the edges of which are rather crudely reinforced with boards held upright by pegs pounded into the ground. During the sixteenth century raised beds were often fenced with boards or railings and these were just as often polychromed in vividly coloured chevrons or stripes and topped by gilded finials. One hundred years later, William Lawson in his *Countrie House-wifes Garden* continued the practice of growing flowers on raised square beds to aid drainage, but recommended that they be edged with shrubby herbs. However, he considered raised beds unnecessary for pot herbs (vegetables), but thought it still wise to grow them in separate beds: 'yet you must have your beds divided, that you may go betwixt to weed'.

Raised beds were favoured by early gardeners, for their use greatly improved the cultural conditions under which the treasured flowers, vegetables, herbs and fruits were grown. In the county of Cheshire 'butts', the vernacular for raised beds, were common in kitchen gardens and were widely used until at least the late 1940s. Fields were also cultivated in 'butts', using heavy horses pulling a specially devised plough to turn the earth into raised beds.

In this illustration, notice also the vine trained up into the tree and the pots of gillyflowers supported by cuffs of bent withies, a style of garden ornament popular throughout the sixteenth and seventeeth centuries.

Above In the *jardin potager* at Barnsley House, Gloucestershire, where in sowing and setting out vegetables and herbs, Rosemary Verey exercises the same ingenious use of plant form and colour as she does in the rest of her intensely inspiring garden. Individual beds are separated by two-colour brick paths. Such paths are fairly easy to construct if the soil underneath is first well-firmed and covered in a layer of sand. Set the bricks into this and then sweep dry ready-mix concrete into the cracks. If it doesn't rain within a day or two, sprinkle with water. Each spring, check over the paving, keeping it clear of moss, which makes bricks slippery, and topping up the 'mortar' between the bricks as necessary.

Opposite Beaten gravel paths around raised beds edges with larch poles. Gravel is difficult to keep in place, but the logs help to prevent the path merging with the vegetable beds.

The prospect of having to dig over an entire kitchen garden plot every autumn proves too much for many people. Raised beds must also be dug, but only when they are prepared. Thereafter the height is maintained by the rotted manure and garden compost which is added to the soil during the course of the growing year. In conventional kitchen gardens the space between the rows as well as the planting area is also fertilised and dug over; but it is a waste of time and resources to cultivate and feed soil which will only be walked on. In a raised-bed garden the walkways are permanent and only the beds are cultivated.

Raised beds are also more productive than conventional beds – a quality we all wish for when growing our own vegetables and fruit. Because the level of the soil is raised it is better drained; and since the beds are never walked on, the soil is not compacted so it is better aerated, which causes it to warm more quickly so that crops can be put in earlier, taking advantage of the full growing season (useful in cool regions). Raised beds, with their geometric ordering and system of narrow pathways, can also be an attractive feature of the garden and integrate easily into the domestic landscape – an important consideration when most of us have to include our vegetable plots in the garden behind the house. Even the smallest garden can have room for one or two beds on which to grow out-of-the-ordinary vegetables and herbs.

MAKING A RAISED-BED GARDEN

Individual beds are usually no more than 90–120cm (3–4ft) wide, in order that the centre may be easily reached from the pathways on either side. This is important, since a feature of raised beds is that they are not walked upon: you must be able to work the centre comfortably; it is very tiring to have to stretch and balance as you weed or dig.

Raised beds can be any length, but it is much more efficient to have a system of short beds either side of a central path. Short distances are less tiresome to walk; with over-long beds the temptation would be to leap across to reach the other side, no doubt landing on the nice loose soil or squashing a seedling underfoot. So walk gently around the beds and save the gymnastics for another time. The central path is the main runway up which wheelbarrows are trundled, and should be wider than the paths dividing the beds; allow at least 45cm (18in) for the width of these pathways, and up to 90cm (36in) for the central path.

When siting the garden, try, if possible, to put it close to a water supply, and in a good sunny spot away from overhanging trees and hedges, whose roots would compete with the crops for nourishment; a sheltered position is preferable, although if that is not possible, windbreaks of trellis or fencing can be improvised.

To take advantage of sunlight, which most crops need for good growth, arrange the length of the beds on a north–south axis so that both sides will receive equal measures of sun.

The beds do not, however, have to be rectangular in shape. An alternative is to use circles, triangles and squares arranged in patterns like the blocks of a patchwork quilt. But should you choose this option, do not make the layout too complicated or you may find that wheeling a barrow or taking a hose into the garden becomes a tiresome chore as you navigate an intricate system of paths.

Planning advice for the conventional vegetable garden recommends planting for crop rotation, so that a crop is not repeatedly sown on the same area. To do so would deplete

Work methodically when preparing a garden of raised beds: the soil from the first trench you take out will be used to fill in the final trench in the last bed you make, so barrow the soil over to that bed and leave it in a tidy mound ready for eventual use.

Fork a thick layer of manure into the bottom of the trench and then cover it with the soil from the second trench. And so on to the end. Any annual weeds can be scraped into the bottom of each consecutive trench, but perennial weeds should be grubbed up and burned. Turn the spade as you shift the soil so that each spadeful is inverted; don't simply pitch the soil on to the ground before. Aim to keep the surface level, flat and with gently sloping sides, as shown in the cross-section above.

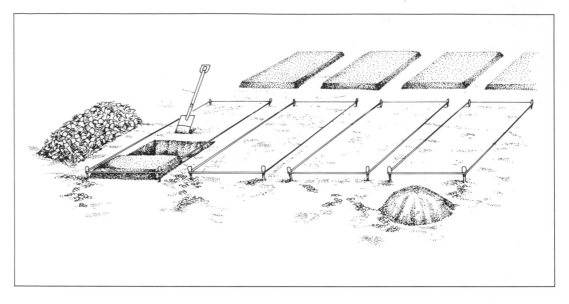

the soil, since each group of vegetables removes certain nutrients from the soil: leafy crops use nitrogen, roots consume potash. Repeated sowing of some crops in the same place, particularly the brassicas, invites soil-borne diseases.

Traditionally, the garden is divided into three according to vegetable groups: 1. legumes and salads that require freshly manured soil; 2. root crops that do best in last season's manured soil with a fresh dressing of general-purpose fertilizer; and 3. brassicas that like fertiliser and a touch of lime. They follow each other in this order on a rotational scheme.

Crop rotation is just as important in the raised vegetable garden and the system should be followed. As an *aide-mémoire*, draw up a scale plan of the garden and indicate each yearly variation within the system of beds so that you will not get confused about where each group of vegetables should be planted.

Then there are permanent plantings of vegetables such as asparagus, Jerusalem and globe artichokes, strawberries and so on. Incorporating beds for these into the garden rotation plan gives you four areas. This means that you can arrange the garden on the old-fashioned 'quartered' system, with central paths running north–south and east–west dividing the groups of beds. How many beds in each quarter depends entirely on the space at your disposal and the amount of food you intend to produce.

In the conventional garden, seeds are sown in long rows, often with the result that you grow twice as much as you need – lettuces are the usual overstock. On a raised bed, seed can be sown in short rows across the bed, or in blocks, or broadcast, or station-sown, with the result that you are much more likely to grow what you need, rather than just to fill the space. Yet on raised beds, because of the excellent growing condition, crops can be grown more closely together, so that you get higher yields from less space.

Digging the Beds

Autumn is the best time to begin work on a new vegetable garden. Try to time the digging to begin when the soil is neither too wet nor too dry.

If you are making the garden on previously uncultivated land, mark out the overall area and remove all turf and perennial weeds. Use a herbicide or a mechanical digger to skim off the turf (taking care not to remove the topsoil as well).

Use a garden line and stakes to mark out the main pathway(s), then the beds and dividing paths. Arrange to have a goodly supply of well-rotted manure and compost near by and commence digging: across the plot, not end to end.

Some wonderfully heated arguments can be engendered by raising the vexed question of single versus double digging: is it better or even necessary to cultivate the soil to two spade depths or is one spade depth sufficient? Certainly on heavy, compacted soil there is a case for improving the quality of the soil to a depth of 60cm (2ft) or more, but for the purposes of a domestic vegetable garden, a single digging to 30–45cm (12–18in) is all that is needed for most of the crops you would wish to raise. Anything else – fruit trees, asparagus and similar – can have its own space specially prepared for it.

Take out the first trench of soil, put it in a wheelbarrow and dump it at the end of the last bed to be dug.

Fork in a layer of manure at least 30cm (12in) deep. Dig the next trench, turning the soil over onto the manure so that the top layer of the soil is now at the bottom and any annual weeds are buried. Continue trenching and manuring to the end of the plot. Fill the last trench with soil from the first trench of the next bed. Work up and down the beds. Don't break up the clods of earth as you work, but do watch for perennial weed roots and remove any you find for burning later.

Tidy around the edges with the spade, gently tossing the soil neatly into the centre and making a narrow gutter around each bed to catch rainwater and prevent it puddling the path. The surface will look quite bumpy, but the action of wind, rain, and – most of all – frost will work on the soil to break it down to a nice crumbly texture by the following spring. When that season arrives, lightly fork over the top surface, rake the beds into a good shape – even, gently sloping sides and flattish top – and fine tilth. The beds should have settled to about 10cm (4in) above the soil level. Scatter a general-purpose fertiliser on top and you are now ready to sow.

If you are changing over from a flat-earth bed to raised beds you can do it either in autumn or in spring; if the latter, you can sow the beds as soon as they are prepared.

Paths

The paths between the beds can be a problem – if you let them. Constant traffic on the paths will probably beat the soil into a firm floor, and although few pests would call such a path home, weeds may need sporadic attention. Straw, treated woodbark and sawdust are usable, but can get tacky underfoot. Gravel has a way of not staying where you put it and brick is expensive. Some people use old carpet offcuts, but rain-sodden muddy strips of fraying nylon pile do nothing for the aesthetic appeal of a kitchen garden.

Green Manure Crops and Mulching

Once a bed has finished cropping, fork it over and cover with a mulch of farmyard manure, compost, grass clippings, or soft leaves.

Alternatively, sow a winter-cover crop to be turned over into the soil in the spring. This practice, known as green manuring, helps to keep weed levels down, and prevents erosion and the run-off of nutrients which might otherwise occur through the action of rain and melting snow.

Raised beds from the 1656 edition of Thomas Hylls's *Gardener's Labyrinth*.

Chives are used to edge the path surrounding apple tree 'goblets' and strawberry plants cover the soil within the bed; both are good companions for apples and also serve as a living mulch, preventing weeds from taking hold.

It is also an excellent method of adding organic matter to the soil. There are few gardens that would not benefit from this. A green manure crop turned over into sandy soil will improve its ability to hold water; on clay soils, the added organic matter helps to break up the heavy structure of the soil, improving aeration and drainage. Most importantly, green manures have the ability to fix nitrogen from the air and add it to the soil through their roots. Earthworms appreciate the fresh food you till under with a green manure crop and as they munch their way through the meal you've provided they deposit casts which are rich in many of the minerals important for good plant growth.

Among the crops suitable for winter-cover crops are winter rye, mustard, rape, field beans, crimson clover (best in mild districts) and hairy vetch. Annual rye grass is most versatile. Sown early in the autumn it will make good growth before being cut down by frost. Leave the dead grass mulch in place, then till it under in the spring.

Green manure seeds are broadcast onto the beds – roughly 35g per square metre (1oz per sq yd) – after they have been cleared of vegetable crops and raked over. Lightly firm the seed into the soil with the back of the rake and water if necessary until the seed germinates.

When the time comes to turn the cover crop under, mow it down first then turn it over by hand. Then rake and sow your first vegetables as soon as possible, applying a granular nitrogen fertiliser first.

If the cover crop is turned under when still quite young the soil will receive the greatest mineral benefit; older growth provides the greatest amount of additional organic matter.

Other mulches Mulches conserve moisture in the soil and suppress weed growth. A wide variety of materials may be used for the purpose.

A mulch layer is best put in place when the soil is starting to warm and has been thoroughly moistened by seasonal rains. It can be put in place around seedling plants when they are more than 7.5cm (3in) high; otherwise put the mulch in place then plant well-grown seedlings through it. The mulch should neither come right up to the plant stems, nor be so far away that weeds have a chance of getting in.

Peat and woodbark are familiar mulching materials, but they have no nutritive value and should really be conserved for the flower garden. In the vegetable garden you want the mulch to serve a dual purpose, adding food to the soil as well as reducing the amount of garden work you have to do. Spoiled straw, leaf mould and grass clippings are good organic mulches which can be dug into the soil after they have served their original purpose.

A straw mulch, about 7.5–10cm (3–4in) thick, will suppress most weeds; some may get in, but the looseness of the soil makes it easy to remove them by hand. It is especially useful around low-growing crops like lettuce and strawberries.

Grass clippings should really be given a chance to dry out slightly before being spread, as fresh green clippings can go slimy. They are high in nitrogen content and therefore good for the soil. Leaves add minerals to the soil as they decompose and ideally should be shredded before use. Use both of these in layers more than 7.5cm (3in) thick for adequate weed control.

Newspapers are an inexpensive, readily available source of mulch, but must be used with a covering layer of grass or straw to prevent the sheets – three or four pages should be used – from blowing away. But this mulch is good all season, will rot down in a year and can then be turned into the soil.

Inorganic mulches, namely black plastic or opaque and clear polythene sheeting, are wonderful for large, thick-stemmed vegetables like tomatoes and zucchini. While organic mulches keep the soil cool, plastic mulches help it to warm more quickly, control weeds brilliantly and, in the case of tomatoes, the constantly moist soil helps to prevent blossom end rot.

Plastic mulching can be bought in rolls or as folded sheets. Plastic garbage can liners cut down one side and across the bottom can also be used with some measure of success, but this is a more makeshift approach to this method of mulching.

When the soil is warm and moist, stretch the sheeting across the bed, burying the edges in shallow trenches and cover with soil. Cut tiny crosses through the plastic at each planting position and then introduce the plant through this. At first the plastic will look fairly ugly, but it will soon be covered by leaf and be hardly noticeable.

Plastic mulched crops do better and produce higher yields than organically mulched beds, and the maintenance is much lower, since an organic mulch may need topping up, and some attention may have to be paid to keeping it in place through the growing season. The disadvantage is that after a plastic mulch is removed, the soil below will be dry and may be quite hard, and this would have to be corrected before another crop was sown or planted.

Making leaf mould This is simple enough: just make a bin 90cm (3ft) square, by stretching wire mesh netting around four posts. Fill with leaves. Water it occasionally to assist rotting, but you needn't turn it or add an activator. All deciduous leaves are good for the purpose, but oak and beech are traditionally the most highly valued.

THE COMPOST HEAP

One of the few things upon which all gardeners agree is the importance of the compost heap. This was not always the case, however; for many the heap has been replaced by a reliance on chemical fertilisers. But now we are realising the imbalance that such a dependence can create in the environment and are at long last returning to the time-honoured methods of returning to the soil that which comes from it.

Compost is organic matter that has been broken down by the collective metabolism of an enormous community of micro-organisms. Like most living things, these invisible life-forms require warmth, water and oxygen to thrive, as well as a supply of organic waste in the form of manure, grass clippings, vegetable waste from the garden and most especially from the kitchen. Most homes produce a couple of pounds of tea leaves, potato and other vegetable and fruit peelings, every day; egg shells and even dust collected by vacuum cleaners and natural-fibre cloth rags (no man-made fibres, please) are usable ingredients for the heap. There is a gratifying symmetry about reusing the detritus of daily living to produce food for the table. However, there are certain things that shouldn't be added to the heap. Any man-made/inert materials, bones, diseased garden wastes (brassicas with clubroot for example) and fallen leaves. The latter may sound surprising but leaves, especially oak and beech, are best given their own heap, since they decompose through fungal rather than bacterial action, and leaf mould is used chiefly as a mulch or soil conditioner rather than as a plant food.

But a compost heap is more than a pile of rubbish in the corner, and must be carefully constructed to prevent it turning into a heap of putrid slime. The balance between the

Black polythene sheeting is a positively useful mulch around moisture-loving vegetables such as spinach, tomatoes and cucumbers as it helps to keep the soil evenly and constantly moist. A blanket of straw, or in this case, dried pine 'needles', serves as camouflage for the plastic and as another mulch layer.

amount of air and water in the heap is critical. A well-made heap is *aerobic*, the micro-organisms having adequate air to provide the speedy decomposition necessary for successful composting; too much moisture and not enough air and the process becomes *anaerobic* – slow and smelly.

Making a Compost Heap

Compost bins and boxes can be made from scrap building materials, metal-mesh fencing, or anything that will make four walls. Two bins are necessary so that you can have one heap ageing while a new one is collecting; each should be approximately 1m (3ft) high and a minimum of 1m (3ft) square – enough for the small garden – and can of course be made larger if you feel your family generates, or you have access to, enough waste to fill it.

Earthworms are essential to a compost heap, so it must be built on soil. Air should enter the heap from the bottom and move through it, so the base should be raised slightly off the ground and the top should be open. The heap is raised in layers; the first should be stout branches and sticks 5–10cm (2–4in) thick. Once the heap has reached maximum height, cover the top with a sheet of heavy polythene in which holes have been punched.

Add the waste in layers alternately with farmyard manure (if you have difficulty obtaining manure, a scattering of sulphate of ammonia at 15g per square metre (½oz per sq yd) will substitute) or an organic fertiliser like blood and bone meal, and soil. Each layer should be 15–25cm (6–10in) deep. Large objects such as cabbage leaves, flower stems and woody stalks should be broken up, egg shells should be crushed and so on. Before being added to the heap, all the various types of waste should be mixed together so that their distribution is even throughout the layer. Sprinkle with water and then fork onto the heap, making sure that the layer is level. Cover with soil and manure and add another layer of waste.

Once the heap is complete it will rapidly start to heat and the composting action begins. You will notice the heap settle, and it then starts to cool. After several weeks, it is necessary to turn the heap, bringing the top to the bottom and the sides to the centre in order that all parts of the heap are heated. Do this by forking the heap into the empty second box; don't do this vigorously, but control the distribution across the layers; take care to put the outside portions to the centre by inverting each forkful.

During hot dry summer days, it will probably be necessary to water the heap every day; give it a light sprinkle.

Garbage-can Composters

If space in the garden is at a premium, or if you require only a small amount of compost, use large plastic garbage cans to contain the heap. These composters can even be used indoors, in a shed, garage or basement.

Made this way, the compost is anaerobic, and so does not require turning; but it does need earthworms. Outdoors the worms will enter naturally; indoors they will have to be introduced and a shovelful of soil containing 'red worms' will establish a colony.

Use a small wood saw to remove the bottom of the bin. Then bury the base of the bin about 10–15cm (4–6in) deep to keep it firmly anchored. If the bins are being kept indoors, punch a few holes in the base of the bin rather than removing it, and put a tray beneath it to catch liquid run-off. (This liquid should be odourless and can be used to feed houseplants.)

As the layers of refuse reach 10–15cm (4–6in), cover with a 2.5cm (1in) layer of soil, shredded leaves or grass clippings. Don't forget to water occasionally, and keep the lid on between additions.

With garbage-can composters only soft refuse should be used, as woody stems will not break down. It helps to speed the process, in both conventional and garbage-can heaps, to break up the refuse into small pieces; run a lawn mower over garden refuse to shred it and chop up kitchen wastes. Be sure to include coffee grounds as these are a natural deodoriser.

The chopped leaves of stinging nettles and of Russian comfrey are an excellent addition to a compost heap and even more beneficial if made into a liquid compost. This is done by stuffing a large container such as a barrel with comfrey leaves, and then adding water. Make a hole in the base of the barrel and stand it on blocks to raise it off the ground. As the leaves decompose a rich inky liquid drips from the hole, an excellent liquid fertiliser for all crops, particularly those which enjoy feeds rich in potassium.

In the 1571 edition of the *Gardener's Labyrinth* shallow raised beds are arranged in a decorative pattern around two much higher beds, raised behind what appears to be wooden retaining walls, with turned finials at each corner. Such high beds were frequently made of brick, but wood or animal bones were also favoured.

PLANTING RAISED BEDS

The important point to remember about raised beds is that you can sow and plant closer and earlier.

To plant closer, arrange the beds in square blocks rather than rows, and put all the plants of one variety equidistant from each other so that ultimately the leaves of each plant touch its neighbour, in what is known as a quincunx: one plant in each corner and a fifth in the centre. This makes a much more economical use of space than a straight row, but does mean that it is almost impossible to use a hoe for weeding. However, good mulching and close leaf cover from the growing crop should prevent this from being a headache; in any case, the loose texture of the raised bed means that weeds are easily pulled out by hand.

Using this plan you can also control the eventual size of the crop: onions sown 45cm (18in) apart give champion size bulbs, yet the closer together they are planted, the smaller they become; 10cm (4in) makes smaller bulbs (and I think more practical ones), but a higher yield in the same amount of space. Beets and kohl rabi follow the same principle (and who wants to eat grapefruit-sized beets?). Small and perfectly formed is best every time.

However, some vegetables would be difficult to grow in blocks such as this; a thicket of peas or climbing beans would be impossible to harvest easily, as they need training up tall supports. These can be grown in rows in narrow beds prepared around the perimeter of the raised beds.

In some instances you will be mixing tall growing crops with those nearer to the ground. In order for them to get full advantage of the sun, plant the tall vegetables at the northern ends of the beds, with the lowest plants at the south.

COMPANION PLANTING

So many parts of the garden can be seen to have empathy for each other that it is hardly surprising that the theory and practice of companion planting is becoming increasingly popular.

Companion planting is a growing partnership, uniting those plants which seem to

Above Sweet peas revel in the rich, deeply dug soil of a raised bed and are here grown up a simple wire trellis arch, to frame the view into the vegetable garden.

Opposite, top left John Parkinson described both broad and narrow-leaved purslane as grown 'in the alleyes of the Garden betweene the beds'. The succulent leaves make a cooling summer salad. For this purpose use *Portulaca oleracea*; it makes a rapid ground cover studded with small, single flowers; *P. grandiflorum* has narrow leaves but much showier flowers.
Opposite, top right Sweet william, a biennial relative of the pink, is a favourite bee plant and should be grown with peas and beans to ensure good pollination.
Opposite, bottom right Lilies grown in the vegetable garden for cutting take the pressure off the flower border, where a basketful cut for arranging would leave a sad bald patch.

benefit each other, to promote healthier growth or as a natural means of pest control. There are a number of excellent books and articles in gardening magazines devoted to the subject, but here I will attempt to provide an overview of the technique and, with each entry in the following chapters, give an indication of the plants which are mutually beneficial and which companionships should be avoided – for there is a down side to the theory: some plants will actually inhibit the growth of the wrong neighbour.

The greatest benefit from companion planting is to be found in pest control, and there are four main ways that this may be achieved.

Aromatic flowers and herbs can be interplanted to confuse the scents given off by a crop that would otherwise attract damaging insects, since certain pests find their food by smell.

Some plants give off a fragrance that pests find unattractive. The Elizabethans used to scatter branches of herbs such as lavender, rushes, sage, tansy and hyssop on their floors as 'strewing herbs' in order to control invasions of household pests; the herb southernwood was called *garderobe* by the French who used it and lavender to prevent moth in wardrobes. We can take this ancient practice into the garden and use these aromatic herbs in neat clipped edgings around the vegetable beds as natural pesticides.

French marigolds are possibly the most popular flowering plant to grow amongst vegetables or as a flowering border. The gay flowers and foliage have an astringent smell which, when mixed with the scent of tomatoes, camouflages the smell of the food crop. Its root system also exudes a substance that puts off soil nematodes that can invade root crops.

Finally, certain flowers are especially attractive to insects which feed on garden pests: hoverflies feed on pollen and nectar from flowers and their larvae feed on aphids, so it is worth planting open-faced flowers like daisies from which hoverflies can easily feed.

Members of the onion family are especially useful in the kitchen garden and can be interplanted with carrots, beets and the cabbage tribe to good effect. Alternatively, an effective repellent spray can be made by pouring hot water over a jarful of chives, garlic peelings, or onion skins. Leave it to steep in a sunny window for a day or two, drain and dilute with water on a ratio of 3:1, and then use the liquid as a spray against aphids, carrot fly, and powdery mildew.

It has been shown that a weed-free plot where there is wide spacing between rows is more liable to infestation because some insects find their food supply by sight; a stand of cabbages clearly outlined against weed-free soil attracts more aphids than cabbages whose outlines are blurred by intercropping, or even weeds left to cover the soil. Weed cover may decrease the yields slightly, and obviously it is not a good idea to allow rapacious perennial weeds to flourish, but many annual weeds can be left to provide soil cover without competing with the crop plants for food.

WAYS OF SOWING SEED

Under glass The advent of peat pots and blocks has made it possible to raise most vegetables from seed in the protection of a cold greenhouse or frame, or with heat in the case of melons, tomatoes and so on. These little pots can then be put directly into the ground so that there is no root disturbance to retard the development of the vegetable. But care must be taken to harden them off adequately before they are planted out, i.e. by exposing the seedlings daily to sun and air by removing them from the protected

atmosphere of the greenhouse or coldframe. This gives the plant a head start, and is usually practised with tomatoes, cucumbers, zucchini, sweet corn, dwarf French and runner beans, and most of the brassica tribe. Pot-grown seedlings are the easiest to use with plastic mulching.

The alternative to this is to sow the seed in a specially prepared nursery bed, where the soil has been raked to fine tilth, and then prick the seedlings out into their growing positions on the bed. Take care to water the seedlings after transplanting. I find that it helps to do it on a still day, so that there are no drying winds, and in the early morning when there may be some moisture in the air.

Broadcasting Many of the leafy, salad-type vegetables can be sown simply by scattering the seed over the prepared bed, just as you would with grass seed, and then gently raking the bed over to cover the seeds with soil.

The young leaves of spinach, lettuce, rocket, chicory and dandelion, are particularly delicious: something the Italians are well aware of, for in their marketplaces I have seen boxes of small saladings, neatly packed in rows according to variety, fresh and moist, for sale by weight. After that it was hard to look an iceberg lettuce in the face: I brought home some Italian seed, mixed the young leaves together with some red-leafed lettuce, a dash of dill and sprinkle of fresh shredded coriander. Delicious.

You can pull up the young seedlings, thinning and munching as you go, or cut off the young leaves (not too near the soil) and allow them to shoot again – a technique known as cut-and-come-again. Most seed merchants offer a ready-mix seed for this purpose, commonly known as 'Saladisi'. If you do this, feed the plants between each cut with a liquid fertiliser high in nitrogen.

Station-sowing To achieve a quincunx planting you do need to be able to control where

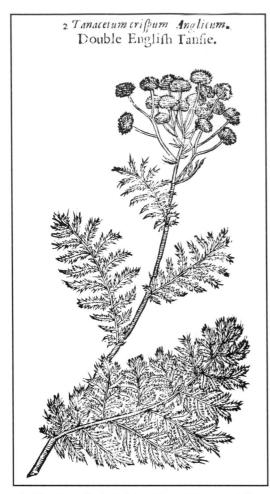

2 *Tanacetum crispum Anglicum.*
Double English Tansie.

In his *Grete Herball*, John Gerard illustrated five sorts of tansy, a plant with a bitter taste and strong, but not unpleasant smell. He deemed the 'Double English Tansie', *above*, to have the strongest odour. In the modern garden, fragrant herbs like this can be used to mask the scent of vegetable crops and so confuse pests that follow their 'noses' when searching for food.

the seed falls: it could be wasteful to sow a long row and then have to thin it out. Station-sowing means sowing small numbers of seed in the growing positions, and is easiest with large-seeded vegetables like beetroots or onions. The seed of many other smaller-seeded vegetables can be lifted with a fingernail and dropped into the planting hole.

If you station-sow ball-rooted carrots, beetroots, and kohl rabi, you can dispense with thinning as the roots will push each other apart. Otherwise, thin each station to one plant to allow it to develop normally.

Intercropping In my experience, the Italians are canny vegetable gardeners; they seem to have an innate sense of how to get the most from the least. It is stimulating to see how not one centimetre of space is wasted in their gardens; flowers, fruits and vegetables are cheek-by-jowl. Even balcony gardens are shaded with tomato plants trained up trellises and underplanted with salads and herbs. Cleverest of all are the vineyards, where the vines are trained into arbours, and tomato plants are then led up bamboo rods between each vine, with cabbages at their feet. The broad cabbage leaves cool the roots of the taller plants which in turn shade the cabbages.

We can achieve the same in our own gardens by combining in our rows those plants which mature quickly with those which are slower off the mark. By sowing a leaf crop, say lettuce, between onions, you make the best use of the space, and provide a living mulch (the lettuce) while the onions mature. Spinach and beans go together, and, on the American-Indian principle of growing pumpkins with sweet corn, zucchini, dwarf French beans, bush or trailing cucumbers will appreciate the regular watering sweet corn requires, and in return shade its roots.

Sowing in fluid Finally, ingenuity is one of the good gardener's main characteristics, and the fluid-sowing of pre-germinated seed is one of the more recent innovations.

The chief advantage of this technique is that, when ultimately sown in the beds, the vegetable seedling has a head start on any ungerminated weed seeds (raking over the seed bed a day or two before planting takes care of any of those). Also, you can get a more even distribution of miniscule seeds. The technique described below is based on *Practical Guide No. 5*, published by England's National Vegetable Research Station.

First of all, the seed must be germinated in a warm, moist environment. Take a plastic box with a lid and line it with paper towelling. Sprinkle it with water until it is well soaked. Tip the box to strain away any excess water.

Scatter the seed evenly over the bottom of the box. Close the box and put it in a moderately warm place, 20°C (70°F) maximum.

Check the seed daily: when small-seeded varieties have roots 6mm (¼in) long, and large-seeded ones are 10mm (⅜in) long, wash them very carefully into a fine-mesh strainer.

Mix to half-strength a packet of cellulose wallpaper paste that does not contain a fungicide. Put half the quantity into a small polythene bag and add the seedlings. Add the remainder of the paste and mix together lightly with your finger.

Seal the bag with a wire twist-tie, clip off a corner of the bag and you are ready to squeeze a line of germinated seed into a prepared seed bed, tray or growing position in the vegetable garden.

It is best to organise yourself so that you can sow all the prepared seed in one day. If the seed becomes ready and it's not possible to sow, you can store it for a couple of days in the refrigerator. NVRS calculates that 150ml (¼ pint) of paste will sow a 9m (30ft) row.

F. Chauueau . in.et fe.

This seventeenth-century engraving, from John Evelyn's translation of *Le Jardinier François* by Nicolas Bonnefons, shows five gardeners preparing an elaborate system of wall supports against which fruit trees will be trained. He described four methods of support, the most substantial of which was a quincunx of wooden laths fixed to wooden blocks set in the wall; the laths could be easily replaced when rotten. The beds at the foot of the wall underneath the fruit trees were to be interplanted with quick-growing crops like lettuce, purslane and young cabbages for transplanting, since this would serve to keep the soil open and fertilised and frequently watered to the benefit of the trees, but he cautions against sowing anything with too large a root system.

The regular layout of oblong beds was to be edged with the sort of plants used to make knots, box, thyme and so on, and these could be cut into whatever 'figure' one wished.

CHAPTER ONE

CABBAGES AND POTAGES

Above Brossica Sabauda, Savoy Cabbage.

Opposite Detail from *A Kitchen Interior with Two Maids Preparing Food* by Gillis De Winter (1650–1720). *Reproduced by courtesy of Jenny Van Haeften.*

Our MEDIEVAL ancestors conducted their lives within a rigid social structure, with the individuals at each level owing fealty to those above them; villein, lord and king – the pecking order was established. But the ultimate end of the chain was the Church, to which even the King was subservient.

It is difficult, perhaps, for us to comprehend how important a role God's emissaries on earth, from the Pope to the least monk in his solitary monastic cell, played within the medieval community. Besides caring for the spiritual needs of the people, the monasteries were active in the temporal world, providing places of refuge in what were exceedingly troubled times, hospital care for the lay community, shelter for the poor and needy, and a great deal of employment for local people. The monasteries were, above all else, seats of learning, where the skills and knowledge of the classical world were carefully preserved after the fall of Rome and the withdrawal of its legions from occupied territories.

Gardening was one of the Romans' most important legacies to Britain (and to much of the western world). During the Dark Ages, a time of constant skirmishing between rival lords and threats of invasion from hostile neighbours, there was little space for a large productive garden within the battlemented walls of the castle, and the occupants had concerns other than the cultivation of plants (although there would have been a small enclosure of wild flowers, herbs and roses as a retreat for the ladies). The monastery was comparatively an island of peace, protected by its very nature as a house of God; and it was the monks who preserved the Roman horticultural skills.

Although some religious communities were destroyed by pagan Vikings, the majority tilled the soil undisturbed and grew the crops necessary to support the monastery. Many of these were Roman introductions: onions, garlic, leeks, grapes and nettles, to name a few.

At this time, the garden was chiefly practical, with vegetables, herbs and fruit grown for medicinal purposes or for the table or 'pot' (whence the name 'pot herb' for all edible plants). Aesthetics did not influence garden design until the reign of Elizabeth I, and if flowers were grown they were for altar decorations on holy days, or for physic.

It is likely that the layout of the earliest gardens would have followed the Roman pattern, and that beds would have been made following Pliny's advice: laid out in a regular pattern, with sloping banks, paths for the gardener to follow and irrigation channels. Such a garden was uncovered at Pompeii, and today one can see similar layouts in the gardens of nearby villages. The plan for a kitchen garden, or *hortus*, at the Benedictine monastery of St Gall, drawn up in AD 820 or 830, demonstrates the ideal: either side of a long central walk leading from the gardener's lodge, there are nine narrow beds, each planted with a separate vegetable including onions, dill, and coriander.

The monks were also responsible for introducing new methods of gardening and new plants, for there was a great deal of traffic between monasteries as the brothers criss-

Above and opposite Root vegetables from John Parkinson's *Paradisus in Sole*: parsnips (2), turnips (4), skirrets (1), carrots (3), and a long-rooted turnip (5) known as the 'navew'.

crossed Europe visiting the outposts of their orders: a garden-loving monk would be no different from any modern touring gardener, observing, hunting out new plants.

What of the common people? Many had a small parcel of land (or *curtilage*) attached to their dwellings, which encompassed any cart sheds, pigsties, chicken coops (bacon and eggs formed a major part of the common diet) and so on. There are frequent listings of *horti* and *hortuli* – gardens and little gardens – in the Domesday Book, so we can assume that any spare space was used to raise vegetables to supplement what could be obtained from other sources. There was not much to choose from; one of the earliest English garden treatises, *The Feate of Gardening*, an instructive poem and one of the few early English gardening texts extant, written by Jon Gardener in 1440, lists seventy-eight herbs, including spinach and cabbage.

But vegetables and herbs were used most to flavour food, and not as a food in their own right, although potage was the mainstay of the poor man's diet. This was a vegetable soup/stew of leeks, cabbage, barley and so on, and would often be made in the liquid in which a piece of meat had been boiled. Andrew Boorde wrote: 'Potage is not so much used in al Crystendom as it is used in Englande'. Potage was the mainstay of the common diet throughout Europe and survives in many national cuisines: Italian minestrone, Hungarian borscht, French garbure and English pease pottage.

Further up the social ladder, the variety of foods in the daily diet improved: more fish was eaten, beef and mutton appeared on the table, lettuce and beetroot were eaten raw in simple salads and the quality of the bread was better. But even the nobility neglected vegetables. This may have been due to popular attitudes regarding what guaranteed health. Medical practice at the time was based on the classical writings of Hippocrates and Aristotle, as interpreted by Galen: that all things are made of elements whose characteristics, when combined, produce humours and complexions. The elements and characteristics of fruits and vegetables were for the most part thought to be suspect if not downright dangerous. Many of our ancestors must have unknowingly suffered from scurvy and other diseases incurred by poor diet.

The medieval kitchen consisted of an open hearth; food could be cooked directly in the ashes and embers, or in pots resting on tripods set over the coals. Small ovens were created by setting a pot in the fire, inverting the pot lid and covering it with hot coals. Frying and fritters were popular, and vessels of hot oil were set among the coals for frying – which must have been a fire hazard. There was a grill for toasting and a spit for roasting meat, and most importantly, a large cauldron. This single vessel hung over the fire, and in it food was boiled with little regard for separating flavours. Only the wealthy had ovens; otherwise the village baker would take in baking for his neighbours: pies were extremely popular, and a stout crust enclosing meat and gravy was a convenient method of food presentation at a time when food was cut with a knife but eaten with the fingers, from a trencher of hard bread rather than from a china or metal plate.

The Church calendar was a busy one, full of days of fasting and penance. This, combined with the seasonal nature of the food supply (and peculiar notions about diet), often led to great dietary hardship; the period of Lent must have been the hardest to weather. At other times of the year one could substitute fresh fruit and vegetables for the missing animal fats and proteins, but Lent came when the new season's crops had not been sown, and the stored supplies were hardly palatable. White meats (eggs and cheese) which on the other, more ordinary fast days provided an alternative, were also forbidden.

Even if one had been allowed to eat it, the salted and preserved hams and red meats were at the end of their shelf-life.

When he wasn't looking after his soul, the medieval gourmand put a great deal of effort into pleasing his tastebuds. Quite honestly, medieval blends of spice and savour, sweet and sour, are extremely attractive; and while manuscript cookery books give recipes for disguising tainted food, I'm sure that the main reason for the tremendous vitality of their cooking was to alleviate the rather repetitive nature of the ingredients. Good food was a precious commodity, and great care would have been exercised to maintain its quality for as long as possible. Household manuals of the time describe at length how to preserve food by salting, drying, pickling, in honey syrups and occasionally sugared, and any householder who mastered these techniques was highly skilled indeed.

There was a strong Middle Eastern influence, due to the holy crusades of the twelfth and thirteenth centuries when European communities were introduced to unfamiliar vegetables and fruits like aubergines, lentils and chick peas, oranges, lemons and bananas. As early as the thirteenth century dried fruit was being imported from Portugal and the Eastern Mediterranean countries, so that by the fifteenth century a prosperous household always had a supply of 'datys, fieggs and great raysyngs' to fill out the Lenten menu and make delicious puddings at other times of the year. The story of how our mincemeat pies originated is too familiar to bear repetition.

When a crusading army marched, then as now it travelled on its stomach, and returning knights and foot soldiers brought with them a set of newly acquired tastes; their womenfolk travelled as well. Certainly they would have been observant enough to research the recipes and cookery methods of the foreign lands they visited. Perhaps this is why so many of the earliest food combinations and methods of presentation call to mind Middle and Far Eastern cuisine. Merchants, too, played their part: reaching out for new markets, men like Marco Polo spent years in the Orient and Indian sub-continent. He is popularly credited with having introduced pasta to Italy from China. But it may have come via Arab traders to Italian ports; the Italians then taught the Chinese to cook pasta.

Medieval palates were fond of sharp flavours, richly spiced food and blends of sweet and sour. Vinegar and verjuice, the unfermented juice of grapes or crab-apples, were extremely popular flavourings, and also served to tenderise tough meat. For sweetness honey was most commonly used; sugar was available, but expensive until the discovery of the New World, and until the eighteenth century was largely confined to medicinal use (this was a characteristic of the times, that rare and unusual ingredients were regarded as medicines). Verjuice, honey or sweet dried fruits like raisins were often combined in a recipe to give a tangy sweet-sourness.

Cinnamon was the most widely used spice, with ginger, mustard and saffron. These highly expensive imported spices were prized for their sourness, and in the case of saffron and cinnamon were also valued as colouring agents. Medieval food presentation was a highly visual event and lurid colours were introduced to provide a feast for the eyes as well as the stomach. Sorrel and spinach juice were also used to give dishes a greenish tinge – a much loved finish for sauces – and gold and silver leaf were used to gild pastries formed in the shape of coats of arms, crenellated castle walls and other similarly grandiose confections. Almond milk, made by steeping ground almonds in water, was used as a milk substitute on fast days, for making puddings, sweet and savoury, and for poaching fish, and on meat days it was frequently used with chicken.

Cabbages, Spinach, Onions, Garlic, Shallots

Chief among the medieval vegetables are all the many species of the brassica, descended from the wild cabbage plant that grows freely along the warmer coastal regions of much of Europe. 'Colewort' is a word that has been used to describe the whole cabbage family, or to refer to a type of open-leaved non-heading brassica like kale, or borecole (from the Dutch *boerenkool* or 'peasant's cabbage'), which, along with those under the heading 'cabbage', are among the oldest cultivated vegetables.

Cabbages are just one of the many supposed Roman introductions to northern Europe and England; others would credit its introduction to England to a Dorset knight, Sir Anthony Ashley, although it was probably only an exceptionally good variety that he imported, since cabbages in one form or another had been grown as a soup vegetable for centuries: coleworts were cultivated by the Saxons and the Celts, whose word for it, *bresic*, gives the genus its name, *Brassica*. It features among the seventy-eight herbs and vegetables included in *The Feate of Gardening*, which recommended successional sowing for a year-round crop; as part of the daily diet, this was important.

Cabbages were among the first vegetables introduced to America; in 1540, Jacques Cartier sowed a patch in Canada and by 1779 the American Indians included cabbages in their vegetable gardens.

Brassicas crossbreed with a shocking facility, and with each new generation, improved forms appeared which led to the development, through selection, of cauliflowers, broccoli – sprouting and heading – Brussels sprouts, and the many forms of cabbage we know today.

We still make successional sowings, beginning in the early autumn, in order to have spring cabbage, and again throughout the spring to provide cabbage during the rest of the year. Cabbage will grow in almost any soil that has been richly fertilised and limed, with the exception of autumn-sown varieties which do better on soil that has been manured for a previous crop. Seed for early crops can be sown under glass for transplanting. In either case, in order to avoid contamination by the pernicious fungal disease, clubroot, dust the seed drill with clubroot powder, and never plant cabbages in the same piece of ground two years running.

Cabbage roots are easily damaged by hoeing, and a straw or black plastic mulch which helps to keep down weeds will also give the plant the cool moist conditions it enjoys. A mulch will also help to regulate the water supply; too much causes heads to split, and if you notice this happening, just give the plant a gentle twist, about a quarter-turn, to root prune and thus reduce the uptake of water. Cabbages can be planted on a quincunx to make best use of the available space. This means that they are set more closely together, which has to some degree the same effect as a mulch.

Most people like to leave a cabbage to make a sizeable single head per plant, but if you cut the head when it is about the size of a grapefruit and leave several leaves on the stem, small cabbages will form from each lateral bud. This only works with summer-cropping cabbage; later varieties wouldn't have time to make new heads.

In classical times it was believed that cabbages grown in vineyards had an adverse effect on the wine eventually produced, but the Italians must have overcome this prejudice, for, as mentioned earlier, I have seen cabbage interplanted with grapes in a number of rural Italian kitchen gardens, benefiting from the shade of the vine. Aromatic herbs, like southernwood, hyssop and thyme, will put the cabbage white butterfly off its scent, as do tomatoes and onions planted among the cabbages; chilli pepper water will have the same effect on rabbits. Underplanting with lettuces, or allowing certain 'non-aggressive' weeds to grow, will camouflage the cabbage's silhouette, so protecting it from aphids and whitefly. Slugs can be killed by sprinkling the plants with strong salty water.

Spinach is a delicious vegetable, despite what children think. It is a native of Persia and probably advanced into Europe through Spain by way of the Moors, who held it in high esteem – 'a prince of vegetables'. It was recognised as a fast-day food by the Christian community and one of its earliest appearances, under the name 'spynoches', was in the fourteenth-century cookbook *The Forme of Cury*, although many sources credit William Turner's herbal, first published in 1551, with its first description in England: 'Spinage or Spinech is an herbe lately found and not long in use, but it is so wel knowen amongst al men in al countreas that it nedeth no description'. In 1597, John Gerard, who owned a garden in Holborn, wrote his famous *Herbal*, naming spinach as a medicinal pot herb that was eaten boiled and 'used in sallades when it is young and tender'.

In 1629, Parkinson described three sorts of spinach: lesser and greater prickly seeded sorts and one smooth-seeded, and

Top The all-season savoy cabbage and *below* a winter drumhead.

recommended frequent cutting to obtain continuous cropping.

Spinach needs rich, moist soil, so that it grows quickly and begins effective cropping before it runs to seed. The first seed can be sown in place in early spring, with successional sowings made every two weeks or so until hot weather and then again in late summer for a fall crop. Sow a small amount each time, and endeavour to keep the weeds down and the soil well watered.

Winter spinach (prickly seed) is really a capsule of many seeds, and can be grown where there are not extremes of cold or hot weather. Winter spinach prefers raised-bed cultivation since the plants resent waterlogging. Begin sowing in mid-summer and finish at summer's end. If the winter is especially harsh, cover with twiggy branches, bracken or similar, to break the worst effects of frost.

All varieties of spinach can be sown in wide rows or bands, 25–30cm (10–12in) across the width of the bed. This will help to keep the soil cool and moist – essential for good spinach. Thin the seedlings (use them in salads) to 7.5cm (3in) and cut the leaves off cleanly when there are only five or six on the plant. Small leaves are more tender than big, which encourages the plant to keep producing, rather than run to seed.

In summer spinach can be used for inter-cropping, particularly if you sow it where neighbouring plants will shade it, and as a catch-crop (a fast-maturing vegetable sown to take advantage of temporarily vacant ground) among slower maturing vegetables – as long as they won't take all the water! Spinach will do well in a strawberry bed or catch-cropped with garlic, particularly if you sow winter spinach with autumn-planted garlic.

In her book *Gesunder Garten Durch Mischkulturen* Gertrude Franck recommends using spinach as an instant compost; the technique applies to the traditional flat-bed vegetable garden, but could be adapted for raised beds. She sows an early crop of spinach, then cuts the leaves to rot where they fall, leaving the soft root systems to decompose underground. All this takes just a few days, and the rotting vegetation provides food for beneficial micro-organisms in the soil. Once the rotting is complete, the soil is cultivated, the spinach row becomes a footpath and another type of crop is sown; there is a constantly changing order of spinach rows and crops

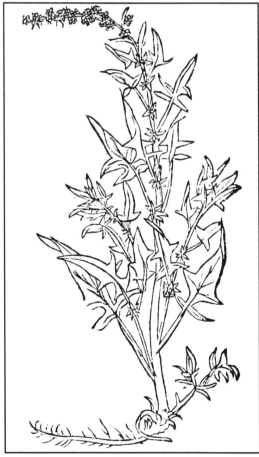

Spinach, from the 1578 English translation of Rembert Dodoens's *Newe Herball*.

and the entire garden is completely mulched and cultivated.

What direction the flavour of our food would have taken without the many species of the genus *Allium* is hard to imagine: onions, shallots, leeks, chives, garlic, Welsh onions and Egyptian tree onions have been cultivated and used to savour cuisines all over the world from the earliest times.

In 5000 BC the Chaldeans used **onions** for casting spells; the Egyptians venerated the onion among their numerous deities, using it as a motif in many tomb paintings. Wherever man settled, onions were cultivated. Gerard described how it 'is cherished everywhere in kitchen gardens: it is now and then in beds sowne alone, and many times mixed with other herbes, as with Lettuce, Parseneps, and Carrets', and remarked that according to Pliny it should be sown with the herb savory as it 'prospereth the better, and is more wholesome'. Overtones of its ancient mystical qualities were long reflected in its attributes: Gerard said that onions pounded with salt, rue and honey were efficacious against the bite of mad dogs, and the juice could restore hair to bald heads.

Onions require a light, rich, well-drained soil and a sunny, open position. Since they can be raised on the same ground year after year, it is worth taking time to prepare the beds well, correcting heavy soils by adding sand or other aggregates, and incorporating leaf mould, well-rotted compost and so on to light soils. Onions disdain fresh manure, so be sure to plant on ground manured for a previous crop.

There are two ways of raising onions: from seed, with the first crops sown in early spring, or from sets (small bulbs). From seed, start thinning as the bulbs form (using the thinnings in salads). In either case, the more space between the bulbs, the greater their eventual size will be. The minimum is about 15cm (6in) apart. Sets should not be buried: leave half the bulb exposed.

Birds have great fun tossing the bulbs out of the ground, but black thread drawn over the bed will prevent this. Take care not to disturb the bulbs when weeding, nor should soil be drawn up around the developing bulbs. Water them regularly but lightly until the end of summer, when the ripening process begins. The tops will keel over naturally and when about half the crop is in this state, push the remaining tops over to expose the bulbs to full sun. When the tops turn brown, pull the bulbs from the ground and leave them on the bed with their roots exposed to dry naturally. Choose a time when you can be sure of sunny warm weather to do this. Finally, gather the bulbs, rub off the dirty outer skins and roots and store them in a dry airy place; dampness in storage will start the bulbs into growth.

Japanese onions are useful for early crops. The seed is sown in the autumn and the onions are ready for use fresh from the ground by mid-spring.

To the list of Pliny's recommended companions for onions add beets and strawberries, and all the various alliums can be grown together, which is probably how they were grown in medieval gardens; peas and beans should, however, be kept apart from all members of the onion family.

Garlic is a love-hate vegetable. Our medieval ancestors were passionate about its pungent flavour which could do wonders to a bowl of mashed beans; along with pepper and peony seeds it was one of the hot spices offered to Piers Plowman. In the seventeenth century, John Parkinson remarked on its 'very strong smell and taste, . . . passing either Onions or Leekes, but exceeding wholesome withall for them that can take it'. Indeed.

Garlic is a scaly bulb, the individual cloves or segments being the scales from which new plants are propagated. Some gardeners recommend planting the cloves in early spring; however, autumn planting is often more successful, especially in cold climates, and will give fresh supplies earlier

in the year. Garlic requires the same soil and situation as onions, but the cloves should be planted 5cm (2in) deep, about 25cm (10in) apart. There is no need to water them and when the leaves turn brown the garlic can be lifted. Tie the desiccated foliage into bunches and hang the garlic in a cool dry place, taking bulbs as necessary.

Garlic planted among roses will protect them from black spot, and some people say that the fragrance of the flowers is also improved and the garlic of a finer quality. This may be due to the rich annual dressings of rotted manure received by a well-tended rose bed.

Shallots are as easy to grow as garlic and of similar habit, in that one bulb produces many. Tradition has it that shallots were introduced by the crusaders, and take their name from Ascalon, where, in 1192, Richard the Lionheart defeated Saladin's army.

Sow shallot bulbs in early spring, protect them from birds and push any bulbs lifted by late frosts back into the soil. Plant them as you would onions, about 20cm (8in) apart. Bend the leaves over as they wither and then lift and store them as for onions.

Leeks have always had a place in English kitchen gardens, and have been so popular in Wales that the leek is one of its national emblems; *leac tun* was how the Saxons described a cottager's vegetable patch. It has a reputation as a poor man's vegetable and was a grateful addition to the potage during Lent, no doubt to substitute for the onions, supplies of which by that season would have been running short. In common with many other highly valued crops, fantastic theories regarding the cultivation of leeks sprang up about how to achieve the biggest and best. But leeks are among the easiest plants to grow, not fussy about soil and unbothered by pests and diseases.

Sow the seed in shallow drills in a nursery bed in early spring. When the seedlings are large enough to handle easily, transplant them by dropping them into dibbed holes 15–22cm (6–9in) deep. Do this in rainy weather if possible, otherwise water them in. The action of occasional hoeing and watering will gradually fill the holes as the plants mature. Cut the weak, long leaves back by half their length as you transplant.

Don't plant leeks onto ground that has been occupied by other members of the onion family, but do give them soil that has previously been manured. They like a rich soil, and will benefit from a liquid manure feed every two weeks.

Leeks and carrots benefit each other; and they can also be planted with celery.

Japanese bunching onions, **scallions** or **spring onions** are similar to each other in form and the bulbs and leaves are used in salads. Successional sowings made from late spring throughout summer will ensure a continuing crop.

Welsh onions, like chives (see page 50), are herbaceous perennials, frequently used as a border plant; however, they come into leaf earlier than chives and for this reason are marginally more useful. They don't form bulbs, and it is the green mild-flavoured leaves which are used in salads and as a flavouring for sauces. Welsh onions can be propagated by division of the clumps in the spring, or annual sowings made in autumn.

Tree onions, sometimes called Egyptian tree onions, are a curiosity, as the onion bulbs form in tight clusters at the top of the hollow stem, where one would normally expect to find flowers. They are extremely hardy and of the easiest cultivation; a bulb will grow where it falls, which can lead to dense overcrowding. The tiny onions are mostly used for pickling and have a very strong flavour.

Beans, Peas, Mange-touts, Good King Henry, Chard, Cardoon, Scorzonera

Beans, in particular the **broad bean**, or fava bean, have long been a chief source of nourishment, perhaps since the Bronze Age and certainly since the days of the Pharaohs. The Greeks and Romans cultivated the broad bean, and in some instances worshipped it, and by the time of the Roman withdrawal, broad beans were an established food crop in Britain. The diet of the common poor during the Middle Ages relied heavily on starch for substance. Except for bacon, other meat was for the rich man's table, and he in turn disdained beans as fodder for the masses; an attitude which prevailed until well into the seventeenth century, when Parkinson recommended beans as 'serving for foode for the poorer sort for the most part'. Faint praise for such an important food.

Because they were used in such quantity, these beans were field cultivated, unless they were grown in kitchen gardens belonging to the big estates, in which case they were always the largest crop, used to feed the lord's retainers. No doubt beans made it onto the high table – especially on days of abstention.

Their other attribute is their fragrance, and anyone who has encountered the scent of a bean field wafting on the breeze would agree that it is one of the pleasures of the open countryside in early summer. Elizabethan ladies distilled the blossoms for a highly prized sweet water, and beans were also dried and ground to use as face powder.

Today broad beans are sown under glass in winter and planted out during early spring to crop in June; or else successional sowings can be made outdoors in early spring. Sow the seed 5cm (2in) deep in a sunny spot and in light soil that was manured for a previous crop.

Pinching out the growing points as soon as the first flowers set encourages early cropping. You should also take care to remove side shoots, as they will not produce worthwhile beans anyway and their continued growth would weaken the developing plant.

Broad beans are extremely hardy and easy to care for; just keep down the worst of the weeds. Black fly can be a curse, but crops from seed sown directly in the autumn seem to be immune, and pinching out also helps control the insects, as they seem to prefer this part of the plant. Southernwood and garlic may help to prevent invasion, or nasturtiums may draw the black flies' attention. Or try interplantings of summer savory, which is sometimes called the 'bean herb' as it is delicious in a white sauce served with the fresh beans.

Pliny recognised the value of broad beans as a green manure, and plants which have finished cropping can either be put on the compost heap or else cut off at ground level and the roots dug into the soil.

Peas, together with broad beans, were a staple food throughout the centuries, and were probably already in cultivation in Britain when the Romans arrived. There were two main divisions of cultivated pea: the white or field pea, which was dried and widely used for the cottager's potage, and the green pea which was eaten fresh but also had a place in potage, although on wealthier tables, since it was considered somewhat more refined. Thomas Tusser, in his poem *Five Hundrede Pointes of Good Husbandry* (1573), esteemed certain varieties such as the runcival pea as 'fit dainties for ladies' because they were imported rather than homegrown, and thus much more expensive.

The fashionable fortunes of the pea fluctuated dramatically over the centuries, peaking during the seventeenth century, led by Louis XIV, who would annually succumb to his inordinate appetite for fresh green peas.

Nothing is more delicious than early peas, except perhaps the sugar pea or snow pea, known also by its French appellation **mange-tout**. This pea is sown in early spring and gathered when no larger than your thumb, as it is eaten for the pod, not the immature pea inside. Sugar snap is another variety of edible-pod pea. It makes vines up to 1.8m (6ft) tall, whereas the mange-tout only grows to 90cm (3ft).

Peas prefer a light loamy soil over a rich base, so are ideal for raised beds. To make the sweetest peas requires plenty of sun, and the sunny parts of a kitchen garden are the first to warm in the spring, so peas do need to be sown early. They are quite hardy and some varieties, particularly the mange-tout, can go in as soon as the ground can be worked.

Ordinary garden peas are either earlies, second earlies or late varieties. In England these can be sown in sequence beginning in late autumn and carrying on until the following April, or, in cooler climates, all at the same time in early spring for a long cropping period. Over a raised bed the seeds of low-growing varieties can be broadcast sown in wide rows up to 60cm (2ft) wide with at least 3–5cm (1.5–2in) between the

Left Peas and *right* broad beans.

seeds. If the rows are any wider than this it is difficult to pick the crop, and thorough, regular picking is what keeps the plants producing. Alternatively, peas can be sown in single or double rows in 7.5cm (3in) wide drills, firmed at the bottom, with the seeds set in threes.

Tread the seeds in lightly and cover with soil to which a high nitrogen fertiliser has been added.

The title page from Otto Brunfels's *Herbarum Vivae Eicones*, 1532, shows the popular board-and-stake retaining walls for raised beds, and a trellis supporting grape vines and roses.

Prop up low-growing varieties with twiggy branches. Tall-growing varieties can be trained up frames of netting or cane wigwams.

Mice can be a problem with early crops, but if you douse the seeds in paraffin just before planting the mice will stay away. Nicotine sprays are useful against thrips, which are recognised by silvery patches on leaves and pods. Dill is a good herb to sow with peas; it grows quickly and if sown before the peas it will protect pea seedlings from birds. Sweet corn is another good companion; the peas appreciate the shelter of the tall-growing corn and use the stalks as a climbing frame.

Like beans, pea roots fix nitrogen from the soil, and the stalks should always be dug into the soil after harvesting or added to the compost heap.

A common perennial weed found throughout most of western Europe, **Good King Henry** (a *Chenopodium* – pigweed family) was early adapted as a vegetable crop and cultivated extensively in the eastern counties of Suffolk and Lincolnshire. It was valued as a healing poultice for ulcers and festering wounds, as a feed for hens (whence one of its common names, Fat Hen) and as a pot herb, the young leaves gathered to simmer in broth. These many virtues are reflected by the other common names: Allgood, Tota Bona, Good Henry – the latter of which is meant to distinguish it from the German herb, Bad Henry (*Malus henricus*). It is preferred by many to true spinach because the leaves have a milder flavour; the young shoots are not unlike asparagus if boiled and eaten with butter. The finest quality is achieved by earthing up the shoots as they appear in early summer.

'It is commonly found in untilled places, and among rubbish neere common waies, old walls, and by hedges', said Gerard. But grown on good soil and well tended, the tender young shoots are numerous and the leaves of better quality. Good King Henry is simple enough to grow: sow the seed in the spring in a warm position in well-drained soil. Remember, it is perennial, so give it a permanent bed where it won't be in the way; a good plant reaches 60cm (2ft) or more and makes a sizeable clump.

Chard, sometimes called Swiss chard or silver beet, is a near relative of the bee-troot (see page 98), but it was cultivated for its spinach-like leaves and succulent mid-ribs. It has always been more popular in Europe and didn't appear on British tables until the middle of the sixteenth century. Gerard grew it in his Holborn garden and called it red Roman beet, so presumably what he had was ruby chard. He remarked that seed did not grow true to the parent and 'brought forth plants of many and variable colours'. The white sort has a finer taste and both kinds are extremely easy to grow.

Chard is not fussy about soil and can be sown in wide rows, or interplanted with slower-growing subjects or between rows of sweet corn or tomatoes; its broad leaves will help to shade the soil, keeping it cool and moist.

The seed is quite large, so it is easy to station-sow and thus avoid excessive thinning; the plants should ultimately be about 10cm (4in) apart. Make the first sowing in early spring and another during midsummer. Chard is a cut-and-come-again vegetable, and the first cutting can be done when the young plants reach 15–20cm (6–8in). Leave a stump of about 2.5cm (1in); it will soon grow away again.

Chard has a long cropping period anyway, but succession-sowing should take it well into the autumn. In mild districts, chard can be overwintered, but it is just as well to sow a fresh crop each year.

❧ *The Tyme.*

Pou ſhall find it in flower in June and July.   ✳ *The Names.*

This herbe is called in Latine Tota bona: & of ſome alſo Χρυσολάχανον, Chryſolachanó, that is to ſay in Latine, Aureũ olus, for his ſinguler vertue: in Frēch, *Toute bonne*: in high Douch, Guter Hērich, & Schmerbel: in baſe Almaigne, Goede Heinrich, Lammekens ooze, and of ſome Algoede: in Engliſh, Good Henry, and Algood: of ſome it is taken for Mercurie.

❧ *The Nature.*

Algood is drie & abſterſiue or ſcouring.

❧ *The Vertues.*

𝔄 Algood taken as meate or broth, doth ſoften the belly, and prouoketh the ſtoole.

𝔅 This herbe greene ſtamped, and layde to, healeth old ſores, and greene woundes, and killeth and bringeth foorth wormes, that ingender in the ſame. Matthiolus.lib. 2.Dioſcor.Chap.162.Radicis ſuccus illitus ſcabiem tollit, & Cutis maculas extergit, præſertim ſi cum aceto miſceatur. Quidam eam quoque præferunt aduerſus venenoſorum animalium morſus.

Tota bona.

Good King Henry, *Tota Bona*, from Dodoens's *Newe Herball* was highly regarded for its culinary and nutritional value, and was used as a poultice to treat wounds and ulcers.

Spinach or perpetual beet is closely related to chard and is grown and harvested in exactly the same manner. But of the two, chard is distinctly better, chiefly because it has a flavour, but also the leaves are not so leathery and the midrib can be served as a vegetable in its own right.

The **cardoon** is another European oddity; and it really should have a more prominent place in the kitchen as well as the flower garden. It is a variety of artichoke that is grown for the succulent leaf midribs rather than its flowering head; it resembles a head of celery, but with spiky leaves. Cardoons are Mediterranean natives, and were much loved by the ancient Greeks; Dioscorides remarked on the extensive and profitable acreage given to its cultivation as 'this being the way in which we make the monstrous productions even of the earth subservient to our gluttonous appetites.'

The French and Spanish were using the cardoon long before the English were introduced to it some time in the mid-1600s, and the plant had colonised vast stretches of South America not long after it arrived in the New World. By 1806, it was included in a list of American esculents and said to have been in cultivation a long time for use in soups, salads and stews. But the English never really took to it, perhaps because of the hostility of its spiny leaves. The preferred form, *cardon de Tours*, which was the most popular type in Paris, is quite mean and difficult to work with, but has the best quality midribs; it is hardier than others and less likely to run to seed. The Spanish type, *cardon d'Espagne*, is much less awkward and was the type listed in America.

Cardoons are best raised from seed sown under glass in the spring. The seedlings are then transplanted to prepared beds. It was the practice to plant them into trenches 45cm (18in) deep, including a 15cm (6in) layer of manure at the bottom of the trench. In the modern kitchen garden in mild climates, they can be grown in raised beds around the perimeter of the garden; each plant needs 45cm (18in) and as they are a winter vegetable they are in the ground a long time.

As the plants grow, give them plenty of water and a liquid feed every two weeks or so. They will be slow to grow at first, but after midsummer cardoons take off, and this is when they most require water and fertiliser.

To make the tender leaf stalks, the plants must be earthed up like celery. Trim away any wilting leaves or dead stalks. Gather the leaves together neatly and secure in a bunch with a twist of raffia. Then wrap a tube of corrugated cardboard around the base of the stem allowing the top 30cm (12in) to emerge at the top. Tie securely and if necessary, fix to a cane to keep the plant upright. Mound the soil up around the base of the plant.

After 1½–2 months, the cardoons will be ready for cutting. Lift them gently from the bed with a garden fork and trim away the roots. Cardoons are tender, so any not consumed before the first frosts should be lifted intact, their leaves left on, and stored in a cool dry place. One method is to lay the plants, with a good ball of earth still around the roots, in a box and cover them with dry sand.

Salsify, Turnips, Swedes, Skirrets, Parsnips, Carrots

Scorzonera, salsify and turnips all originated in southern Europe and the countries bordering the Mediterranean, and it is in these regions that the three remain most popular, although the turnip made an earlier and more lasting impression in Britain and northern Europe. It was grown by the Romans and probably travelled with them, since it was known and eaten in Saxon times.

The black-skinned **scorzonera** was introduced from Spain some time in the early sixteenth century and was commonly known as viper's grass, since the milky juice was supposedly an antidote to snake bite; it was also used against plague, epilepsy and 'giddiness of the head'. Gerard remarked that as a food the root, roasted, boiled or raw, 'doth make a man merry, and removeth all sorrow'. Later, in the seventeenth century, the root was often served candied; Parkinson said that was how he enjoyed it as it was good to 'comfort and strengthen the heart and vitall spirit'.

It was and is extremely popular with the French; Louise XIV's gardener, de la Quintinye, described it as being full of nourishment and of excellent flavour. However, in England at least, it remained a novelty and after the eighteenth century, when some delicious ways of serving it were contrived, it passed into a culinary twilight zone.

The Italians were probably the first to recognise the food potential of **salsify**; when it first appeared in England is unknown, but Gerard grew it at Holborn and called it goat's beard or Go to bed at noone, because he noted that the flowers closed at twelve o'clock and did not reopen until the following midday. He seems to have grown it for the flowers, but recommended the roots boiled in water and 'buttered as parseneps and carrots' as having a 'delicate taste far surpassing parsnep or carrot . . . and strengthening those that have been sicke of a long lingring disease'. We know it today as the vegetable oyster, but the supposed fishy flavour is not that pronounced.

But in spite of all this virtue, salsify has suffered the same fate as scorzonera. This may be due to the mistaken habit of peeling the roots before cooking, which entirely destroys their flavour. To this day these are vegetables grown only by the discerning few, which really is too bad, since both roots are of easy cultivation and contribute to the cook's repertoire.

Both vegetables should be grown in a loose moisture-retentive soil that has been manured for a previous crop. Sow the seeds in spring about a 5mm (¼in) deep; because of their long tap roots, neither vegetable transplants successfully, so take care to sow the seed thinly.

When weeding, do not disturb the plants, as this could cause them to fork, and a forked root is useless from the cook's point of view. Hoe gently or else sow lettuces or a similar crop between the rows to keep weeds down. Alternatively, grow large-leafed vine crops like ridge cucumbers or pumpkins; the leaves shade the ground, keeping the soil moist and relatively weed free.

Salsify and scorzonera are ready for use in late autumn and early winter; salsify cannot be lifted and stored, but the green tops can be cut down on any roots left in the ground, and will shoot again to make a tasty leaf in mid-winter. The roots can also be left in the ground over winter and the crop used at will or harvested in the early spring. Scorzonera, however, can be lifted and stored in sand, but it is extremely hardy and so can be left in the ground and lifted as required. But do take care to lift each carefully without damaging the root.

Turnips, as mentioned earlier, are one of the oldest root crops. In AD 42, Columella noted that the turnip was especially popular in France and used as a food for both man and beast; the Romans knew several varieties. By the fifteenth century, the Flemish were improving upon the strains of cultivated turnip, and these sorts were introduced to England sometime in the mid-sixteenth century, probably by Flemish immigrants.

The turnip was one of the earliest Old World introductions to North America; Jacques Cartier sowed seed in Canada and it was among the first crops of the Virginia settlements.

Turnips like limy soil and will do well on raised beds, since they appreciate the deeply dug, well-drained soil and bottom layer of rotten manure.

Sow the first early crops in early spring; be sure that the surface soil has been worked to a fine tilth; humus incorporated into the top of the bed will give the plants a good start. Sow the seed thinly, and just cover it with soil. Make successional sowings as necessary until the end of spring. Winter crops can be sown in early summer for harvesting throughout winter to early spring.

As the first seedlings appear, thin carefully. The aim when thinning is to allow the large mature leaves ready access to air

Left to right Turnip, black-skinned scorzonera and salsify.

He round Rape or turnep at the beginning hath great rough rode leaues, whiche leaues in the ende next the stemme , are deepely cut and iagged vpon both sydes : and towards winter, it will haue a round stalke , vpon the which grow small yellow flowers, which bring foorth small browne seede in litle coddes or huskes lyke Cole-wurtes, to whiche the Rapes are muche like in flowers, huskes, & seede. The roote is rounde and thicke, white both without and within, somtimes as great as a mans head, sometimes no bigger then ones fiste, and sometimes smaller.

There is another kinde of Turnep or Rape, yet not that sorte, whiche some men call the red Rape or Nauew , whereof we haue alredy spoken in y Chapt. of Beetes: but another kinde very like to the round Rape or turnep aforesaid, in rough leaues, stalkes, flowers, coddes, and seedes : and and differeth but onely in this , that his rootes or Turneppes are not white but red, in all thinges els lyke to the other, as I vnderstande by some Herboristes, who haue declared vnto me, that the noble and famous Queene Douager of Hungarie and Bohem, doth cause them to be set and planted in her most ryche and pleasant gardens.

Dodoens's portrait of a turnip, which he identified as 'round rape'; distinct from the 'long rape' or 'navew', with white flesh and ranging from the size of a man's head to that of his fist, or less.

The origins of the **skirret** remain shrouded in the mists of time, but by the mid-sixteenth century it was a highly esteemed root vegetable, perhaps because it had a reputation as an aphrodisiac: viz. Gerard, 'they are something windie, buy reason whereof they also provoke lust'; 'The women in Suevuia . . . prepare the roots thereof for their husbands, and know fell well wherefore and why, & c.'

Skirrets continued in popularity until the end of the eighteenth century at least but have now become a vegetable dinosaur.

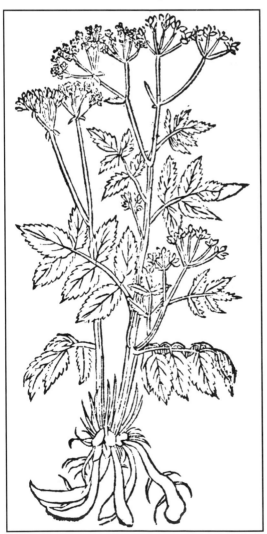

Skirrets were a medieval delicacy, but today they have vanished from the garden scene.

and sunshine, so the leaves must never be crowded. Eventually the plants should be 15cm (6in) apart. Turnips are nicest when no larger than an apple, or even smaller. Short squat seedlings are more likely to succeed, so take out the long lanky ones and eat them as a tender green (in the southern United States, turnips are grown primarily for their leaf and never make it to root stage). Water only if the weather is particularly dry.

Spring-sown turnips are good partners for peas and can be raised between the rows; interplantings of lettuce or spinach can help to keep tiresome infestation by destructive flea beetles to a minimum.

Swedes, or rutabagas, are a variety of turnip commonly cultivated in fields, but the garden sorts are much sweeter and finer in texture. They probably originated in Scandinavia, were introduced to Scotland in the late eighteenth century, and occurred in American gardens at the beginning of the nineteenth century.

Sow the seed in early summer about 3.5cm (1.5in) deep and thin to 30cm (12in) apart. Their culture is the same as that for turnips. Swedes are hardier than turnips, so can be left in the ground over winter and pulled as needed.

I include them merely for curiosity's sake, but the early recipes for their use can be applied to parsnips, salsify and scorzonera. The plant has compound leaves and flower umbels similar to those of parsnips, but the edible roots grow in clusters, each one finger-thick, 'sweet, white, good to be eaten, and most pleasant in taste'.

Skirrets are a winter vegetable and were most successfully propagated by root division or cutting; again, Gerard on the subject: 'This Skirret is planted in Gardens, and especially by the root, for the greater and thicker ones being taken away, the lesser are put into the earth againe: which thing is best to be done in March or Aprill, before the stalks come up, and at this time the roots which be gathered are eaten raw or boiled'.

Parsnips are native to Britain and much of Europe and need no introduction. It may be that early on the wildling was found to improve by good cultivation and by selection of seed from the best plants. In 1850 the variety 'Student' was developed; it was an immediate success and is available today, retaining its popularity as a show variety.

Pliny wrote that parsnips were highly regarded by the Emperor Tiberius, who had them as tribute from the Rhineland. During medieval times parsnips were a fast-day food, particularly popular with the poor. The Elizabethans admired the sweetness of the flesh and it was among the Virginia colonists' Old World introductions.

Like all roots, parsnips appreciate the conditions afforded by the raised-bed system; but plant them on a bed that has been manured for a previous crop, since fresh manure causes the roots to fork.

Parsnip seed is slow to germinate and does so unevenly; only fresh seed should be used. It is large enough to station-sow, a few seeds to each hole. This may help when it comes to weeding, since it is important to keep the rows free of weeds until the first leaves are well established.

Sow the seed in early spring; sow shallowly, as the germinating seed is weak compared to others. A few radish seeds or a small-heading lettuce mixed with the parsnips will germinate first and so mark the sowings, and do the hard work of opening the soil surface for the sprouting parsnips. Keep the soil moist, but don't puddle. When the seeds have made their first true leaves, thin to one plant per station; shoulder-to-shoulder plants will intertwine and be deformed as a result. Plants should be 15cm (6in) apart.

If you want to grow 'beautiful' parsnips, or if the soil is stony, station-sow into 'bores' made with a broom handle. Make holes about 30cm (12in) apart and up to 60cm (2ft) deep. Move the handle around in a circular motion so that the bore is cone-shaped, and 15cm (6in) wide at the mouth. Fill with potting compost then ram the soil firmly into the bore with the end of the handle. Sow the seed and lightly cover with soil. This is the traditional method of obtaining show-quality produce.

The flavour of parsnips is matured by a good frost, so don't start harvesting until the winter has set in. They can be left in the ground and lifted as required, but usually they are lifted and stored after several sharp frosts, when the foliage has died down. Just as it is difficult to spot seedlings in the early days, a leafless parsnip easily gets lost in the vegetable garden during winter.

Parsnips are relatively free from disease; unlike carrots, which can be ruined by carrot-root fly, but there is a way around this. First a word about their history and cultivation.

The **carrot** is native to much of western Europe, and had a small following in classical antiquity. It was known by the thirteenth-century Chinese as it came from western Asia, but in England it was only during the reign of Elizabeth I that it achieved any notoriety; probably because it was sweet and the Elizabethans were quick to latch on to anything with this characteristic. This was not its only attribute, however. In 1599, carrots saved the lives of many poor people who were starving; a few years later John Parkinson recorded that 'The leaves in Autumne turne to be of a fine red or purple, the beautie whereof allureth many Gentlewomen oftentimes to gather the leaves and sticke them in their hats or heads, or pin them on their armes in stead of feathers.' Flower arrangers take note.

To obtain long tapering carrots you need a loose sandy loam, but the stubby-rooted and ball-rooted varieties do well on clay. Again they are ideal for raised beds as any manure, and only well-rotted, should be out of reach of the roots.

Carrot seed can be sown in early spring under cloches; maincrops can be sown after the soil has warmed. Sow in rows 10–15cm (4–6in) apart, 12mm (½in) deep. If you mix the seed with silver sand it will make it easier to sow thinly and also mark the row, which helps when it comes to weeding. Make successional sowings so that you can begin harvesting the carrots when they are quite small without robbing yourself of a mature crop at the end of the season. Carrots should be thinned gradually to 7.5cm (3in) apart and if you time this right, you can have bite-size carrots for salad. Alternatively, mix the seed with radishes and as you pull the radishes you thin the carrots.

Carrot-root fly is the worst pest but ringing the bed with chives or other onions, sage, or scorzonera, or interplanting with beetroot, seems to help. Tomatoes, peas and lettuce are good companions.

RECIPES

Because much medieval fare was prepared with salt-preserved meat, it was necessary to include salt-absorbers such as dried peas or beans, whole grains and, in some instances, crumbled toast, which also served to thicken the gravy. Spices like ginger, cinnamon and pepper were used by wealthier people to relieve the relentless blandness of much medieval cooking, although in some instances its chief purpose may have been to disguise foods that were past their best.

Sauerbraten (Serves 8)
This German dish combines the crumb-thickening qualities and spice in the ginger biscuits which give it its character. The sauce for the meat is similar to the popular fourteenth-century sauce called *carmeline*; according to the *Forme of Cury*, a cookery book of the period, this was made from powdered cloves, cinnamon and ginger, raisins, nut kernels, salt and vinegar, with bread as an optional ingredient.

Rub salt and pepper well into a 1.8kg (4lb) piece of chuck steak. Lay the steak in an earthenware dish over a bed of sliced onions, 2 bay leaves and a teaspoon of whole black peppercorns. Heat equal parts of vinegar and water – there should be enough to cover the meat – and sweeten to taste with brown sugar. Pour over the meat, cover the dish and leave it to marinate for 3 days.

Put the meat, onion and 125ml (4fl oz) of the marinade into a casserole and brown the meat well in a hot oven 220°C (425°F). Reduce the heat to moderate 160°C (325°F), cover the dish tightly and cook gently for 3 hours or until the meat is tender. Add more liquid during the cooking time as necessary to keep the meat moist.

Place the meat on a serving dish and keep it warm while you make the sauce. Strain off the cooking liquid and skim off most of the fat. Melt 4 tablespoons of brown sugar in a heavy-bottomed sauce-pan then slowly add the strained liquid, a handful of raisins and 6 crushed ginger biscuits. Stir the sauce until it is smooth then pour over the meat and serve. Add a tablespoon of soured cream if desired. This dish is traditionally served with egg noodles.

Garbure
For 4 people, coarsely chop 2 onions, ½ a large cabbage, 2 potatoes, 3 carrots, 3–4 small turnips and a fat clove of garlic if desired. Put all the ingredients into a large saucepan and cover. Add a couple of handfuls of dried peas (unsoaked) or haricot beans and 225–350g (8–12oz) of gammon cut into large pieces. Cover with water or chicken stock, season with pepper, summer savory or thyme and a bayleaf or two. Bring the garbure to the boil, then reduce the heat and simmer gently until the meat and vegetables are tender.

Vegetable and preserved-meat stews like garbure reflect the fare of the rural poor on festival days; at most other times of the year the stew would consist of vegetables only. The potatoes and haricots are 'modern' ingredients; leave them out and substitute cracked wheat and dried peas for medieval authenticity.

This recipe is based on Hilda Leyel's, as given in *The Gentle Art of Cookery*. She suggests that the syllable 'garb' refers to the need to eat such a dish with a fork. However, medieval diners ate with their fingers, and with one hand would remove chunks of vegetable and meat from the communal bowl, place it on their trencher of bread and then take it with the other hand to eat it. That way the fingers which were in contact with the mouth did not make contact with the communal bowl. For this reason it was exceptionally bad etiquette to scratch at the table.

Split Peas and Bacon (Serves 4–6)
Tie 225g (8oz) of split green peas in a muslin cloth. Put them into a pot with a 1kg (2lb) piece of bacon, 1 onion stuck with 2 cloves, a piece of garlic, several peppercorns and a bayleaf. Cover with water. Bring to the boil and then simmer until the bacon is tender.

Turn the pea pudding out of the muslin into a dish, add melted butter, salt and pepper to taste and serve with the bacon, sliced, and brown bread.

You could prepare this recipe leaving the peas out of the muslin and make split pea soup.

Dorothy Hartley, in her book *Food in England*, quotes a fourteenth-century recipe for beans and bacon:

Take benes and drye hem in an oven and grynde hom and winnow oute the hulles, and take and wash hom clene and do hom in a pot and seth hom and do thereto gode broth and ete hom wyth bacon.

Pea Potage
This recipe uses fresh peas; adjust the quantities to suit your needs.

Substantial dishes with a medieval taste include Garbure, with a bacon and cabbage base, Fried Parsnips dusted with cinnamon and Bean Tansy, sweetened with sugar and candied lemon and orange peel.

Shell a Quart of green Peas, and boil them in two or three Quarts of Milk, adding beaten Pepper, Salt, Mint, and sweet Marjorum powdered, and a little spice beaten. Boil it until the cream rises, and then stir and serve it hot.

From *Adam's Luxury and Eve's Cookery*, 1744

Leek and Oatmeal Soup (Serves 2–4)

This is an Irish dish, a porray of vegetable and grain. Melt 1 tablespoon of butter in 1 litre (2 pints) of liquid, half milk, half chicken stock. Bring the liquid to the boil and add 55g (2oz) of oatmeal and 6 leeks, well cleaned and coarsely chopped. Use the green leaves as well as the white. Cover and simmer until the oatmeal is cooked. Season with salt, pepper and parsley.

Garlic Vinegar

This flavoured vinegar is a delicious condiment to have on hand and a teaspoon can be added to stews or casseroles while you are softening the onions.

Bring 300ml (1 pint) of white wine vinegar to the boil. In a bowl crush 2 cloves of garlic with a teaspoon of sea salt. Pour the vinegar over the garlic. Cover and leave the vinegar to steep for several weeks before straining it off into a bottle.

Fettunta

This traditional Italian form of garlic bread, is made from large circular coarse white loaves and is superior to that made from French baguettes. It makes a flavoursome 'trencher' for sopping up tomato sauces.

Toast both sides of as many slices of bread as necessary. Crush cloves of garlic under the blade of a knife and rub the garlic over the bread on one side only. Place the bread on a flat serving dish and dribble best-quality olive oil over each slice. Scatter a little coarsely ground sea salt over the bread and serve.

Parsnips have had a bad press for far too

long, and again a culinary leaf can be taken from the old cookery manuals about how to serve this sweet root.

A kitchen *c.* 1516. Earthenware pots steam at the hearthside and a cauldron boils above the flame.

Roasted Parsnips

One of the tastiest accompaniments to a roast of beef is roasted parsnips. Use baby-sized roots, or cut larger ones into quarters, blanch them in lemon water, then put them into the fat below the roast during the last 45 minutes of cooking.

Parsnip Fritters (Serves 4)

Boil 250g (½lb) of parsnips until they are tender. Peel them and then cut them in half to remove the core which runs down the centre.

Purée the parsnips. Add 2 tablespoons of flour, 3 eggs, a tablespoon of milk, a teaspoon of sugar, a pinch of salt and a grate of nutmeg to make a stiff batter.

Heat 2mm (⅛in) oil in a frying pan and drop the batter in by the spoonful. Fry each fritter on both sides until golden.

This recipe is based on one in *Adam's Luxury and Eve's Cookery*, which recommends serving with a sauce of 'Sack and Sugar with a little Rose-Water or Verjuice. When you serve 'em to Table strew Sugar over them.'

Fried Parsnips

Take the large Roots, boil them, and strip the Skin. Then slit them long-ways into pretty thin Slices; Flower and fry them in fresh butter till they look brown. The Sauce is other sweet Butter melted. Some strew Sugar and Cinnamon upon them. Thus you may accommodate other roots. [The dusting of cinnammon is a good idea. Allow one large root per person.]

From *Acetaria*, John Evelyn 1699

Spinach and Bacon (Serves 2)

We have advanced a few centuries with the last recipes, but returning to a medieval theme, this uses either spinach or chard in a sweet-sour sauce.

Fry some fat bacon, 4 slices to 1lb of spinach, slowly so that the fat is rendered and the bacon crisp.

Add a chopped clove of garlic, and the washed and picked over spinach. Sauté gently; don't let the spinach burn. When it has wilted add 1 teaspoon each of vinegar and sugar and 2 teaspoons of cold water. Blend into the wilted spinach and serve hot.

Roasts, stews, and thick porridgey mixtures of grain made with almond milk and eggs were the main categories of food presentation in medieval times, but pies, fritters and other foods that could be served as individual food parcels and easily eaten with knives, spoons and fingers enlarged the cook's repertoire. Stuffed vegetables came into this category.

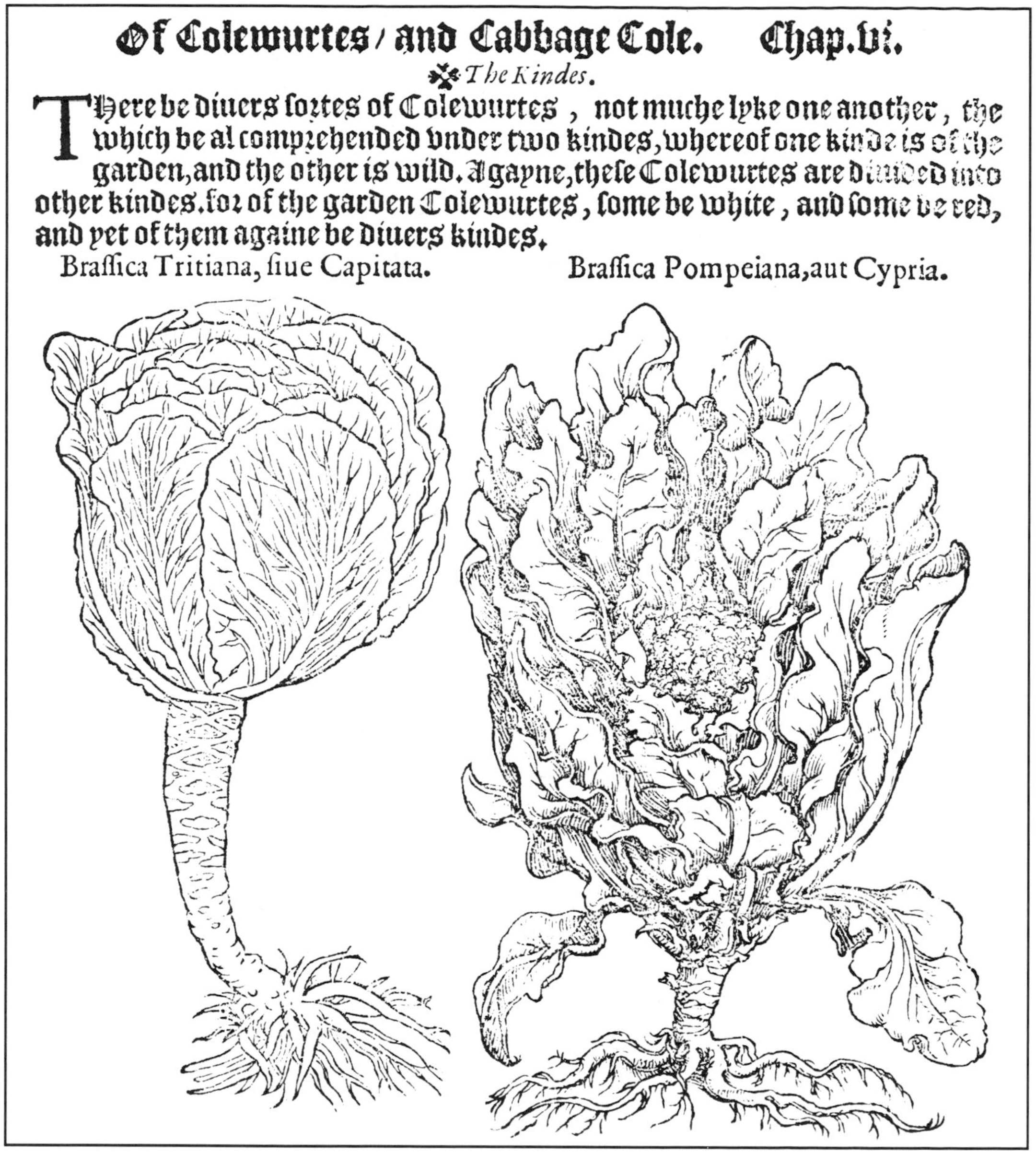
Of Colewurtes/ and Cabbage Cole. Chap.vi.
The Kindes.
There be diuers sortes of Colewurtes, not muche lyke one another, the which be al comprehended vnder two kindes, whereof one kinde is of the garden, and the other is wild. Agayne, these Colewurtes are diuided into other kindes. for of the garden Colewurtes, some be white, and some be red, and yet of them againe be diuers kindes.
Braſſica Tritiana, ſiue Capitata.
Braſſica Pompeiana, aut Cypria.

Dodoens's engraving of round-head cabbage, '*capitata*', and '*Brassica Pompeiana*': Gerard later copied this engraving exactly in his *Grete Herball* and identified it as 'Cole-Florie'.

Stuffed Cabbage (Serves 4–6)
Blanch a large cabbage in boiling water until you can separate the leaves easily but without breaking them, keeping the cabbage whole. Make at least ½kg (1lb) of stuffing from equal parts of minced veal and boiled ham, 125g (4oz) mushrooms, shallots and garlic, parsley, pot marjoram and thyme, salt and pepper to taste. Bind the mixture together with fresh bread-crumbs and 2 egg yolks. Pack the stuffing between the leaves, wrap the cabbage in a muslin cloth with a knob of butter, and steam it in a bain marie in a slow oven 150°C (300°F) until cooked through: a large cabbage will take at least 2–3 hours.

Bean Tansy (Serves 2)
A tansy is a sweet or savoury egg dish, rather like an omelette. The following uses either broad beans, peas or French beans (which did not appear in Europe until the seventeenth century).

Boil 250g (8oz) of beans until tender. Purée or process for a coarser texture. Blend into the beans 55g (2oz) of bread-crumbs, 2 whole eggs and 2 egg yolks, 1 tablespoon of sweet sherry and 25g (1oz) caster sugar.

Melt a tablespoon of butter in a heavy-bottomed frying pan. Pour in the tansy mixture and cook gently over a low heat until firm. Invert on to a warm serving dish and scatter candied orange and lemon peel over the top.

Carrot Torte (Serves 4)
Sweet-flavoured vegetables were highly valued and early cooks made far more imaginative use of carrots and parsnips than we do today. Their treatments may have been basic, but the flavours they chose to combine can give inspiration to modern cooks.

Boil 250g (8oz) of carrots until they are tender. Allow them to cool, then grate them finely. Separate 4 eggs; reserve the whites and beat the yolks until they are thick and creamy; then gradually add 250g (8oz) caster sugar. When all the sugar has been incorporated, add 250g (8oz) of chopped almonds, the grated rind and juice of half an orange and a few gratings of nutmeg. Mix these well in, then fold in the stiffly beaten egg whites.

Pour into a greased spring-form cake tin and bake in a moderate to slow oven 325°F (160°C), for almost 50 minutes, or until the centre is firm to the touch. Do not overcook or the torte will be dry.

Chill for several hours before serving with whipped cream.

CHAPTER TWO

HERBS AND SPICES

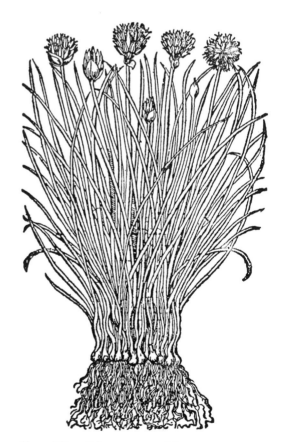

Above Allium Schoenoprasum, chives.

Opposite Detail from *Spring* by Lucas Van Valkenborch. *Reproduced by courtesy of Christie's.*

A S ENGLAND moved into the sixteenth century, priorities changed. The dissolution of the monasteries during the reign of Henry VIII moved their wealth and lands into the secular hands of minor nobility and commoners, whose service to the king was rewarded by the bestowing of manors and estates. These were gentler times, culminating with the prosperity and stability of the Virgin Queen's reign, which provided a new economic mobility for the people. With less threat of internecine war, the people were less reliant on the castle and had the confidence and the space to create unfortified homes and larger gardens. Like all new property owners, these people sought to improve their acquisitions and turned to the ideals of Renaissance Italy, where the theory and practice of garden design had reached a degree of sophistication unknown in England, but beginning to be felt in France.

The same was true of cookery. For nearly three centuries, recipes, methods of preparation, preservation and presentation had remained virtually unchanged. But as attitudes to health and diet changed and the medieval mantle fell away, a new approach was adopted. This mood of enquiry was promoted by the work of burgeoning scientific bodies (one of the earliest, founded in Italy in 1609, was called the Academia dei Lincei) and most importantly, by the invention of the movable-type printing press. Books were no longer the domain of the extremely wealthy or the monastic orders; hundreds of copies of a work could be made to satisfy a growing market, and, by making information about improved methods in both fields available to a broader spectrum of people, the press helped to revolutionise horticulture and cookery. There was now abundant information on the cultivation and preparation of new food crops, many being introduced from the New World.

Vegetables were still treated with suspicion, but fruit was gaining in popularity. The decorative face of the garden was changing, with refugees from Italy, France and Holland bringing their various skills to England; but the appearance of the kitchen garden remained much the same. The orchard, however, altered radically and the science of grafting and cultivating the finest fruit became a major concern of the ardent gardener.

Today, for most garden-lovers, considering the notion of an old-fashioned herb garden is as comforting as donning a much-loved and aged pair of slippers. Is this nothing more than nostalgia and a yearning for the simpler, calmer days which are gone forever? Or is it more complicated: has the herb garden, as the earliest form of domestic garden and the source of healing medicines and delicious scents and tastes, woven itself into the collective gardening memory, so that our affinity for it is inexplicable and unshakeable?

Certain gardens may be made of herbs, some with trees and yet others of both, when consisting only of herbs they require a poor and solid soil, so that they may produce fine plants which greatly please the sight . . . and it should be planted with fragrant herbs of all kinds, such as rue, sage, basil marjoram, mint and the like . . . let

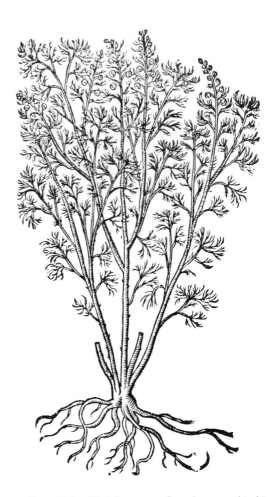

Gerard identified five sorts of southernwood in his *Grete Herball*, of which two, the female and male, *above*, known respectively as the greater and the lesser, were the most widely used for physic and for creating knot gardens.

there be a higher piece of turf made in the fashion of a seat, suitable for flowers and amenities; . . . behind the turf plot let there be a great diversity of medicinal and aromatic herbs, which not only please by the odour of their scents, but by their variety of flowers refresh the sight, among which rue should be mingled in many places for its beauty and greenness, and its bitterness will drive away poisonous animals for the garden.

From *Opus Ruralium Commodorum*, Petrus de Crescentiis, ed. 1486

This work, written at the end of the thirteenth century, described in detail, first, 'the trees and herbs according to their existing uses to the human body'; second, 'according to the pleasure they afford to the mind, consequently preserving the health of the body as the state of the body affects the mind'. It remained the foremost work on gardening and garden design until the end of the fifteenth century.

Medieval gardens were of two types: the orchard and the herb garden, which was their kitchen garden. The orchard was not a grove of fruit trees as we know it today, but a small space set aside within the castle walls; the earliest were simple patches of turf dotted with wild flowers – the flowery mede – upon which one lolled in the company of friends and lovers. This eventually transmuted into the pleasure garden of the Renaissance, with four divisions according to function: 'Potager, Bouquetier, Médicinal, Fruictier' (Olivier de Serres, *Le Théâtre d'Agriculture*, 1603).

In the potager, or kitchen garden, the tradition of growing herbs and vegetables in beds was continued: 'In such a place as the Sunne shineth upon at noone, you shall provide your beds, somewhat raised, and well mingled with Earth and Horse-dung.' The description of its siting and layout given by Estienne and Liebault in *Maison Rustique* (1570), and later translated by Gervase Markham, is curious, given later developments. It was to be separated from the pleasure grounds by a 'great Alley' three fathoms wide, surrounded by a quickset hedge. The kitchen garden was to be placed so that it could be seen from the house windows 'for pleasure', and far from the threshing floor and barn so that the crops would not be damaged by dust and chaff.

Beds, or 'floores' as they were called, were given to monocultures of beets, turnips, spinach, orach, rocket, parsley and sorrel, onions, garlic, scallions and carrots. There were also to be floores for

slips [cuttings], to be set upon as well as for maintaining a Plat of sweet flowers as well as for borders, and for winter pot herbs. To this end prepare a bed for sage, hyssop, thyme, marjoram, lavender, Rosemary, Southernwood, Savorie, Costmarie, Basil, Spike, Balm, Pennyroyal and Camomill for to make seats and a labyrinth. Also, shape out . . . a Physic garden near to the enclosed ground for fruit for Physick Herbs [which included asparagus].

Knots, neat clipped hedges of herbs set in patterns and infilled with coloured earth or flowers, were primarily emblematic – the devices of allegory – a style of literary reference much loved during the Renaissance. The knot garden had its roots in the gardens of classical Italy, where hedges of box and topiary were considered essential to a garden's design; the Latin word *toparius* described a gardener, and knots gained popularity in English gardens during the fourteenth century. But the knot garden's greatest period of popularity was during the sixteenth and seventeenth centuries. In his book *The Country Housewife's Garden*, the first gardening book written expressly for women, William Lawson declared: 'the number of formes, Mazes and Knots is so great, and men are so diversely delighted, that I leave every Housewife to her selfe, especially seeing to set down many, had been but to fill much paper'. In other words, there were so many patterns of knots in

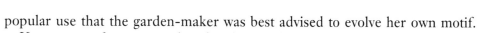

A knot garden of individual beds
edged and divided internally by clipped hedges of scented shrubs
is shown in this illustration from the frontispiece of
the 1597 edition of Gerard's herbal.

The female, or greater southernwood from
Gerard's herbal. He described how this plant,
'with careful manuring' would 'grow to be as high
as a man', in contrast to the low-growing 'male'
sort shown opposite.

popular use that the garden-maker was best advised to evolve her own motif.

Knots were of two types: closed and open. Closed knots had lines of shrubby herbs like rosemary, thyme or hyssop forming the motif which was picked out in flowers or coloured gravel with paths between the beds. Closed knots had no paths and consisted of monocolour flower infills between the lines of herbs.

So herbs were cultivated for the pot, as we know, and some had moved out into the decorative garden; but their most important use remained as medicine or 'physick'. More books and treatises were appearing on gardening and cooking, but each plant description was accompanied by an outline of its virtues: which afflictions the herb could treat. The medieval guilty conscience about anything done purely for pleasure was hard to appease.

Women, then as now, took the lead in caring, nourishing and providing for the daily family wants. The sixteenth-century housewife's knowledge of physic was considered her most valuable quality. In her stillroom she prepared the balms, infusions, poultices and unguents to cure her family and servants (and livestock, in the case of a country housewife); her second most vital ability was a 'perfect skill and knowledge in Cookery'; for which the 'first step thereunto is, to have knowledge of all sorts of Herbs belonging to the Kitchin', and she should also know how to sow and grow each (Gervase Markham, *The English Housewife*, 13th edn., 1576). She was doctor, chef and gardener.

Sage, Clary, Rosemary, Bay, Hyssop, Thyme, Savory

An Arabian proverb asks, 'How can a man die who has **sage** in his garden?', and in 1699 John Evelyn remarked, 'Tis a plant, indeed, with so many and wonderful properties as that the assiduous use of it is said to render men immortal'. Gracious! and most of us think that its only use is to flavour pork.

The veneration of sage as the immortal herb goes beyond pre-history and circles the globe. The Dutch found, much to their pecuniary satisfaction, that the Chinese were willing to trade three pounds of tea for one of sage. In 1772, Sir John Hill recorded the case of one old woman whose great age labelled her a witch. She had a small walled enclosure of five yards square at her front door, full of sage, which was her only food.

As well as the familiar grey-green-leaved garden sage, *Salvia offincinalis*, there is the red-leaved variety, *S. off. purpurea*; this type was the most highly prized in olden times; there is also the white-flowered *S. off. alba* and the cream-and-pink variegated *S. off. tricolor*. All these sages are evergreen shrubs that thrive in full sun and light sandy soil. Plant in spring about 45cm (18in) apart; they reach about 45–60cm (18–24in) in height, but the plants are best kept trimmed to keep them from going straggly. Clip off the new shoots as they appear. Use some fresh, dry others and use some to propagate. Soft cuttings, about 10cm (4in) long, will root easily inserted in sand under glass under shady places. Trim off the bottom leaves and insert them in rooting compost to half their depth. They will be ready for planting out by the following spring.

Plant sage with cabbages and carrots, but keep it away from cucumbers. 25g

I *Salvia maior.*
Great Sage.

Salvia major, the Great Sage, from Gerard's herbal. He also described the variegated or painted sage which we know as *S. tricolor*, crediting John Tradescant with its introduction.

(1oz) each of sage and China tea infused in 1 litre (2 pints) of boiling water, and then reduced to a third of the original quantity, make a rinse for dark hair.

Salvia sclarea, or **clary sage**, is mainly a herb for physic; its other common names of eyebright and clear eye are a good indication of its properties, but it can be used to flavour soups and stews. It has highly aromatic leaves and pale blue-and-white flowers.

Clary is a pretty flower to include in the kitchen garden. It is a biennial and grows

to 75cm (30in). Sow during the spring in a well-drained sunny site, in well-prepared soil. Sow the seed 2.5cm (1in) deep and thin the seedlings to at least 30cm (12in) apart. Clary transplants easily, so it is easiest to raise stocks in a nursery bed to plant out in flowering positions in the spring. Harsh winters and cold heavy soils may kill off young plants.

'Make thee a box of the wood of **rosemary** and smell to it and it shall preserve thy youth', says Banckes' *Herball* of 1525. Rosemary defined the renewal of waning energy in the French language of flowers, and also is the symbol of fidelity between lovers, due to its designation as the herb of remembrance. It is native to the western shores of the Mediterranean, was used by the Greeks and Romans, and by Arab physicians in thirteenth-century Spain, and was first noted as a flavouring in the late fifteenth century, as a common seasoning for salted meat.

But it was the Elizabethans who cherished rosemary far beyond the other garden herbs and flowers. Brides wore it wreathed in their hair; it was given with orange pomanders at New Year; and in gardens where it clothed the walls, trained against a wire trellis, its abundance indicated that the mistress ruled the roost: conversely, where it waned, the master dominated. Apparently, some hen-pecked husbands were bold enough to engage in some clandestine pruning to throw neighbours off the scent.

There are many forms of rosemary, including prostrate and upright-growing

Left to right Rosemary, bay and sage

varieties, and ones with gold and silver variegated leaf; the gold is hard to come by and has to be protected from cold frosts but it is worth having for its uniqueness.

Apart from its value in the kitchen, rosemary is a valuable decorative shrub, its spiky habit and subtle grey-green leaves making a distinctive hedge or wall covering. It is a true sun-lover and needs a sheltered spot in cold gardens. It likes limy soil that is well drained, but it needn't be particularly rich. For a hedge, plant 60cm (2ft) apart. Semi-hard-wood cuttings taken in late summer and inserted in sandy soil in shade will root easily; take these about 10–15cm (4–6in) long. Hard-wood cuttings can be taken in early autumn. The best plants, though, are raised from seed sown in a warm sunny spot in spring.

Sage and rosemary grow well together, but otherwise rosemary is a plant to grow for its beauty and flavour alone, and to benefit honey bees.

Longevity from sage, vigour from rosemary – and strength from **bay**, for bay was the ancient symbol of valour and victory. The Romans sealed dispatches announcing victory with a bayleaf and the heroes of war were crowned with laurel; in Greece prize-winning athletes and scholars wore diadems of bay.

Laurus nobilis denotes its regal connotations; and Parkinson remarked that 'It serveth to adorne the house of God, as well as of man . . . to crowne or encircle as with a garland, the heads of the living, and to sticke and decke forth the bodies of the dead; so that from the cradle to the grave we have still use of it, we have still neede of it.'

Bay is not to be confused with Portuguese laurel, which is toxic. Crushed bay leaves have the distinctive spicy aroma; laurel leaves are duller, softer and more pointed than the glossy bay leaf.

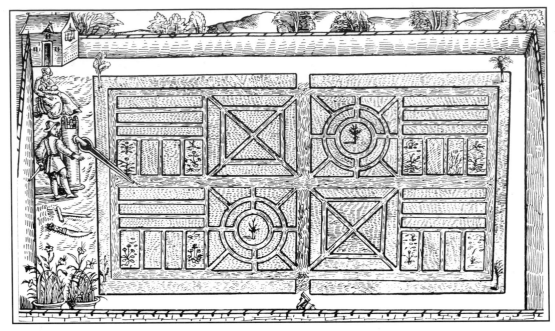

Thomas Hyll's *Gardener's Labyrinth* (1577) featured several ingenious methods of watering the beds, including this irrigation system using the paths surrounding the beds, fed from a hand-pump.

Bays are evergreen natives of the Mediterranean and will succumb to cold dry winds in times of heavy frost. The best place for a bay is against a warm wall. Bays can be trained against the wall if the back branches are kept clipped, but free-standing specimens are the ideal. Given time and a chance to establish, a bay will reach a maximum of 15m (50ft), but we commonly see them in gardens as clipped accent shrubs; little balls atop straight-arrow trunks, pyramids and so on.

Plant any time from mid-autumn to mid-spring in rich peaty soil. Bay is easily propagated from hard-wood cuttings in autumn, rooted in sandy soil under glass.

'Purge me with **hyssop**, and I shall be clean; wash me, and I shall be whiter than snow', is just one of the many biblical references to this resinous herb. Its name is of Greek origin, from *azob*, meaning 'holy herb': it has held its spiritual connotations at least since classical times. Originally, the cleansing qualities of the resinous leaves were valued above any culinary contributions. Among the Elizabethans it was a favourite strewing herb, and hyssop oil was used for personal delousing. In the knot garden the shrub was much used for constructing low hedges, for it stands hard clipping in autumn after its soft mauve, pink and white flowers have faded; hyssop will bloom for the entire summer.

The whole plant is highly fragrant with a curious and not unpleasant blend of spice and camphor. The young shoots and flowers featured in early Italian and French cookery, but it is a flavouring to be used with discretion. It is native to southern Europe and the Middle East and therefore prefers a sunny position and well-drained soil.

Hyssop plants can be raised from seed sown in spring, either under glass or *in situ*; the preferred method is by taking cuttings of new growth in the spring and lining them out in a coldframe. Alternatively, use pieces pulled from the base of old plants; these may have roots and can be planted out to continue growth. New plants should be planted in the spring, at about 45cm (18in) apart for hedging. Hyssop is a hardy evergreen that requires little attention once established. Keep it tidy by regular clipping; harvest before the flower petals open.

Bees and butterflies adore hyssop, and for this reason alone it is worth having a bush or two in the garden. It is traditionally planted with grapevines to improve yields. Planted with cabbages, the fragrance will discourage white fly.

Thyme gives you courage, or so the Roman soldiers believed: they bathed in thyme-scented water before battle. To be told that you smelled of thyme was high praise in ancient Greece – it meant that you had style; they also burned thyme to cleanse their temples. The Romans introduced the herb to northern Europe and it was immediately popular, used as a strewing herb, in tussie mussies and sweet powders, and in the kitchen. That this herb should be given such powerful attributes is not altogether surprising, for in the kitchen it is one of the most flavourful herbs and should be used sparingly.

There are over a hundred species of thyme, all descended from wild thyme, *Thymus serpyllum*, commonly called 'mother of thyme'; the culinary variety is *T. vulgaris*, although the lemon-scented *T. citriodorus* can be used successfully with fish and poultry, and is the hardiest for gardens in cold climates.

'Beneath your feet, Thyme that for all your bruising smells more sweet'; there are many forms of creeping thyme, some with shiny dark leaves, others woolly or variegated gold and silver. Used at the front of a border or near pathways, these herbs will spread out and scent the air as you pass, crushing the leaves underfoot. One of the great pleasures of summer is to catch a whiff of sun-warmed wild thyme growing in an open meadow or next to the road.

Bees are attracted to thyme, and the famous Greek Hymettus honey is highly prized for its spicy flavour, derived from the thyme which flourishes on the sides of Mount Hymettus.

Garden thyme has a neat habit, is evergreen and can be used as a path edging. It enjoys a sunny spot in well-drained light soil, enriched with well-rotted manure. On heavy soils it doesn't perform so well, or smell or taste as strongly. Plant in the spring about 15cm (6in) apart. Thyme plants use up the goodness in the soil quickly, so an annual manure mulch is a good idea. Otherwise, renew the stocks every three to four years from seed (in the right conditions it self-sows readily), or by dividing mature plants in the spring. As with hyssop, pieces pulled from old plants may have roots and can be planted out. Harvest branches for drying when the flowers first appear.

Lemon thyme is cultivated in much the same manner, but try to propagate from those plants which have the strongest scent; self-sown seedlings may not be up to scratch.

One variety of thyme that is worth having as a curiosity is *T. herba-barona*, which takes its name from the tradition of using it to season a baron of beef. It is a creeping groundcover, tasting strongly of caraway.

Thyme is reputed to discourage mice, and an infusion of the leaves sprayed on members of the cabbage family will help control white fly.

The annual **summer savory** (*Satureia hortensis*) and the evergreen **winter savory** (*S. montana*) are common to European and American gardens. The former is of the greatest culinary value, although I find that winter savory, if a little coarse, has a pleasing sharpness useful for making cheese.

Savory was introduced to England by the Romans, who made with it a vinegar sauce similar to today's mint sauce, and soon found a place in native cooking. Virgil described savory as the best fragrant herb to be grown near beehives, and both savories were included in John Josslyn's list of plants grown in the new American colonies to remind the settlers of home.

Summer savory was used like parsley to garnish dishes and is commonly called the bean herb, particularly to be eaten with broad beans. A 'handful of sliced horse-radish-root, with a handsome little faggot of rosemary, thyme and winter savory' is the *Compleat Angler*'s choice of herbs for trout; a trifle overpowering I'd have thought.

Sow the seeds of summer savory in early spring in a prepared bed in drills 6mm (¼in) deep, then thin the seedlings to 15cm (6in). The seed is slow to germinate, so it might be advisable to sow in trays and prick out into a nursery bed. Give this savory sunshine and well-drained manured soil.

Winter savory is a shrubby perennial that does best in sunshine in a poor soil. Plant and propagate in the spring; soft cuttings will root easily in sandy soil in a coldframe.

Harvest the leaves before the flowers appear in midsummer; cut the plant back hard to encourage a second crop. Plants are good for four or five years if trimmed in the autumn and mulched with well-rotted manure. They make a good low hedge or border.

Sow summer savory with beans and onions, and use winter savory against aphids. Both winter and summer savory are excellent bee plants and, curiously, an old remedy for bee or wasp stings is to rub the spot with crushed fresh savory.

Borage, Chive, Tansy, Lovage, Horseradish, Southernwood, Wormwood, Rue

Borage is most famous for the mild cucumber freshness imparted by its young shoots and flowers, blue as a summer sky with a tiny black eye. They are a welcome addition to salads and summer drinks, especially Pimms. But among Elizabethan needlewomen the flowers were a favourite embroidery motif, probably because it was one of the Cordial plants and so an emblem of happiness, 'cordial' implying the sense of happiness and contentment imparted by the plant. According to *The Tresurie of Hidden Secrets and Commodious Conceits* (1596), 'conserve of Borage is especially good against melancholie; it maketh one merrie'. This conserve and a distillation of the flowers were often given to invalids and those of weak spirit: as the old saying goes, '*Ego Borago, Gaudia semper ago* – I, Borage, Bring alwaies courage'.

The flowers were also candied or dried to use in pot-pourri, and the young top growth was frequently used as a pot herb or salad green. Dried and burned, the ashes were used as a gargle to clear mouth ulcers and borage syrup made from the leaf juices was used to treat fevers and jaundice.

The Romans probably introduced borage to Britain where it is now a common wild flower. Borage was among the plants grown by Columbus's crew on Isabela Island and so was one of the earliest imports to the New World.

Borage is a hardy annual that grows readily from seed sown in the spring; in fact, one you have a borage plant you can allow it to seed itself, which it will do wherever the seed can reach. It will grow in any soil but prefers one that is loose, gravelly and slightly alkaline. Borage will flower throughout the summer and until it is knocked down by the frost.

Bees are extremely fond of borage and for this reason it should be planted amongst fruit trees to aid pollination. The leaves are a rich source of potassium and thus a useful addition to the compost heap.

Chive is a member of the allium family, being *Allium schoenoprasum*. It is a hardy perennial that grows easily from seed sown in the spring. Chive plants are often recommended as border plants in the garden, but they are not evergreen, so if you decide to use them in this fashion, do so where you do not wish a permanently defined line, as you would, for example, in a knot garden.

Once a clump is established you can begin gathering for use by cutting bunches of leaves close to the ground. This encourages the clump to spread and grow more densely. Most people who grow chives for seasoning pinch out the flower shoots as they appear; allow the plants to flower, however, if you are growing mainly for decoration, as the small bright pink flower umbels are an extremely pretty addition to the garden, and to salads – they are also edible.

Chive is one of the few herbs traditionally more valued as a condiment than as a physic, appearing in a fifteenth-century cookery manuscript, noted by Gerard as a 'pleasant Sawce and good Potherb', and continuing in popularity until the mid-1700s when it was noted that chives were widely grown in London nursery gardens. One hundred years later, Loudon remarked that chives' chief purpose appeared to be as a food additive for young guinea fowl and chickens. Such are the whims of culinary fashion.

Related, but with an entirely different flavour, is the Chinese or garlic chive, *Allium tuberosum*. Its leaves are flat and more grass-like than the hollow tubular blades of chive and the taste is distinctly garlicky. It is raised easily from seed sown in spring and is almost evergreen.

Chive is an invaluable companion plant to be used with carrots against carrot fly, among roses against black spot and in strong infusion as a spray against powdery mildew.

Tansy is a tall-growing perennial herb that can spread quite quickly, so it needs to be kept in check in the herb garden. It has compound feathery leaves and in late summer clusters of bright yellow button-like flowers. It was long thought to be a purifying herb, used for strewing and as a fly repellent; the ancient Greeks thought that it preserved dead bodies, and it gave Ganymede immortality. In the sixteenth century, William Turner described how 'Our weomen in Englande and some men that be sunneburnt and would be fayre, eyther stepe this herbe in white wyne and wash their faces with the wyne or ellis with the distilled water of the same'.

The purifying tradition carried over into the kitchen; from the sixteenth century, tansy cakes were eaten to purify the body after the Lenten fast. Eaten on Easter day, tansy was said to recall the bitter herbs of the Israelites. But the herb cake was accompanied by ham to indicate in no uncertain terms that the household was not Jewish. From this, no doubt, springs the baked ham that is traditional Easter fare in many households.

Eventually, as we have seen, tansy came

Left to right Tansy and borage.

The scentless but large-flowered Great Unsavorie Tansy from Gerard's herbal.

to mean any egg-based dish to which green herbs or other flavouring was added, rather like an omelette and either sweet or savoury: Isaak Walton gave a recipe for Minnow Tansy, but I think that recipes for tansy as 'boiled Herbaceous Dishes' are more pleasing.

Tansy does best in moist ground; wild tansy grows by ponds and in marshy places and has a better aroma than garden-cultivated plants. But it is rampant, so keep it confined to the border surrounding the kitchen or herb garden.

Lovage is another border plant and, with angelica, is one of the more stately herbs, reaching 1.8m (6ft) or more. It does well in semi-shade and likes moist soil for its deep-reaching roots. Lovage can be raised easily from seed sown in a nursery bed in early spring, and then planted out into the garden wherever vertical emphasis is needed the following year. It self-sows easily, so watch for seedlings to replenish stocks, as the plants should be replaced every 3–5 years. The foliage is quite attractive in the garden, and in the kitchen the shiny green leaves are a good substitute for celery in stews or salads. Unfortunately, lovage is a martyr to black aphids, so spray with insecticide at the first sign of attack.

The stems were once candied like angelica and the seeds have a hot, peppery flavour. In spite of the fact that it is one of our oldest garden herbs, it has little mythology attached to it, although medically it was used as a gargle to ease sore throats, and lovage tea was taken to soothe rheumatic joints.

Horseradish should also be grown in a perimeter border, in well-cultivated soil enriched with plenty of manure. It is propagated by root division in early spring; drop the roots into dibbed holes 38cm (15in) deep and about 30cm (12in) apart. Sprinkle some fine soil into the hole around the roots, then draw in garden soil to fill the planting hole, and firm well. Keep weed-free and water occasionally. A bed of horseradish is a permanent feature and the roots will spread rapidly if not controlled; regular harvesting should keep it in check, and the roots can be stored in boxes of dry sand for use during the winter.

The volatile oils of horseradish which give it its hot taste are released only through grating; this heat was much valued as a stimulant taken internally or externally. Raw horseradish was often used as a poultice or plaster to relieve neuralgia, chilblains and gout. Infusions made with milk were used as facial cleansers, and in vinegar to clear freckles. Children suffering from whooping cough were treated with the vinegar infusion diluted with water and sweetened with honey, since horseradish aids breathing and helps to clear congestion and improve the circulation; it was often prescribed to patients recovering from heart attack. But its chief attribute is as a digestive stimulant, and for this reason grated horseradish mixed with vinegar or cream is often served with oily fish and red meat, like mackerel or smoked salmon, and most famously with roast ribs of beef.

Horseradish was not recognised as a condiment in England until the end of the sixteenth century, when Gerard commented that 'the Horse Radish stampled with a little vinegar put thereto, is commonly used among the Germans for sauce to eat fish with and such like meates as we do mustarde'. But by the eighteenth century, John Evelyn was calling it an 'excellent, universal condiment' used as mustard in salads and with any other dish.

There is a tradition that horseradish is detrimental to the healthy growth of vines; yet setting clumps at the foot of potato beds is reckoned to be beneficial to both.

The genus *Artemisia* provides us with one of our most delicious flavouring herbs, **tarragon**, *A. dracunculus*, which is a herbaceous perennial, and two attractive evergreen shrubs, southernwood, *A. abrotanum* and wormwood, *A. absinthium*.

To begin with tarragon: this is the herb which John Evelyn advised should never be left out of salads: ' 'Tis highly cordial and friendly to the head, heart and liver.'

Tarragon is a native of Siberia, and had made an impression in Europe by the late Middle Ages. The thirteenth-century botanist, Ibnal Bayter, names it *tarkhun* or little dragon. The French word *estragon* also meant little dragon and so the name came down to us. It was first noted in English gardens during the Tudor period

Draco herb.t.
Tarragon.

Tarragon, called *Draco herba* by Gerard, from his herbal.

and Gerard had it in his garden at Holborn. He referred to it as *Draco herba* and said that it is cherished in gardens.

Describing its form Gerard compared it to couch-grass, with roots which are 'long, fibrous, creeping farre abroad under the earth ... by which sprouting forth it increaseth, yielding no seed at all'. From this we know he grew true French tarragon which is almost always sterile. This is not true of the other sort, Russian tarragon, *A. dracunculoides*. It is coarser in texture and has less taste than the French sort. So be on your guard when purchasing plants.

Tarragon needs a warm site with some shelter and light rich soil. The roots should be planted at least 7.5cm (3in) deep in the spring. If the winter is likely to be very harsh, it is worth lifting a few roots to overwinter. Lay them in sandy soil in a shallow box and store in a cool, frostproof place. Alternatively, give the tarragon bed a thick mulch blanket after the stems have been cut back to ground level at the end of the season.

Propagate by root division in the spring or else by soft stem cuttings taken in early summer. Prick the cuttings into a box and put them in a shady place. The young plants should be ready to plant out the following spring.

Fresh tarragon can be had during the winter by forcing roots in the same manner as for mint; dried tarragon loses much of the herb's subtlety.

Tarragon is chiefly valued as a culinary herb, although the root was said to soothe toothache. Its sister plants, however, are age-old physic herbs, esteemed for their antiseptic qualities. The Greeks and Romans numbered **southernwood** among the aphrodisiac plants and it was used, as was **wormwood**, as a vermifuge, strewn on floors and in linen cupboards to ward off fleas, lice and all the other nasties which plagued our ancestors. (Hence its French name of *garderobe*.) Branches of these herbs were included in the tussie mussies carried by judges and others to ward off gaol fever and the plague. Southernwood's astringent smell was sufficiently stimulating to prevent people dropping off during interminable Sunday sermons, so our ancestors carried bunches of it and lemon balm to sniff while they munched caraway or dill seeds to be sure of staying awake. However, in 1772, Sir John Hill recommended southernwood tea as being pleasant and 'it always disposes persons to sleep'.

In the herb or kitchen garden these two shrubs make admirable edging and are ideal for clipping to form knots. They enjoy a sunny spot and well-drained soil and should be planted about 25–30cm (10–12in) apart. Clip them over in the spring to keep the shrubs neat. The clippings can then be used for propagation; they should be about 12cm (5in) long and will root easily in light sandy soil. Remove the leaves from the lower half of the stem, trim the end to just below a leaf node and arrange the cuttings around the perimeter of an earthenware flowerpot, spaced about 2.5cm (1in) apart. Put the pot in a shaded place and keep watered.

Rue is another useful edging herb with distinctive blue-grey foliage. It can be left to form a rounded bush but regular clipping encourages better shape and foliage. It will grow in the poorest soils as long as it has plenty of sun and can be easily propagated by soft cuttings as described above.

Rue is a Mediterranean native and was much used by the Greeks and Romans as a culinary as well as a physic herb. It has the same antiseptic attributes as the artemisias and was also used in tussie mussies. Rue was Shakespeare's 'sour herb of grace' (*Richard III*) and it was the herb of repentance, used in the Middle Ages to sprinkle holy water during the contrition which preceded Holy Communion. Rue was meant to be an antidote to lethal poisons and to counteract the spells of witches. More commonly, a nibble of rue was meant to ease eye strain and indigestion; crushed rue leaves applied externally were said to relieve the pain of sciatica, and held against the temples cured headache. Italians include rue in salads, but other than that its modern culinary applications are few.

Use either of these shrubs near cabbages or fruit trees in order to repel moths and caterpillars.

Mustard, Marjoram and Mint

Many of us use prepared mustard without a great deal of thought, yet since the days of the Roman Empire **mustard** has been one of the most popular condiments and herbs for physic, and mustard plasters are still considered efficacious against chest infections like bronchitis. In the Middle Ages, mustard achieved its greatest success as a sauce, and its sale was so universally profitable that it soon gained the attentions of unscrupulous merchants, whose profligate adulterations caused legislation in France, and a plea for similar regulations in England, to control the quality.

There are three distinct species of mustard: *Brassica nigra*, or black mustard, which was the most widely used type until superseded by *B. juncea*, the brown or Indian mustard, which is a smaller plant and better suited to mechanical harvesting, and *B. alba*, known in England as white mustard and in America (where it is most widely used) as yellow mustard.

B. alba makes a small plant (it is the one originally used in the mixed-salad sprouts 'mustard and cress', now replaced by rape). In China the green leaves are pickled for winter use, and the young leaves of this species, and those of *B. nigra*, cut close to the ground shortly after they emerge, are delicious in salads. It really isn't practicable to grow seeds for home use; but do try sprouting them on a damp cloth for use in salads.

> O bind them posies of pleasant flowers,
> Of marjoram, mint and rue.

The fragrance of **marjoram** has long been admired; Theophrastus included it in his list of perfumes and the Elizabethans counted it amongst their most useful strewing herbs. Parkinson wrote: 'The sweete Marieromes are not onely much used to please the outward senses in nosegayes, and in the windowes of houses, as also in sweete pouders, sweete bags, and sweete washing waters . . . .'

Marjoram had magical powers: if young people anointed themselves with the herb blended with powdered marigolds, thyme and wormwood on St Luke's Day, they would dream of their future spouse.

The most popular sort was sweet or knotted marjoram, *Origanum majorana*, which is hardy only in its native Mediterranean countries. In cool climates it should be treated as a half-hardy annual, sown under glass in early spring, hardened off and then planted out in early summer in light, well-drained soil in full sun in the warmest part of the garden. It makes a tall plant, up to 60cm (24in).

Pot marjoram, *O. onites*, is lower growing and is a hardy perennial, so it is more often grown in northern gardens. It can be propagated by seed or division and enjoys the same conditions as its sister.

In cooking, pot marjoram has the stronger flavour, and knotted marjoram should be added only at the last moment to perfume the dish as well as to lend its distinct flavour. The flowering shoots of both types can be dried for winter use.

Wild marjoram, *Origanum vulgare*, is the **oregano** of Neapolitan cookery, and without which pizza could not exist. It is so redolent of Italy that it is hard to believe that oregano grows wild on the chalk cliffs of southern England. But it is the Mediterranean sun which gives the herb its flavour; in northern gardens and in England, it loses its zing and is simply an attractive creeping herb.

Mints, however, thrive in cool moist soils, and bring a warmth and freshness to summer dishes and beverages. Spearmint, *Mentha viridis*, is the species most common to kitchen gardens, but the space would be better used by *M. rotundifolia*, also known as Bowles or apple mint, which has round, furry leaves and a finer flavour.

Early on, the medicinal qualities of mint were legion; Gerard gives no less than forty maladies soothed by various preparations of the herb. It was used to perfume bath water and as a strewing herb in churches; and the smell alone was enough to improve memory and banish headache. Oil of peppermint, *M. piperita*, is used in preference to the actual leaves for flavouring syrups and candies, as well as the liqueur crème de menthe.

All mints increase by means of creeping roots and are invasive. Parkinson complained of all the mints that 'the rootes runne creeping in the ground, and . . . will hardly be cleared out of a garden, being once therein, in that the smallest peece thereof will growe and encrease apace'. For that reason, mint is often planted in a bottomless tin bucket sunk into the bed which helps to contain the roots.

Nothing compares to fresh mint, and if it is grown in a sheltered spot, there should be leaves throughout winter. Otherwise, lift a few roots and plant them in a box kept under the greenhouse staging for a supply of fresh shoots.

Dried mint leaves are said to repel rats and mice, but the plant's invasive qualities limit its use as a companion in the kitchen garden.

Left Mint, *top* mustard seed sprouts and *right* marjoram.

Coriander, Parsley, Carrot

Coriander, sometimes known as cilantro or Chinese parsley, is a Middle Eastern native with pungently flavoured sour leaves and spicy orange-tasting seeds esteemed for their medicinal properties and in cookery; over 5,000 years ago the Chinese used the roots and the seeds; and the manna received by the Israelites is described in the Bible as 'like coriander seed, white; and the taste of it was like wafers made of honey'. The leaves are used in soup by the Egyptians, and are much used by the Chinese, Peruvians and Mexicans, but their flavour is not to everyone's taste: it can have heavy overtones of bath soap. But used with a light hand in stuffings for lamb or pork it makes a pleasant change from the standard herbs. The Romans introduced the herb to Northern Europe and today the seeds are used to flavour liqueurs, candies and seed breads.

Coriander is a hardy annual that likes full sun and rich soil. Since you need to use so little of it there is no need to give it much space. Sow the seed shallowly in the spring and thin to 15cm (6in). It germinates easily and crops quickly. Make a second sowing in the late summer or early autumn; coriander is fairly hardy, and late-sown crops will not run to seed but make more and finer foliage. Don't use the seed fresh: its flavour is only palatable when dried, so leave the seedheads on the plant to mature and harvest when the shells go papery brown. If left to fall to the ground, coriander will self-sow. It is a good bee plant, and does well if sown with anise. Aphids dislike coriander, so use it among roses and fruit trees.

Parsley should be in every garden, yet many people are chary of sowing the seed in the superstitious belief that for them it will not germinate: and wait for some gifted friend or relative to perform the deed. The seed is notoriously slow to germinate; it has to go seven times to the Devil and back first. In 1577, Thomas Hyll gave a technique which involved soaking seed in vinegar and covering the bed with a woollen blanket (among other things), so that the seed would appear in an hour. I hope none of us is that anxious; but some gardeners swear by boiling water, using it to soak the seed, or pouring it onto the seed bed. Others recommend patience; too many people give up when there are no seedlings in evidence after a week. This method serves me well, but I do like Aunt Marjorie to sow the seed! It is believed to be unlucky to transplant parsley. Perhaps this herb's association with death accounts for the many taboos; its earliest known use was by the ancient Greeks, who used it for funeral garlands.

There are two main types of parsley: the moss or crispy curled, with which we are most familiar, and the broadleaf or Continental parsley (also identified as either French or Italian!), which has a much more distinctive and pervasive flavour, retained even when dried, which is more than you can say for common moss parsley.

Sow the seed in the spring in a shady sheltered spot in rich moist soil. Sow it shallowly and thin the plants to about 25cm (10in). For winter crops make another sowing at midsummer; winter-grown plants may require cloche protection.

When picking parsley, don't rob one plant of all its leaves, but gather from several. Parsley makes an attractive edging to paths and flowerbeds, and in this way, with patience, you will be assured of a ready supply. Parsley is also meant to repel onion and carrot-root flies and is a companion plant for asparagus and tomatoes.

Chervil has a finer flavour than parsley and is one of the classic *fines herbes*. It is not particular about soil, although early crops prefer a sunny spot, while those sown in summer like some shade. Chervil preceded parsley into Britain; the Romans brought chervil, while it is suspected that parsley didn't appear until the mid-1500s. Chervil was the more popular of the two; the Dutch had a dish called *warmus* flavoured with chervil and Gerard recommended the boiled roots for use in salads. (There is also a parsley known as Hamburg parsley which is grown for its root.) The herb was meant to be especially good as a restorative tonic for the elderly. Today this

Parsley grown in a hanging basket makes an attractive patio-garden feature.

mildly aniseed-flavoured herb is more widely used in France than either England or America.

Chervil is one of the few herbs that prefers a semi-shaded position, and so can be interplanted with taller crops, among tomatoes, beans or sweet corn, for example. It self-sows readily, which is handy since only the freshest seed is likely to germinate. Chervil is remarkably hardy, so a few plants left to make seed will keep the kitchen supplied through the winter.

In her book *Culinary and Salad Herbs*, Eleanour Sinclair Rohde describes how cottagers made parsley baskets: 'These baskets were made by lining a wire basket with moss and filling it with good soil, and then about a dozen parsley roots were pushed in at the top, bottom, and sides and the soil made very firm.' The parsley baskets were hung in a sunny window and a well-tended, regularly picked basket made a ball of dense green foliage. This is a particularly useful idea for city dwellers, whose window sills may already be crowded with well-stocked boxes of other herbs.

Most herbs are ideal subjects for window-box cultivation and, provided that the box is well made and well tended, the plants will thrive, since the window-box provides them with exactly the growing conditions they desire – sun and fertile, well-drained soil.

This title-page engraving from Lonicer's *Botanico* of 1565 shows a gaggle of apothecaries haggling with a herb dealer, while at the far right a gardener harvests herbs from a raised bed. To the left in the foreground, herbs and roots are being sorted and pounded in a mortar while alembics distil the medicos' potions to be administered to the bed-ridden patient.

BOTANICON.

PLANTARVM HISTO=

RIAE, CVM EARVNDEM AD VIVVM ARTIFICIOSE EXPRESSIS ICONIBVS, TO-mi duo, per ADAMVM LONICERVM, Medicum Phyſicum Francofortenſem.

ADDITA SVNT

Animantium Terreſtrium, Volatilium & Aquatilium breuis deſcriptio.

Item : *De Gemmarum, Metallorum, Succorumⓠ concretorum uera cognitione, delectu & uiribus.*

Præterea : De ſtillatitiorum liquorum ratione, & inſtrumentorum ad eam artem præparatione, compendioſa tractatio.

POSTREMO

ONOMASTICON, *quo uariæ plantarum nomenclaturæ ex diuerſis linguis, item uoces, quarum frequens in deſcriptioni-bus uſus eſt, explicantur.*

OMNIA DE NOVO RECOGNITA. Indice adiecto Quintuplici.

Cum Gratia & Priuilegio Imperiali.

FRANCOFORTI, APVD HAEREDES *Chriſtiani Egenolphi,* 1565.

Dill, Basil, Angelica, Costmary, Caraway, Anise, Fennel

Dill may be similar in appearance to fennel, but its flavour could not be more different: clean and refreshing and utterly unique. Today it is most used in the cuisines of eastern Europe, Russia and Scandinavia, although in the sixteenth century it was often grown among the cabbages and pot herbs in English gardens. We tend now to associate it with gripe water; this dill infusion is an old remedy for colicky babies, and it was long valued as an aid to digestion, as well as being used as a charm to ward off the spells of witches: 'Therewith her Vervain and her Dill, that hindereth Witches of their Will.' But witches also used it to concoct love potions. More usefully, the flowering heads, just as they set seed, are an essential ingredient for pickled cucumbers.

Dill is a hardy annual that grows quickly and easily from seed sown in early spring. Succession-sowing will ensure a ready supply of young plants which should be used in preference to the tall, up to 60cm (2ft), mature plants. Set aside part of the crop to make seed. Dill does well in the shade of taller growing plants and so is useful to interplant with corn, climbing beans, among onions or cucumbers. Dill is also a good bee plant.

No kitchen garden should be without **basil**, in spite of the fact that in cool northern gardens it never makes the kind of growth it would in sunnier climes. Nevertheless, good crops can be had by sowing under glass or in pots on a sunny windowsill. It is a tender annual and should be sown indoors in the spring for planting out when the soil has truly warmed in early summer. According to the Greeks, basil must be sown while shouting harsh words of abuse or it will not flourish

(gardeners usually save such tantrums for couch grass or bindweed). Pinch out the flowers as they develop to make the plants leafier.

Gerard names this Great Basill *Ocimum magnum*; we know it as *O. basilicum*.

There are several varieties of basil identified by the size of the leaves and also by colour, for as well as the standard green sorts, there is a dark-purple-leafed basil, 'Dark Opal'. Recent innovations have led to the All-America Selection of 'Purple Ruffles' raised by Burpee Seeds, and a

sister plant, 'Green Ruffles', both with large, deeply serrated, crinkly leaves. Another American innovation is 'Silver Fox' with pale leaves edged in white.

Gerard's Citron Basill, *Ocimum medium citratum*, with a 'most odoriferous smell' of lemon.

Not surprisingly, the greatest variety of basil is to be found in Italy, and the sort known as lettuce-leaf is worth looking for if you are fortunate enough to holiday in

Left to right Basil and dill.

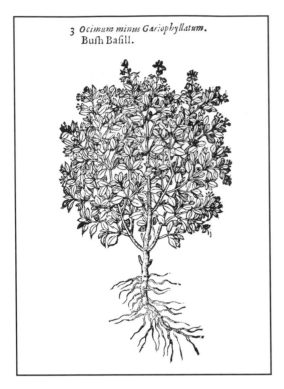

3 *Ocimum minus Gariophyllatum.*
Bush Basill.

‡ 4 *Ocimum Indicum.*
Indian Basill.

Gerard's Bush Basill is the same as our *Ocimum minimum.*

Gerard's Indian Basill is described as being dark purple, like our variety 'Dark Opal'.

that country. There is also a basil that bears its leaves in small clusters, *Ocimum minimum*, or bush basil.

It is thought that basil was introduced from India to Europe via the overland trade routes of the Middle Ages. The species known as *O. sancta* was one the holiest herbs of the Hindu religion and its name derives from the Greek *basilikon* or 'royal'. The plant was said to turn into scorpions if handled too roughly or to breed scorpions in the brain of those who inhaled its perfume; to turn into wild thyme if given too much sun; to protect from the evil eye; to capture the object of a man's affections. Quite a collection of dubious attributes.

There is an old tradition that basil and rue should never be planted together, but basil does well with asparagus and tomatoes; with the latter it makes a most delicious salad. Basil leaves should be shredded by hand, never chopped with a knife or snipped with scissors.

Angelica is probably the tallest herb we grow and there are equally tall tales connected with its history. It has long been considered one of the most valuable of all herbs for physic; according to Parkinson all the parts of the plant were used variously for improving the condition of the heart and stomach and protected these organs from infection; the powdered root was used to control 'the rage of lust in young persons' and to assist digestion and clear congestion of the lungs. Angelica was said to be an infallible antidote for poisons and numerous infections. One legend tells that an angel revealed that the herb cured plague; while another tradition held that since it bloomed on the holy day of St Michael the Archangel it countered the spell of witches and the evil eye.

Modern usage is more parochial; we

like its stems candied as cake decoration. The plant does have considerable sweetening qualities and pieces of stem cooked with rhubarb or tart apples improves the flavour of these fruits in pies or simply stewed and served with cream.

Angelica is a herbaceous perennial, but it rarely survives longer than two years, probably because it makes such copious growth, reaching 1.5m (5ft) or even 1.8m (6ft) during its second year. Thus it should be raised from seed sown in late summer, immediately after the seed has ripened. It requires rich deeply dug soil and partial shade to do well. Self-sown seedlings can be lifted and transplanted; plants should be at least 60cm (24in) apart.

Chrysanthemum balsamita is the botanical name for **costmary** or alecost; the latter name refers to the antique practice of using the leaf to strengthen the flavour of ale. Sprigs of costmary were used by the pilgrims as Bible bookmarks, hence the other common name, Bibleleaf.

Costmary is a herbaceous perennial, similar in appearance and habit of growth to tansy. It is upright and tall-growing, to 90cm (36in), and has small yellow flowers in late summer. The foliage is a pleasant green and feathery-looking. Give it a dry soil for preference, but costmary will grow just about anywhere you care to put it. Propagate it, if necessary, by divisions of the creeping roots.

Gerard recommended a strong infusion of costmary for 'disorders of the stomach and head', and its primary use seems to have been as an aid to digestion, and to treat worms in children. The dried leaves are a valuable addition to pot pourri, having a lemon-mint perfume. Fresh sprigs can be added to stews and soups or laid in the bottom of a cake tin before baking to flavour sponges.

Some herb plants should be included simply for their seeds. **Caraway** and anise are two such plants. Caraway, *Carum carvi*, is a biennial of easy cultivation, growing in any good soil and full sun. Sow the seed at the end of summer for cropping the following year; or else sow in spring, cut back at the end of autumn and the plants will flower and set seed the following summer. Harvest when the seed pods are ripe. Cut the entire stem to ground level and hang it upside-down in a dry place. When the plants have dried thoroughly, crush the pods gently to extract the seed.

Caraway has been used as a flavouring since the Stone Age. The Egyptians used it as a funeral offering; the Romans, who introduced it to northern Europe, valued it as a digestif; and today caraway seeds are the basis of the German liqueur *kummel*. In fact caraway is distinctly Germanic, appearing in German meat stews, cabbage dishes, sausages and cheese.

While it was popular enough in England during the Middle Ages, the leaves used to flavour broths and to garnish salads and the seeds to spice cakes, and among the Elizabethans – Falstaff enjoyed a dish of caraway and pippins, roasted or baked – its popularity has declined. But it is worth recalling its digestive properties and using the seed to flavour rich meats.

Caraway seed tisane is helpful after a heavy meal; and in his *Niewe Herbal* (translated from the original Dutch by Henry Lyte and first published in 1578), Rembert Dodoens said of caraway, '[it] is very good and convenient for the stomach and for the mouth ... it swageth and dissolveth all kind of windiness, blastings of the inward parts, and to conclude, it is answerable to Annis seed in operation and vertue'. He also commended the roots boiled and eaten like carrots.

Anise has a strong taste of liquorice. The seeds were used by the Romans to flavour cakes eaten at the end of the banquet to assist digestion. Anise-flavoured drinks are popular in Mediterranean countries, particularly in the south of France where they are known collectively as *pastis*, taken either before or after meals or at any time, to cool the heat of the day.

As a physic anise had a reputation for soothing coughs and breaking up congestion; at one time the seeds were smoked, and small children were given cool infusions of aniseed for chest infections, colic and hiccoughs. Dodoens advised that the scent of anise could cure a headache, and that a small sachet of the seed kept on the pillow prevented bad dreams.

Anise is a native of the Near East and Northern Africa and as such requires the sunniest, warmest spot in the garden to set seed. It is an annual that enjoys a light, limy soil. If you are not able to provide these conditions outdoors, you can raise anise in pots in a warm window. Sow the seed in spring and thin the seedlings to 12cm (5in) apart. Keep the plants free of weeds. After the seedheads have formed, lift the plants entire and put them in a sheltered place to dry. Don't collect the seeds until they are completely dry.

Fennel was a necessity in every colonial American garden. According to S. G. Goodrich in his *Recollections of a Life and Times* (1856),

A sprig of Fennel was in fact the theological smelling bottle of the tender sex, and not infrequently of the men, who from long sitting in the sanctuary – after a week of labor in the field – found themselves too strongly tempted to visit the forbidden land of Nod, would sometimes borrow a sprig of Fennel, and exercise the fiend that threatened their spiritual welfare.

But it was held in high repute long before the New World was discovered, and in Europe during the Middle Ages, fennel was one of the most popular herbs used to give flavour to salt fish. The green stalks and feathery leaves have a pronounced aniseed taste and today the herb is still used most often with fish in sauces, court bouillon and as an integral part of the Provençal *grillade en fenouil* in which fish is cooked on a bed of dried fennel branches over an open fire.

Parkinson wrote: 'There are two sortes of Fenell, whereof two are sweete ... ordinary sweete Fenell [and] Cardus Fenell by those that sent it out of Italy.' He noted that the Italians would blanch the stems to make them tender and 'more delightful to the taste', while ordinary fennel 'is of great use to trimme up, and strowe upon fish, as also to boyle or put among fish of divers sorts, Cowcumbers pickled, and other fruits, &c. The rootes are used with Parsley rootes, to be boyled in broths and drinkes to open obtructions. The seed is of much use with other things to expell winde. The seede also is much used to be put into Pippin pies and divers other such baked fruits, as also into bread, to give it the better taste'. That about sums it up, but also an infusion of the seed makes a soothing eye wash, and gives tomato sauces or pork dishes a delicious piquancy.

Fennel is a perennial, but it is only successful as such if it is not allowed to flower, which in turn means no seed. But it grows easily from seed sown in early spring in any good soil in the sun. The leaves are as finely cut as those of dill, but the foliage is denser; there is a bronze-leafed variety that is frequently seen in herbaceous borders. It makes a tall plant about 1.3m (4ft) high and seedlings or young plants should be set at least 30–38cm (12–15in) apart. Soil is drawn up around the young shoots which emerge from the base of the plant to blanch them for use in salads.

This herb is not a good companion in the kitchen garden, so fennel should be cultivated in its own bed. It is said that coriander and the artemisias have an adverse effect on fennel, inhibiting its growth and the setting of seed.

RECIPES

Herbs are our oldest medicines, and a study of the antique herbals reveals the wide range of plants which were regarded as efficacious against an equally wide range of ailments. Some of these remedies are, in the light of modern knowledge, patently absurd; however, there are quite a few which form the basis for modern treatments and drugs, and others which warrant serious investigation. For example, tansy is now known to give relief to some migraine sufferers; and it has recently been discovered that oil of evening primrose can do much to alleviate the misery of rheumatoid arthritis. Nevertheless, modern practitioners of what was once our only form of medicine work hard for recognition in the face of established scepticism.

On the home front, the simple use of herbs has never been completely abandoned and there are a great many people for whom a soothing cup of herbal tisane takes the place of chemical 'attitude adjusters'; who find relief in herbal steams and baths; and whose other homely remedies afford them all the comfort they need. There are a number of preparations for the various herbal remedies; some require grain alcohol, the sale of which is restricted in Great Britain, but others, given here, are easily achieved so long as the basic rules are followed. Much of the information given here is based on the excellent book *The Herbalist*, compiled by Joseph E. Meyer.

Infusions are made just as you would tea; with 15g (½oz) of dried herb to 500ml (1 pint) of freshly boiled water. Honey can be used to sweeten infusions of bitter herbs.

Decoctions are made by boiling hard materials like roots and seeds for some time to extract the goodness.

Syrups are made first as an infusion, then boiled, strained and blended with 30ml (1fl oz) of glycerin.

Mascerations are made by steeping the soft herb leaves in a sweet oil, such as almond oil.

Ointments are made from eight parts of vaseline to two parts of herb.

Poultices are hot compresses used to soothe or draw. Bread soaked in milk or water is a common poultice.

Fomentations are made by wringing out a cloth in a herbal infusion or decoction which is then applied to the affected part.

Plasters are made by sandwiching the crushed or bruised herb leaves between single layers of a thin cloth like muslin.

TISANES AND SOOTHING WATERS
Note: Make herb teas only in crockery or china, never metal.

Sage Tea

For coughs, colds and fevers, this drink also benefits the liver.

To each cup of boiling water add ½ to 1 teaspoon of dried sage leaves. Pour freshly boiled water over the leaves and cover closely; if the tea is being made in a cup, use the saucer. Leave to infuse, then strain and drink sweetened with honey.

Sage Gargle

Brew a pot of strong sage tea. To half a pint of infusion add one tablespoon each of honey, salt and vinegar. Bottle the mixture tightly and use as a gargle.

Thyme tea relieves chest and nasal congestion; mint tea, especially made with peppermint taken every morning and evening, improves the digestion; parsley tea is mildly diuretic.

Hyssop is largely regarded as a decorative herb, yet in the sixteenth and seventeenth centuries it was valued in salads and for physic. Hyssop tea made from the green shoots was taken to relieve rheumatism.

Hyssop Tea

To make Syrup of Hyssop for Colds. Take a handful of Hyssop, of Figs, Raysins, Dates, of each an ounce, French Barley one ounce, boyl therein three pintes of fair water to a quart, strain it and clarifie it with two Whites of Egges, then put in two pounds of fine Sugar and boyl it to a Syrup.
From *The Queen's Closet Opened*,
Sir Kenelm Digby, 1655

The following remedies are gleaned from Rembert Dodoens's *The Niewe Herbal*, which was one of the earliest attempts to catalogue plants systematically, and presents formulae in a much more straightforward, and believable, fashion than many of the herbals which appeared both before and after it.

Hyssope sod in vinegar and holden in the mouth, swageth toothache.

The seed of [lovage] warmeth the stomache, helpeth digestion and is pleasant to the mouth and taste.

He goes on to say that it was used as a pepper substitute. Caraway, anise and cumin were also valued as digestives.

Borage boiled with honied water is very good against the roughness or hoarsenesse of the throte.

Southernwood steeped or soked in oile, is profitable

From left to right Hannah Glasse's 'Olive Pye', Green Sauce, Rosemary Snow, Seedy Cake, and cooling Lemonade with Borage Flowers.

to rub or annoint the bodie, against the benumming of members taken with cold.

If Wormwood be taken fasting in the morning, it preserveth from dronkennes that day.

Herbal sachets added to hot baths can stimulate or relax, depending on the herb, or simply be used as an aid to beauty. Ninon de Lenclos, the notoriously beautiful Renaissance courtesan, preserved her looks with herbal baths, so that at the age of seventy her estranged grandson fell in love with her. (Fortunately, he discovered the true nature of their relationship before things got out of hand.)

Ninon's muslin sachets contained a handful each of lavender flowers, rosemary leaves, dried mint, comfrey flowers and thyme. Steep the sachets in boiling water for ten to fifteen minutes and then add the water to a hot bath. *Bonne chance.*

The fragrance of sweet herbs and flowers was meant to be just as beneficial as the actual ingestion of the leaves and petals, and the fragrant steam of a herb bath is part of its healing pleasure.

Anise seed, knotted into a hankie and held to the nose, was meant to prevent nightmares and give a good sound sleep. (I wonder how the bag was held to the nose during sleep?) Richard Banckes' herbal of 1525 recommends the regular inhalation of rosemary to 'keep thee youngly'. Marjoram and anise had the same quality.

Such simple herbal remedies can do little harm, and the pleasure of their use may be all the benefit they afford.

HERBS IN THE KITCHEN

The purpose of herbs and spices in the earliest recipes was to provide a contrast to the blandness of preserved foods, and to balance the sourness which could arise from the combined flavours of fruit and vegetables used in single-pot cookery.

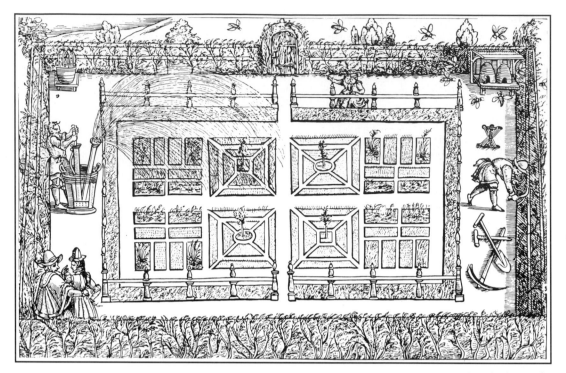

This garden is similar to the one on page 48 except that it is fenced round with a quickset hedge and watered by 'a great Squirt of Tin'. Note the beehives in the corner and decorative railings.

Sweet herbs like parsley, thyme, rosemary and chervil and the spices ginger and cinnamon enhanced the native sweetness of apples and pears and gave flavour to grains and starches.

When the style of cookery began to change in the late sixteenth century, led by the Italians, who began to present dishes in which the individual flavours of the ingredients could be distinguished, it became important to use the flavouring with discretion. By the mid-eighteenth century, Hannah Glasse was directing that no single herb flavour should predominate, so that a sauce would have savour, rather than an overriding sweetness or sourness.

Now, we seem to have come full circle, and much modern cookery prides itself on the distinctive quality of its flavouring ingredients; it seems sensible that if you are going to use a herb, let it at least be tasted. But, just as herb and spice blends must be used with care, some single herbs suit certain foods better than others. Fresh green coriander is sour and goes best with sweet lamb but does little for beef; while the reverse is true of thyme. Fish is generally regarded as a sweet flesh and the sourness of fennel and dill suit it well. Fresh root ginger is decidedly sour and one of the most delicious dishes I have ever encountered was brill in a ginger-root-flavoured butter sauce.

Poultry is bland enough to be flavoured either way; while the richness of game is best balanced by sweet herbs and spices such as ginger, clove, cinnamon and mace. These spices can be used with impunity to flavour fruit, but green herbs are generally reserved for vegetables. But in the end it is all a matter of individual taste and an innovative cook experiments with flavour combinations to build up a distinctive culinary dialect.

The following collection of recipes, gleaned from cookery manuscripts and books of this and several centuries, not to mention friends and relatives, will, I hope, inspire experiment.

Rosemary Snow

Whip 250ml (½pt) heavy cream until it is stiff. Whip the whites of 4 eggs until they are stiff but not dry, gradually adding a tablespoon of icing sugar. Gently fold the egg whites into the cream. Lay a branch of freshly picked and washed rosemary on a platter. Pile the whipped cream mixture over it and sprig with twigs of rosemary which the guests use to scoop up the cream. It can be messy, but the cream takes on a delicate flavour of rosemary.

Lemonade with Borage Flowers

Borage flowers impart a subtle fragrance of cucumber to fresh lemonade and the clear blue of the flowers contrasts prettily with the yellow fruit slices. My thanks to Jean Parrish of Chicago, Illinois, one of the great cooks of our time, for drawing my attention to this simple but elegant refreshment.

Squeeze 1 lemon per person into a jug. Add a generous tablespoon of sugar per lemon and then pour over 300ml (¾ pt) boiling water per serving. Mix together well and set aside to cool. Serve it over ice with thin slices of lime and lemon and a scattering of borage blossoms.

Seedy Cake

Separate 3 eggs and beat the whites until they are stiff. Continue beating as you add 150g (5oz) of super-fine sugar, until the sugar has dissolved. Lightly beat the yolks and blend them into the egg whites.

Sift together 175g (6oz) self-raising flour, 2 tablespoons of cornstarch and a pinch of salt. Gently fold the flour mixture into the eggs.

Melt 1 tablespoon of butter with 2 tablespoons of orange juice and 1 tablespoon of water. Pour the liquid into the egg and flour mixture and then gently fold it in, with a generous tablespoon of caraway or anise seed. Bake in a well-greased square cake tin in a fairly hot oven 190°C (375°F) for 20 minutes. Scatter caster sugar over the cake while it is still hot. Leave to cool and then cut into 2.5cm (1in) square cubes.

Olive Pye

Veal Olive Pye was Hannah Glasse's name for meat rolls stuffed with an egg, oyster and spinach farce, then baked in a pie crust. Chestnuts and artichoke bottoms were optional extras. The result was a more sophisticated version of a standard beef pie in which the meat is cubed. This is a modernised version.

Sauté 125g (4oz) chopped mushrooms in 25g (1oz) butter until the juices begin to run. Add 250g (8oz) chopped spinach and cook until the spinach is just soft. Take the pan off the heat and season with salt and pepper, thyme, nutmeg and powdered ginger. Add the yolks of 6 hard-boiled eggs, one at a time, blending them thoroughly into the spinach (reserve the whites for the salamagundy on page 102). Finally, add 50g (2oz) of sultanas.

Pound 6–8 slices (depending on the size of the cut) of buttock steak as thin as you can without pulverising the meat. Lay the slices out on a floured board. Put a stripe of stuffing down the centre of each slice, lengthwise, to within 2.5cm (1in) of one end. Turn in the edges and roll up the meat slice towards the non-stuffed end. Secure with a toothpick. Dredge the rolls with seasoned flour.

Heat 1 tablespoon each of olive oil and butter in a frying pan. Add the meat rolls and brown them well. Put the meat in a heavy casserole and deglaze with 1 table-spoon of vinegar. Add 125ml (¼ pint) of rich beef stock to the casserole. Cook in moderate oven 160°C (325°F) for 30–45 minutes or until the meat is tender.

Meanwhile, make 250–300g (9–11 oz) of shortcrust pastry and line a deep pie dish, leaving sufficient pastry to cover the pie when filled. Use a slotted spoon to take the meat rolls from the gravy and arrange them in the pie dish.

Mash several anchovy fillets with the back of fork and mix them into the gravy in the casserole. Pour the gravy over the meat rolls, put the pastry cover in place and bake at 190°C (375°F) for 20 minutes or until the pastry is cooked.

Custard Cream Flavoured with Bay

Make an egg custard, from 4 eggs beaten with 100g (4oz) super-fine sugar and 1 pint of milk that has been heated but not boiled. Put a few bay leaves in the bottom of a baking dish and pour the custard over them. Bake in a moderate oven, 180°C (350°F) for 30 minutes or until set. A light dusting of powdered cinnamon will not be amiss.

Sage Wine

For home wine-making buffs this recipe may be of interest. Our ancestors were accomplished at making delicious drinks from most fruit and many herbs, some purely medicinal, others for the pleasure they afforded.

To three Gallons of Water, put six Pounds of Sugar; boil these together, and as the Scum rises, take it off; and when it is well boil'd, put it in a Tub boiling hot, in which there is already a Gallon of red Sage leaves, ready picked and wash'd. When the Liquor is near cold, put in the Juice of four large lemons, beaten with a little Ale Yeast; mix these all well together, and cover it very close from the Air, and let it stand forty-eight hours; then strain all through a fine Hair Sieve, and put it into a Vessel that will but just hold it; and when it has done working, stop it down close, and let it stand three Weeks or a month before you bottle it, putting a Lump of Loaf Sugar in every bottle. This Wine is best when it is three Months old. After this manner you may make Wine of any other Herb or flower.

From *Adam's Luxury and Eve's Cookery*, 1744

Savory and Apple Jelly

An overabundance of apples one year led to this recipe; it is delicious with roast pork. Any herb could be substituted, but it is a treat to enjoy the warmth of summer savory in the midst of winter.

Wash the apples. Do not peel or core them. Cut them into chunks and put them into a preserving pan with enough cold water to just cover. Add branches of freshly picked summer savory and boil until the apple is pulpy. Put into a jelly bag and leave to drip through into a bowl. Resist all temptation to squeeze the bag to hurry things along – to do so would make the jelly cloudy.

Measure the juice and to every 500ml (1 pint) allow 500g (1lb) of preserving sugar. Return the juice and sugar to the preserving pan and boil rapidly until setting point is reached. Put the jelly into small sterile jars and seal.

Green Sauce

Lavish displays of food presented with brightly coloured sauces added to the grandeur of medieval banqueting tables. Along with carmeline sauce, medieval cooks prepared yellow sauce coloured with saffron and flavoured with ginger, and this green sauce that uses the colour of pounded green herbs and the spices cardamom and clove.

Steam equal parts of *fines herbes*, parsley, chives, tarragon and chervil until they are just soft. Put them through a food mill. Mix approximately 3 tablespoons of purée with a tablespoon of soft butter.

Make 250ml (½ pint) of white sauce in your usual manner, flavouring the hot milk with several cloves and a few crushed cardomoms. Just before serving add the buttered herb purée to the desired strength of flavour.

The purée can be made when there is a glut of parsley and the other herbs. Simply mix it with the softened butter and freeze in usable-sized portions.

Pot marigolds, borage, lavender and dill surround a clipped bay at Farnham Royal Herb Garden.

Roast Chicken with Tarragon

Eat a leaf of fresh tarragon; it's a surprisingly hot taste and makes the tastebuds tingle. But when cooked that sharpness is translated into a mellow richness. One of the finest uses for tarragon is to flavour roast chicken.

Put one large or several small dessert apples and a few branches of fresh tarragon into the breast cavity of the chicken. Shake in some salt and pepper and seal the cavity with a skewer or toothpick.

Roast the chicken in the usual manner; the moisture and aroma from the apples and tarragon will permeate the flesh. Lemons pierced all over with a fork can also be used, but the scent of apples is finer. Use dessert apples in preference to cooking apples that turn to mush.

Tarragon Vinegar

Tarragon vinegar can be made with the fresh or dried herb. It is so simple that it hardly bears description. But it is one of the finest ways of having tarragon, a real summer herb, in the kitchen. As well as using it in salad dressing, try a teaspoon of this to deglaze the pan when making sauces for pork or lamb.

Gather the leaves in midsummer. Use the fresh growth at the ends of the stalks, about 1–2 tablespoons to 500ml (1 pint) of vinegar.

Steep the leaves in wine vinegar, red or white, for not less than a week. Strain it off into clean bottles.

Most herbs can be used to flavour vinegar or olive oil, following the above method. Rosemary, garlic and small red chillies, crushed to expose the seeds which contain the hot oils, added to olive oil makes a tangy baste for summer barbecues; or you can use a few drops to cheer up winter casseroles.

Sweet Herb Sorbet

The service of a fresh fruit or herb sorbet, faintly sweetened, before the meat course, has enjoyed a revival. Certainly it tidies up the taste buds after the introductory courses.

Make a sugar syrup of 150g (5 oz) sugar and 250ml (½ pint) water. Add the strained juice of 1 lemon, return the syrup to the boil and add 2 tablespoons of the sweet herb of your choice: chervil, parsley,

Gravad Lax made with pink-fleshed trout, Herb Olives and Leek and Sage Tart.

mint and so on, finely chopped. Put the syrup into a shallow dish and freeze it until it is just stodgy. Quickly work in the stiffly beaten white of 1 egg. Return the sorbet to the freezer and freeze for several hours. A teaspoon of gin can be added if desired. Allow to soften before serving.

Pure Herb Jelly

Fill a pan with freshly gathered well-washed herbs of any kind. Choose a size of pan to accommodate the quantity of herbs available. Add just enough water to cover, bring to the boil and then reduce the heat and simmer for 30 minutes.

For every 500ml (1 pint) of liquid add the juice and rind of 1 lemon. Strain and measure the liquid into a clean pan, then add 500g (1 lb) of preserving sugar to every 500ml (1 pint) of liquid. Boil rapidly until setting point is reached. Put the jelly into small jars.

Tart of Herbs

An Herb-Tart is made thus: Boil fresh Cream or Milk, with a little grated bread or Naples-Biscuit (which is better) to thicken it; a pretty Quantity of Chervile, Spinach, Beete (or what other Herb you please) being first par-boil'd and chop'd. Then add Macaron, or Almonds beaten to a Paste, a little sweet Butter, the Yolk of five Eggs, three of the Whites rejected. To these add Corinths plump'd in Milk, or boil'd therein, Sugar, Spice at Discretion, and stirring it all together over the Fire, bake it in the Tart-Pan.

From *Acetaria*, John Evelyn, 1699

'Macaron' refers to macaroni, which in Evelyn's day were flat egg noodles and another one of Italy's many landmark contributions to the civilisation of Northern Europe. There is a tradition that egg noodles were first described by Marco Polo, who was thus responsible for the introduction of pasta from China to Italy.

Stillroom maids making confits and sweet waters, from Bonnefons's *Jardinier François*.

But pasta may have arrived from the Near East via Arab traders and slaves before Polo was even born, and there is even a chance that the Italian travellers taught the Chinese how best to prepare and sauce hot noodles. 'Corinths' refers to fine raisins.

Leek and Sage Tart

To 6 leeks, lightly steamed and sliced into discs, add 1 tablespoon of fresh sage, 1 large egg and 125ml (4fl oz) of cream or yoghurt. Lightly fry and coarsely chop 5–6 strips of lean bacon. Add the bacon to the leek and sage mixture. Season with salt and pepper to taste.

Line a shallow baking dish with wholewheat shortcrust pastry. Pour the leek and sage mixture into the crust, pour the bacon dripping over the top if desired, and bake the tart in a hot oven 190°C (375°F) for 20 minutes or until the pastry is cooked.

Herb Olives

Fill a large preserving jar with ripe black Greek olives. Pour in enough olive oil to come half-way up the jar. Add 1–2 cloves of garlic that have been lightly crushed with the side of a knife. 3–4 small red chillies, crushed to expose the seeds, and a teaspoon each of coriander and cumin seeds. Cover the jar and leave for several days before removing the garlic. Turn the jar now and again to mix the spices and chillies throughout the olives.

Gravad Lax

Dill is one of my favourite herbs; it has a clearly defined taste that stands up to cooking, or sparkles fresh in a green salad; nothing is nicer or more refreshing than to munch a sun-warmed frond on a summer afternoon in the garden. The Swedes use dill to make this dish of salt-preserved salmon.

Use a salmon tailpiece or, if you think that a true salmon is too expensive, sub-

Gerard's illustration of Small Sage, *Salvia minor*.

stitute pink-fleshed trout, filleted; prepare several fish at once as the dish improves with freezing.

For 1.35kg (3 lb) of fresh filleted fish, mix together 1 heaped teaspoon each of sea salt and light brown sugar, and ½ teaspoon of white pepper. Lay half the fillets flat on a shallow dish, and divide half the salt mixture evenly between them, pressing it into the flesh of each fillet. Sprinkle 1 tablespoon of fresh chopped dill over each. Lay the remaining fillets over those in the dish and cover them with the rest of the salt mixture. Dribble 1 tablespoon of brandy over the fish, cover them closely with cling film and put a heavy weight on top. Chill for up to three days, carefully turning the fish each day.

Serve in thin slices or pencil thin strips. Traditionally, Gravad Lax is served with a

mustard sauce made by mixing 2 tablespoons of sweet German or Swedish mustard with 1 tablespoon each of light brown sugar and fresh chopped dill. Blend with 2 tablespoons of white wine vinegar and 1 egg yolk. Gradually add 125ml (4fl oz) of sunflower oil as you would for mayonnaise to make a smooth creamy sauce.

Pesto Genovese

Next to dill, basil is one of my most valued herbs and is at its best when eaten raw in salads or used to make the classic Pesto sauce to serve with fresh pasta.

Chop together until very fine 50g (2 oz) each of fresh basil, *pecorino romano* or sardo cheese, and pine nuts, 1–2 cloves of garlic and 1 teaspoon of coarse salt. Gradually add olive oil to make a thick creamy paste.

Tomato and Basil Salad

A plate of sun-ripened tomatoes, freshly picked and thinly sliced, should be dressed with nothing more than a veil of finest olive oil, a grind or two of black pepper, a sprinkle of sea salt and shredded basil.

Herb and Garlic Cheese

To 250 (8 oz) of fresh curd cheese add equal parts of finely chopped herbs, including chives and winter savory, 1 clove of crushed garlic, a teaspoon of paprika, and salt and pepper to taste. Blend well and store tightly covered in the refrigerator.

Cheese of Seven Herbs

To four ounces [125g] of grated cheese [Cheshire] allow two tablespoonfuls of thick cream, three tablespoonfuls of sherry, and two level tablespoonfuls of the following herbs in mixture: finely chopped parsley, sage, thyme, tarragon, chives, chervil, and winter savory, also seasoning to taste. Put all the ingredients into a double saucepan and stir over very gentle heat till the mixture is creamy and pale green in colour. Whilst still warm, fill up small pots with the cheese and use when cold.

From *Culinary and Salad Herbs*, Eleanour Sinclair Rohde, 1940

CHAPTER THREE

FLOWERS

Above Dianthus barbatus, Sweet William.

Opposite Detail from *Still Life* by Jan Davidsz De Heem (1631–95). *Reproduced by courtesy of Christie's.*

FOLLOWING THE UPHEAVAL of civil war, which affected much of Europe during the early years of the seventeenth century, the later half was a more positively exciting time. Scientific discoveries were standing the physical world on its ear; trade with countries that had previously existed only in legend was established and proving highly lucrative; superstition was succumbing to the power of reason; and man was at last beginning to feel the master of all he surveyed.

Agricultural improvements were changing the seasonal quality of the food supply and its quantity. Productivity was raised by rotational cropping, improved methods of ploughing, sowing and harvesting, and the application of efficient manuring and fertilising practices, thereby encouraging farmers to devote less land to pasturage and to increase the tillage of crops. There was an increase in the number of market gardens surrounding urban centres, supplying the growing populace with fresh vegetables and fruit; the Dutch technique of storing root crops for winter feed became accepted practice, which meant that livestock no longer had to be slaughtered at the end of autumn, and so fresh meat was more readily available.

The French had lagged behind the Italians and the English in gardening and cooking, but by the end of the sixteenth century they were catching up. By the end of the seventeenth century, France, Louis XIV and the 'cultural monolith' of Versailles had replaced Italy as the centre of European civilisation, and the French influence brought to England by Charles II (who had found refuge in the French court during the Civil War) could be seen in every aspect of daily life.

All over the countryside new gardens in the French manner were created. Tudor gardens had largely retained the medieval idea of a walled enclosure, but now there was a new-found confidence; and in the garden this was manifested by the dropping of walls and the creation of elaborate parterres and rigidly formalised parks, with the great houses of the nobility and wealthy merchants set like jewels on their grand terraces.

Parterres were knot gardens grown up, and not necessarily the better for it. The intricate patterns of herb hedges remained, although box was taking over for the purpose, and flowers were banished from the design because they would not grow uniformly and would have destroyed the regularity of the pattern.

Claude Mollet, gardener to Louis XIII, was said to have originated the *parterres à compartiments de broderie*, while his son André espoused the virtues of tree-lined avenues. Both ideas were to become signatures of formal garden design, the greatest exponent of which was Le Nôtre, garden architect to the Sun King, Louis XIV.

Le Nôtre laid out vast canals, avenues and parterres of box and coloured gravel; and in the working part of the garden, under the authority of the renowned horticulturalist Jean

Two of the seventeen patterns for knots given in Gervase Markham's translation of *Maison Rustique* showing the increasing intricacy of design as parterres in the French style become more popular.

de la Quintinye (who had charge of the royal kitchen gardens), created the *parterre fleuriste*, a cutting garden to supply posies for the royal table.

Jean de la Quintinye exercised his skill in producing top-quality fruit, vegetables and flowers, and, because of his revered position in the court, influenced the *beau monde* to do likewise, who in turn demanded a wider range of recipes for a wider range of produce.

In the mid-1600s, a two-volume work appeared that married a new approach in cookery to advances in horticulture. Written by Nicolas de Bonnefons, who had been valet to the young Louis XIV, the first was a gardening book, *Le Jardinier François* (1651), the second a cookery book, *Délice de la campagne* (1654). Interestingly, both volumes are dedicated to 'the Ladies', who are assured that not only will their senses be rewarded by the fragrance and beauty of flowers and fruit, but the sale of excess produce will greatly please the family exchequer. He also advertised seeds for sale: 'I will furnish you with all the kinds of plants which you have seen, and I have others sent from Italy, which we do not grow'. This volume was translated into English by John Evelyn and published as *Rapin's French Gardener* in 1672.

In the first part of the book, Bonnefons recommends that the vegetable beds be dug in winter when the rains of autumn have made the ground workable (and when 'labourers are under-employed'); the beds should be double-dug (!) 'three to four feet deep', and in the bottom should be laid six inches of 'the leaves of trees, even to the rotten sticks and *mungy stuffe* to be found under old wood piles . . . whatever you can procure with the most ease and least charge'. Great care should be taken to eradicate couch or 'dog grasse' to the 'very least string' to 'utterly exterminate a *weed* so extremely noxious to your *Garden*'. Fruit trees were to be underplanted with lettuce, purslane, chervil, chicory and young cabbages for transplanting, which would serve to keep the soil open and the trees well watered.

This is followed by descriptions of how to grow each vegetable and fruit, often accompanied by explanations of Italian horticultural techniques; fortunately, their influence was not entirely dead.

What is striking about the cookery volume is the wide variety of vegetables and fruits used, the simplicity of the approach, and the flavours: where medieval foods would have been richly spiced and the separate flavours muddled, Bonnefons's recipes allow the individual tastes to shine through.

Bonnefons was aiming at the simple country cook, though, and his style was in direct contrast to that preferred by the French nobility, who were, after all, the trend-setters, and for whom a plethora of expensive ingredients and complex presentation was a way of displaying their wealth. Their cookery author was La Varenne, whose book *Cuisinier François* marked a clean break with medieval cookery and laid the foundation for what we recognise today as classical French cuisine. Yet throughout the book there are echoes of the Middle Ages: the author shows a love of sweet and sour, and rich spices, but used with discretion.

Food presentation had entered a new era with the use of china plates instead of bread trenchers; forks were now in common use. This meant that sauces could be more liquid, and though crumbled toast was still used as it was in the Middle Ages to thicken sauces, and hashes of meat and vegetable were still popular, smooth gravies and small portions of meat could be used to compose a dish. The order in which the courses of a meal were served now changed: the fish course was put ahead of the meat and after the soup, whereas in Tudor times it had always followed the meat.

Table settings of the period must have looked like scale models of Le Nôtre's garden designs; and at state banquets vast edifices of confectionary were erected, combining hundreds of small dishes of preserved and fresh fruits supported by gilt columns and cornices, garlanded with fresh flowers. By the late seventeenth century this had metamorphosed into the floral centrepiece, but even that was made to look like a Lilliputian flower garden, complete with sugar statuary. Again, this was a method of displaying wealth: the flowers used were often obtained out of season.

If flowers were losing ground in the garden design, they were still necessary in the stillroom for lotions and potions, and in the kitchen as salad ingredients and as garnishes. La Varenne uses a garnish of flowers with his recipe for a pungently spiced and smoked ham; but flowers were also valued for their flavour, and many recipes called for the addition of orangeflower water or marigold petals to colour and warm a broth; and floral as well as fruit-flavoured vinegars were extremely popular (yes, they used raspberry vinegar, too!).

Although many aspects of cookery and gardening have altered over the centuries, the basic practices are little changed since the seventeenth century. The traditions of classic French court cookery and the innovations of La Varenne are largely responsible for the way in which we prepare and present our food today. Had the Italian influence prevailed, our approach to vegetable cookery would have a great deal more character today. At the Italian table, vegetables are served as a distinct course after the meat, resulting in a far more interesting repertoire of recipes. Under the French influence, however, vegetables became mere side dishes or garnishes. Although flowers returned to play a major role in the garden with the revival of the Italianate garden at the end of the eighteenth century, they never regained their position in the cook's repertoire.

Roses, Pinks, Sweet Williams, Marigolds, Lavender, Violets

Gerard wrote: 'the **Rose** doth deserve the chiefest and most principall place among all floures whatsoever'. This has been the general consensus of international opinion from the dawn of horticultural history. There could not be a garden without a rose, and this plant was one of the first to be improved through cultivation and selection; 5,000 years ago, the Sumerian King Sargon took roses as the spoils of war, to grow in his royal garden at Ur. The Romans feasted on cushions stuffed with rose petals and scattered roses at any opportunity; they ate them, drank them and bathed in waters scented by the queen of the flowers. Our medieval ancestors prized the rose just as highly and recognised this, rather more respectfully, by assigning the flower to the mother of Christ.

When the flower garden made its independent appearance as the pleasure or nosegay garden of the Elizabethans, the rose was the first bush planted, and it was probably a damask rose. However, which damask is uncertain, for the term applied to two distinct types. Gerard's damask was *Rosa gallica officinalis*, the 'Apothecary's Rose', which during the thirteenth century provided the basis for a thriving industry at the French town of Provins. The fine crimson petals of this almost thornless shrub rose retain their elegant perfume when dried and were used by the town's many apothecaries to make a highly prized rose conserve. It took the name 'damask' from the tradition that it was a rose brought from Damascus by Thibaut le Chansonnier, Crusader, King of Navarre, Comte de Champagne et Brie and poet, whose verses pay homage to his beloved rose.

However, Parkinson distinguishes between the damaske and damaske province rose.

The Damaske Rose bush is more usually noursed up to a competant height to stand alone, . . . then any other Rose . . . The flowers are of a fine deepe blush colour, as all know, . . . of the most excellent sweet pleasant sent, far surpassing all other Roses or Flowers, being neyther heady nor too strong, nor stuffing or unpleasant sweet, as many other flowers.

Among the uses he gives are 'the super-excellent sweete water it yeeldeth being distilled', and the dried petals for sweet bags. A more prosaic use was rose petal syrup to relieve constipation. Parkinson decided that the scent of the Apothecary's Rose (damaske province) was inferior to that of the damask, but conceded to 'let every one follow his own fancie'.

There are two groups: the summer damasks and the autumn damasks, which bloom twice during the season (unlike many other 'old roses', which flower just once). This group includes the rose, *Rosa damascena bifera* 'Quatre Saisons' and 'Kazanlik' or *R. damascena trigintipetala* which is cultivated for the production of attar of roses. Other roses worth growing are 'Mme Hardy', 'Celsiana', 'Fantin Latour', 'Ferdinand Pichard' with white petals splashed with rosy pink, and 'Rose de Resht'.

The Gallica roses are one of the few old rose groups to appreciate regular pruning and thinning of overcrowded shoots in the spring or else midsummer, when shoots which have finished flowering should be removed. Dress the bed each year with well-rotted manure and feed with potash. Gallicas also sucker if grown on their own roots and this can create a pretty effect if kept in bounds. They are low-growing, to 1.2m (4ft), and can be grown as a hedge

kept trim by an annual clipping each winter. This is how Vita Sackville-West grew the ancient Gallica she discovered growing tenaciously at Sissinghurst Castle. 'Rosa mundi' with crimson petals striped pink is grown as a hedge at Hidcote Manor Gardens in Gloucestershire. Other varieties worth having are 'Tuscany', the 'Old Velvet Rose', 'Belle de Crécy' and 'Cardinal de Richelieu'.

Damask roses make fairly tidy shrubs between 90–150cm (3–5ft) tall. They do not mind a modicum of shade and will grow well even if mixed with other trees and shrubs. Light winter pruning helps to promote recurrent flowering.

All the allium family, parsley, and marigolds are mutually beneficial when planted with roses.

Next to the rose, the most highly valued flower was the **carnation** or **pink**: the clove-gilly-flower of our Elizabethan ancestresses who used its sweet scent for physic, food and the pure pleasure afforded by the flowers. John Evelyn recommended the flowers infused in vinegar to be used in 'time of contagious sickness, and very profitable at all times for such as have feeble spirits'.

Traditionally these flowers were introduced to England by the Normans, who called them *giloflier*, signifying their clove perfume. There were two types: singles, or pinks, evolved from *Dianthus plumarius* and doubles, from *D. caryophyllus*, which give us the hardy border carnations including the old 'Crimson Clove'; according to Parkinson this was the sort 'most used in Physicke in our Apothecaries

Left to right White-flowered pinks and Fantin Latour rose.

shops', because no others were able to give 'so gallant a tincture to a Syrupe'.

Both types are hardy perennials that enjoy full sun and limy soil. They are easily propagated by layering and can be kept neat by clipping over lightly after flowering.

Sweet william, *D. barbatus*, was also prized in cottage gardens. It is biennial and should be sown outdoors during the spring in a nursery bed and then transplanted during the autumn to its flowering position. Like its perennial sisters, sweet william likes an alkaline soil. Remove the flower heads as they fade, although one or two may be left to take advantage of the plant's willingness to self-sow.

Calendula officinalis is the botanical name for the common **pot marigold**, used by the Romans as a saffron substitute and long valued for the warmth of its flavour and the colour it contributes both to the garden and to prepared dishes.

It is a hardy annual and will grow in any soil in a sunny spot. Marigolds are one of the happiest flowers in the garden, but if you choose to introduce them, take care to keep seedheads to a minimum as they self-sow readily.

French marigolds, *Tagetes patula*, are half-hardy annuals which should be sown under glass in late spring; they germinate and grow on quickly and this avoids the plants going spindly. This plant is said to have been introduced from Mexico to Europe by the Spaniards and in the mid-sixteenth century to England by French Huguenot refugees. The species *T. lucida*, also from Mexico, has the finest perfume and grows to 30cm (12in), while French marigolds, which have pungently scented flowers and foliage, come in a wide range of sizes, flower form and colouring. The tallest growing, belied by its name, *T. minuta*, is a natural herbicide. A cover crop of this flower, grown over several years, will clear couch grass. All the marigolds

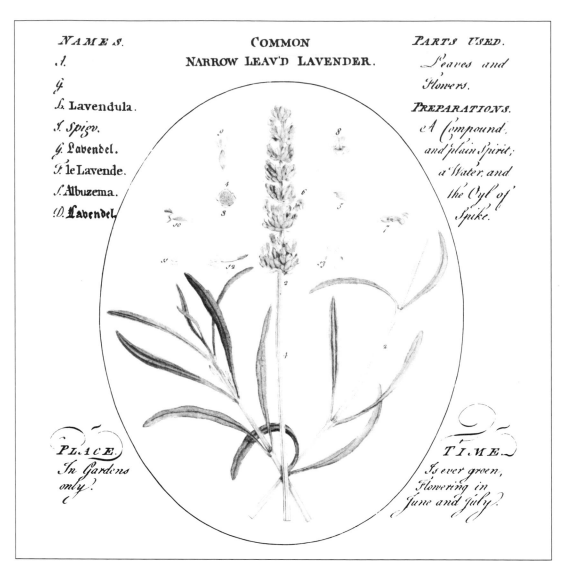

Common Narrow Leav'd lavender from Sheldrake's *Botanicum Medicinale*, 1759: 'Lavender is a warm, Aromatic Plant, and the distill'd Water . . . is used in strengthening Fomentations.'

are useful garden companions and should be used as edgings and interplanted with tomatoes, beans and potatoes.

There must be room in the garden for at least a small hedge of **lavender**; perhaps the deep violet dwarf variety 'Hidcote' or the paler, dwarfer 'Munstead'. Larger gardens will have space for the old English lavender, *Lavendula vera*, or a warm wall to cosset white-flowered lavender, which was the type favoured by Queen Henrietta Maria. Other varieties include *L. stoechas*, the French lavender, which has a neat habit and curious angular dark purple flowerheads; it, too, needs shelter in cool climates.

Lavender and roses have for centuries provided the raw materials for pot-pourris, perfumes and confits. Lavender-scented washing waters and sachets kept moths from the linen cupboard. Lavender wine, according to Henrietta Maria's cook, was a

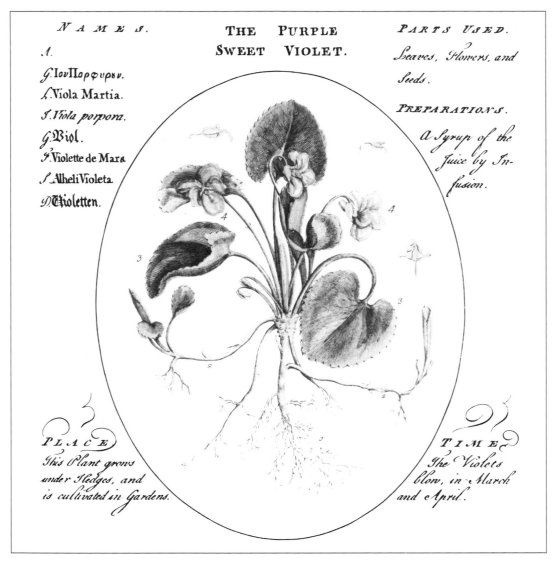

NAMES.

A.

G. ἸουΠορφυρϭυ.

L. Viola Martia.

S. Viola porpora.

G. Biol.

F. Violette de Mara

I. Alheli Violeta.

D. Violetten.

THE PURPLE
SWEET VIOLET.

PARTS USED.

Leaves, Flowers, and
Seeds.

PREPARATIONS.

A Syrup of the
Juice by In-
fusion.

PLACE

This Plant grows
under Hedges, and
is cultivated in Gardens.

TIME

The Violets
blow, in March
and April.

Sheldrake's Purple Sweet Violet: he wrote that the violet was one of the Cordial flowers, as leaves, flowers and seeds could be used to make a laxative syrup.

'great cordiall' made by adding two ounces of lavender and three ounces of sugar to a bottle of sack and shaking the bottle frequently during the week it was left to infuse. Lavender tea and compresses were used to relieve migraine, nervousness and palpitations; a few sprigs enhance the relaxation to be had from a hot bath.

Give lavender a sunny open position in well-drained, preferably alkaline soil. Cut the flower stalks as soon as the blossoms open and hang them upside down in an airy place to dry. Even if you don't wish to gather the flowers, clip the shrubs over at the end of summer or early autumn to stop the plants becoming leggy. Take care not to cut into the old wood and leave about 2.5cm (1in) of new growth. Propagate lavender from the clippings; they will root easily in sandy soil under cover.

The genus *Viola* includes hundreds of species of annual and perennial plants, the most prized of which is *V. odorata*, the **sweet violet**. It has been cultivated in gardens for centuries; the Romans and the Persians sipped violet wine, and to Christians it signified Christ's humility. Francis Bacon wrote, 'That which above all yields the sweetest smell in the air is the Violet, especially the white double violet which comes twice a year'.

Sweet violets are hardy perennials growing from crowns and propagated by runners or division of the crown in early spring. They need rich soil and partial shade.

The **viola**, in particular the dainty 'Heart's Ease', is a hardy annual that self-sows in any good soil in partial shade or full sun. Violas are for the most part unscented, but they have an enthusiastic character, spreading to make vast clumps and rarely out of flower from early spring to mid-winter in a sheltered spot.

Violettas are the result of a cross between bedding pansies and *V. cornuta*, from which they take their fibrous roots and perennial habit. Violettas have small flowers, vanilla-scented and numerous; they were a favourite edging plant in Victorian cottage gardens and should be used as such in the kitchen garden. Give them full sun and well-drained soil, and propagate by division of the fibrous roots in autumn.

Hesperis matronalis, **dame's or damask violet**, is a tall-growing hardy perennial, reaching 60–90cm (2–3ft). The scent, redolent of cloves and violets, is most prevalent in the evening; the double form, *flore pleno*, has the best perfume and should be propagated by cuttings rooted in sandy soil under cover in the late summer. Gerard remarked that the flavour of the leaves was similar to that of the salad leaf, Mediterranean rocket, *Eruca sativa*, for which they were sometimes used as a substitute.

Daisies, Petunias, Geraniums

The **daisy**, *Bellis perennis*, is a plant of the medieval 'flowery mede'; today it is most often looked upon as a common weed of lawns. However, garden cultivation has resulted in some delightful double forms, with white petals edged pink and growing in shapely tufts. Daisies are truly perennials, but when grown as such the plants eventually deteriorate and so should be treated as biennials, sown in the summer and transplanted to flowering positions in the autumn. Use these little daisies as edgings for herb beds and among the fruit trees and shrubs to feed bees and thus aid pollination.

Another member of the *Compositae* or daisy family which has been grown in gardens for the fragrance of its foliage and the physic quality of its flowers is **camomile**. The non-flowering sort is the type to use for lawns and seats; the more it is crushed, the more it will spread. Otherwise cultivate the flowering version of *Anthemis nobilis* and harvest the flowers for soothing tisanes and infusions to serve as rinses for fair hair and facial toners. Dried flowers included in the filling for a dog's bed keeps fleas away.

In the garden camomile is an invaluable companion for cabbages and onions. It is said that an infusion of fresh camomile flowers provides a good spray to help prevent damping off.

To make a camomile lawn takes great perseverance and a vast quantity of plants; they should be set about 15cm (6in) apart, watered religiously and rolled several times through the growing season to help the plants establish. Perhaps a better plan would be to allow the plants to root themselves between the paving stones of paths through the kitchen garden.

A sprinkling jug watering a garden; an action emblematic of patience of the mid-1600s.

Petunias are colourful half-hardy annuals whose colour and flower form add variety to the garden scene. The blossoms have a honey-flavoured nectar much loved by hummingbirds and bees. There are vivid shades of purple, magenta and pink, stripes and bicolours, single and doubles – some so double as to resemble pompons. But the white-flowered sorts, both single and double are a real garden joy. Sow the seed indoors in early spring and plant out when all danger of frost is past. Petunias are native to South America and so appreciate a warm, sunny position. They are especially good companions for all types of beans.

There is one group of plants, the **geraniums**, which, although they provide us with dainty flowers if of the cranesbill sort, or showy bedding if belonging to the pelargoniums, are deserving of a place in the kitchen garden for the fragrance of their leaves. Scented geraniums are usually classed as greenhouse or indoor plants. They are tender, but if given a chance to spread their leaves out of doors during the hot summer months, will repay this kindness with lush foliage and sturdier growth compared to what is made under the shelter of glass.

This group of plants is deserving of collection. There are many sorts, identified by the fragrance of the leaves. Lemon is the most common, but there are also rose, orange, peppermint, nutmeg and musk. The variety of leaf size and shape is great; finely cut, lacy leaves to heavily felted, heart-shaped foliage. Some leaves have pronounced chocolate variegations, others creamy-white markings.

Scented-leaf geraniums were introduced from the South African Cape at the end of the eighteenth century and gained instant popularity among gardeners from all walks of life.

Plant them outdoors after all danger of frost is past, in well-drained soil, and mulch with well-rotted manure. Keep watered in dry weather and pinch out the growing tips to encourage bushiness. As soon as there is a hint of frost lift the plants and pot them up. Bring indoors to a cool room or a frost-free greenhouse. Don't over water during the winter; keep the plants on the dry side and in a bright spot. Too often scented geraniums are put into the middle of a warm room with the result that they go leggy and lax.

They are easily propagated from soft cuttings taken whenever there is enough material. Some varieties, such as the lemon-scented sort, root easily in water or compost. Others, particularly the small-leaved sorts, can be difficult.

Scented geraniums are good companions for roses, brassicas and grapes.

Left to right Daisies and petunias.

RECIPES

Roses are sovereign in the kitchen as well as the garden, and there are hundreds of recipes for using the petals as a basis for sweetmeats, perfumed waters, jams, jellies and cordials. Rosewater was frequently used to flavour foods, and this practice is today common in the Middle East and parts of India. We tend to save our roses for decoration and the mixing of pot-pourri, an amalgamation of dried flower petals, spices and herbs.

Bowls full of fragrant petals and aromatic leaves, carefully gathered and slowly dried to preserve their savour, then blended with sweet spices and pungent oils, once featured in the rooms of many houses where the lady and her stillroom maid used the produce of the herb garden to create delights such as pot-pourri as well as sweet bags and scented waters.

The term pot-pourri is French, meaning 'rotten pot', for the earliest pots-pourris were moist. Also known as scent jars, these use petals and leaves that are not thoroughly dried; more of the natural oils are present so the original floral fragrance is stronger than that of a dry pot-pourri, in which all the petals and leaves must be crisp-dry and to which a scented oil is added to boost the perfume. Moist pot-pourri is kept in lidded bowls and the covers are removed when the fragrance is needed – but some have lids pierced with small holes. Dry pot-pourri is kept in open bowls on tables in a spot where air currents will waft the perfume about the room; it should be stirred occasionally – by hand as you pass the bowl is nice – to arouse the scent.

POT-POURRI FLOWERS AND HERBS

Rose petals are the main ingredient in most recipes for pot-pourri. Certain varieties in particular hold their fragrance well when dried: the Bourbon roses 'Madame Isaac Pereire', 'Parfum de l'Hay', and 'Zephirine Drouhin' have a fruity, raspberry scent; damask roses like 'Gloire de Guilan' and 'Kazanlik' are grown in the Near East for attar of roses; hybrid musks like 'Buff Beauty' and the old 'Apothecary's Rose', *R. gallica officinalis*, will also provide excellent perfume. These are mainly pink or red roses; white roses can be used too, but the petals when dry look more like shreds of paper than sweet flower petals.

Rose petals form the basis for pot-pourri and many other fragrant stillroom recipes.

Lavender is the other ever-present pot-pourri flower. Some recommend only *L. angustifolia*, the old English lavender, as being suitable. But this makes quite a large bush, and the low-growing variety 'Hidcote', is much neater, has as pleasant a scent in flower and leaf, and is a much richer colour.

Pinks, violets, pot marigolds, nicotiana, heliotrope, lily-of-the-valley, woodruff, red valerian and mignonette are also used to provide perfume and colour.

Foremost among the plants used for their leaves is the lemon verbena, *Lippia citriodora*, and any of the scented geraniums: *Pelargonium crispum*, *P. tomentosum*, 'Attar of Roses' and 'Mabel Grey'. Sweet herbs like thyme, marjoram, basil, bay, mint and tarragon are also included.

SPICES AND OILS

Powdered spices are frequently added to enrich the bouquet of a floral mix. Cloves, nutmeg, cinnamon and allspice are most commonly used, but coriander, cardamom and mace can impart an incense-like quality to the mix.

Essential oils, chiefly floral but sometimes derived from exotic leaves and resins such as patchouli and sandalwood, are used to strengthen the overall fragrance, so that the pot-pourri pronounces itself as decidedly woodsy, floral or whatever to taste, or simply to substitute for some ingredient temporarily unobtainable. These oils are available from herbalists such as Culpepers, some health-food stockists and others who cater for 'alternative' living.

FIXATIVES AND SALT

Fixatives are scented powders derived from plant roots and resins. They are used to absorb and thereby hold the fragrant oils in the pot-pourri petals and leaves. Orris root powder is the most common, along with gum benzoin. Sandalwood raspings, patchouli leaves and vanilla-scented tonka beans are also used, but sparingly as they have quite pervasive odours.

Moist pot-pourri recipes usually call for salt in which the petals and leaves are pickled. Old recipes call for 'bay salt'; this

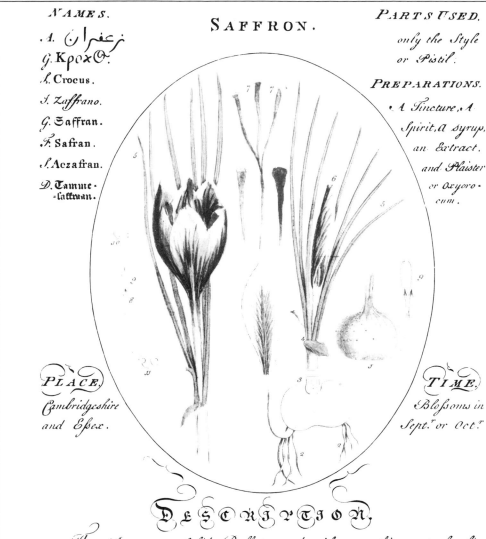

SAFFRON.

NAMES.

A. زعفران (i)

g. Κρος Ο.

L. Crocus.

I. Zaffrano.

G. Saffran.

F. Safran.

S. Aczafran.

D. Tamme-saffraan.

PARTS USED.

only the Style or Pistil.

PREPARATIONS.

A Tincture, A Spirit, a syrup, an Extract, and Plaister or Oxyoro-cum.

PLACE.

Cambridgeshire and Essex.

TIME.

Blossoms in Sept.r or Oct.r

DESCRIPTION.

The Root is a Solid Bulb 1. coverd with many thin coats of a fine Thready matter, and compressed top and Bottom. The Fibres 2. Grow round the bottom of the Root; long, and white as the Root. The Flower rises from the Centre of the Root 3. incompassed with Leaves, inclosed in a Whitish Skin. 4. The Leaves 5. are long, Narrow, of a deep Green, smooth, with a white Rib in the Middle. from the Centre of the Leaves enclosed in a white film rises the flower 6. having Six Leaves of a very light purple at the upper Edges Striped which nearer the Stalk becomes a Deep Rich Shining purple. The Three Styles 7. are red like Velvet open and Jagg'd at the Top but uniting in the Stalk lose their colour and become a Transparent white. The Chives 8. are white at the Bottom becoming purple where they join the Apices 9. which are white, coverd with a Gold Colourd Farina 10. magnified–a leaf cut Transversly.

VIRTUES

Saffron is a high Cordial.

is thought to refer to salt obtained from naturally evaporated sea water. It can be found in health-food shops and can be mixed with equal parts of non-iodised table salt for use. Alternatively, coarse kosher salt can be used.

GATHERING AND PREPARING
FLOWERS AND LEAVES

Always gather petals in the early morning after the dew has dried but before the full heat of the sun has reached the flowers. Choose only those flowers that are in their prime. Pull the flowers apart gently so as not to bruise the petals. Discard any that are damaged.

DRYING PETALS AND LEAVES

Petals must be dried slowly, somewhere out of direct sunlight but where there is a gentle flow of air – under a bed or chest of drawers is ideal. They must be spread flat in a single layer.

Bamboo floor mats, sheets of newspaper spread over wire cake racks and shallow boxes are all suitable. But if you intend to produce quantities of dried petals, take the time to make several net drying racks that can be stacked in a cool, shady corner.

Make a wooden frame out of wood 2.5cms wide by 2cms thick (1in by 2in); the overall dimensions will be determined by the area in which they will be stacked. Artists' canvas stretchers, purchased from art supply shops, can easily be used for the frame.

Stretch sheer curtain netting or butter muslin over the frame. Fix short legs, (10–15cm (4–6in) at each corner.

For centuries, saffron was cultivated in East Anglia; Saffron Walden in Essex was a centre of production. The dried and powdered stigmas of this flower were a prized flavouring during the medieval period, and its liberal use, according to Francis Bacon, made the English a lively race.

Lavender is gathered by cutting the whole stalk. Tie the stalks in small bunches and hang them upside-down in an airy shady place. When dry, the flowers heads can be gently crumbled from the stalks. Herbs can be treated in the same way, but a well-made pot-pourri is as pleasing to the eye as to the nose, so texture is as important as colour: whole leaves of scented geraniums and lemon verbena make a pleasing contrast to smaller particles of leaf and petal. Strip whole leaves carefully from herb branches and dry as you would flower petals.

PRESERVING FLOWERS WHOLE

Whole flowerheads of colourful plants such as marigolds and cornflowers, and perfect rosebuds, can be dried by placing them flat in a box of dry silver sand or silica gel (from chemists). Lay them on the surface of the sand, taking care that they do not overlap, then cover with more sand. Put in a warm place for several days. This method, which preserves the colour and character of the flower perfectly, can also be used to dry roses whole on the stem for dried flower arrangements.

Orange and lemon peel is sometimes included in pot-pourri mixtures, but be sure to use only the rind and none of the white pith. Special citrus zesters are helpful as they produce fine threads of peel which dry easily. Put the peel on sheets of greaseproof paper to dry; paper or muslin would absorb the scented oil.

EQUIPMENT AND RECIPES

All the implements needed will be on the kitchen shelf. For measuring use a pint jug, kitchen scales, a set of measuring spoons and a calibrated eye dropper for measuring out essential oils.

For blending the spices and fixatives, use a glass bowl and wooden spoons. Freshly ground spice is superior to packaged spice powders. Buy whole spice, and coarsely grind it in either an electric coffee mill or by hand in a pestle and mortar.

Large earthenware storage crocks, with ventilation holes sealed, or tall glass sweet jars with screw-on lids are perfect for mixing the pot-pourri. Do not on any account use plastic or metal containers.

Pot-pourri making is a highly personal enterprise, and recipes can only serve as inspiration and are not meant to be slavishly followed, since not all gardens grow the same flowers, and not all combinations of scent are uniformly enjoyed. Keep a notebook when blending a pot-pourri, so that the ingredients of an especially pleasing mix will not be lost; this is how the wonderful antique recipes we can use today have reached us – through *receipt* books, some dating from the sixteenth century, kept for the instruction of still-room maids and gentlewomen learning one of the homemaker's most pleasant duties.

A lavish use of lavender edges the central path enhances the magical quality of a kitchen garden.

Rose and Lavender Dry Pot-pourri

Blend 300g (10oz) of rose petals, 85g (3oz) of lavender flowers, and 85g (3oz) of lemon verbena leaves together. Add 55g (2oz) of orris root powder and 1 table-spoon each of allspice, cinnamon, cloves and nutmeg. Finally, add rose essence; 12–16 drops should be adequate, but the amount will be determined by the fragrance of the rose petals used, so mix and sniff as you add the essence to test the strength.

Cover and leave the pot-pourri to mature for 2 weeks, stirring periodically.

Simple Moist Pot-pourri

Dry 225g (8oz) of rose petals for 2 days. Mix 150g (5oz) each of coarse salt and table salt and combine with the petals in alternate layers of 1.25cm (½in) in a crock. Put the pot-pourri to cure in a cool dry place for 10 days. Stir daily after 5 days. On day 11, pour the mixture into a bowl and add 28g (1oz) or more each of lavender flowers, sweet herbs or scented geranium leaves, 1 teaspoon each of cloves and ginger and 28g (1oz) of orris root powder. Mix well, return the pot-pourri to the crock, cover tightly and leave to mature for at least 1 month. Shake the container occasionally to assist the blending of the various perfumes.

Flower vinegars were the seventeenth-century equivalent to aspirin, and a small sponge soaked in violet vinegar pressed to the anxious brow was a popular headache cure. Herbal and floral vinegars kept noxious odours at bay, and helped to revive our great-great-grandmothers when their stays got the better of their circulation.

Here are the instructions Sir Hugh Platt gave for the making of rosewater and vinegar.

Geranium Leaf Sponge, Eggs cooked with Marigolds, Lavender Vinegar, Pot Pourri and Rose Creams.

Rosewater and Vinegar

Rosewater and Rosevinegar of the colour the Rose, and of the Cowslep, and violet vinegar.

If you would make your Rosewater and Rose vinegar of a Rubie colour, then make choice of the crimson velvet coloured leaves, clipping away the whites with a paire of sheeres, & being through dried, put a good large handfull of them into a pinte of Damaske or red rosewater; stop your glasse well & set it in the sun, till you see that the leaves have lost their colour . . . What I have said of Rosewater, the same may also be intended of Rose vinegar, violet, marigolde, and cowslep vinegar, but the whiter vinegar you chuse for this purpose, the colour thereof will be the brighter, and therefore distilled Vinegar is best for this purpose.

From *Delightes for Ladies*, Sir Hugh Platt, 1602

Oyle of Roses

This recipe is one of the more workable methods for extracting essential oil from rose petals, referred to as 'leaves'.

Take Sallet Oyle and put it into a earthen pot, then take *Rose* leaves, clip off all the white, and bruise them a little, and put them into the Oyle, and then stop the top close with past[e], and set it into a boyling pot of water, and let it boyle one hour, then let it stand al one night upon hot embers, the next day take the Oyle, and straine it from the *Rose* leaves, into a glasse, and put therein some fresh *Rose* leaves, clipt as before, stop it, and set it in the Sun every day for fortnight or three weeks.

From *A Book of Fruit and Flowers*, 1653

Use enough oil (choose a tasteless, odourless salad oil like sunflower oil) to cover the petals. Even a glazed pot will absorb the smell of the roses, so it is best to use an ovenproof glass or a stainless-steel pot. Use a simple flour-and-water dough to seal the vessel and place it in a bain marie in a hot oven, 200°C (400°F), then (assuming you have no embers) reduce the heat to the lowest setting and leave overnight. Strain the liquid into a preserving jar, add the extra petals – about half the quantity of the first maceration – and seal. Strain the mixture into small vials and store in a cool dark place.

Two more patterns for parterres from Markham's translation of *Maison Rustique*.

Oil of Lavender

To make Oyle of Lavender, take a pint of Sallet Oyl, and put it into a glass then put to it a handful of Lavender, and let it stand in the sun twelve daies and use it in all respects.

From *The English House-Wife, A Way to Get Wealth*, Gervase Markham, 13th edn. 1676

Gervase Markham goes on to say that roses and violets can be used in place of lavender, but you must cut away the white part of the rose petals and shred them before adding to the oil.

To make Conserve of Red Roses

Take one Pound of red Rose-Buds, and bruise them with a Wooden Pestle in a Marble Mortar, adding by Degrees, of white Loaf-Sugar powdered and sifted, three Pounds; continue beating them, till no particles of the Roses can be seen, and till the Mass is all alike.

From *Adam's Luxury and Eve's Cookery*, 1744

Another recipe, from *The Tresurie of Hidden Secrets* (1637), also uses petals and sugar in a 3:1 ratio and says that you should remove the white part of each petal and store the conserve in a well-sealed pot. 'Conserve of roses comforteth the stomach, the heart and all the bowels . . .' Other flower conserves can be made in the same manner.

Rose Creams

Sift 225g (8oz) of icing sugar with a generous pinch of cinnamon. Beat 1 egg white until it is stiff but not dry, gradually adding half the icing sugar. Moisten with a sprinkling of rosewater and tint with a few drops of red food colour. Add the remainder of the sugar. Fill a piping bag with the mixture and pipe small star shapes on to a tray lined with aluminium foil. Put the creams in a bright, airy place to harden, which will take several days.

Violet creams can be made in the same manner, altering the colour and flavouring accordingly. Use a pinch of powdered cardamom in place of cinnamon.

Although the flowers of scented-leaf geranium have no culinary value, the leaves can be used to line the bottom of cake tins. When the baked cake is inverted the leaves are exposed; the flavour they impart is mild. Try adding the leaves to apple jelly or to custards as you would a bay leaf.

During the summer I regularly add fresh leaves from scented geraniums in the garden to the bowl of pot-pourri in our hall. There they dry, gently adding their perfume to the rose and lavender petals, and freshening the mixture.

Pot marigolds added to stews and broths provide colour and a pleasant warm savour. The petals can also be used in salads. John Evelyn gave a recipe for a sweet steamed bread pudding made with marigold petals, and for the mint pennyroyal to be served with a sweet butter sauce flavoured with rosewater. Conserve of marigolds was taken to relieve melancholy and ease palpitations.

Eggs Cooked with Marigolds

This recipe would provide an agreeable first course for a summer dinner.

Simply poach fresh eggs over boiling water, scattering bright gold marigold petals thickly over the tops of the eggs before you put the lid on the pan. These eggs are most successful if prepared in a multi-section egg poacher with a nut of butter added to each cup.

Flower pickles were a prized salad ingredient and relish for boiled meat from the sixteenth to eighteenth centuries. Most often they were preserved in a sweet-sour liquid. In his *Acetaria*, John Evelyn wrote that while flowers could be eaten alone or in composition with other salletings, they were 'a more palatable Relish, being Infus'd in Vinegar; Especially those of the Clove-Gillyflower, Elder, Orange, Cowslip, Rosemary.'

To Pickle Flowers of any Sort

Put your Flowers into a Pot with their Weight of Sugar, and to every Pound of Sugar, put a pint of Vinegar.

From *Adam's Luxury and Eve's Cookery*, 1744

To Pickle Any Kind of Flower

Put them into a gally-pot [small earthenware pot used by apothecaries] or double glass with as much sugar as they weigh, fill them up with wine vinegar, a pound of sugar and a pound of flowers . . .

From *The Accomplish't Cook*, Robert May, 1685

Cowslip Pickle

To keep Cowslips for Salates

Take a quart of White wine Vinegar, and halfe a quarter of a pound of fine beaten Sugar, and mix them together, then take your Cowslips, pull them out of the podds, and cut off the green knobs at the lower end, put them into the pot or glasse wherein you mind to keep them, and well shaking the Vinegar and Sugar together in the glasse wherein they were before, powre it upon the Cowslips, and so stirring them morning and evening to make them settle for three weeks, keep them for your use.

From *A Book of Fruit and Flowers*, 1653

Pinks were commonly called clove-July-flowers or gilly-flowers, because of their pronounced spicy scent. Their other name was Sops-in-Wine, since the flowers were often dunked into claret to impart a taste of cloves. There is a recipe in *Adam's Luxury* for pickling currants, by simply warming them in white wine vinegar and adding as much sugar 'as you like', that was also recommended for use with clove-July-flowers.

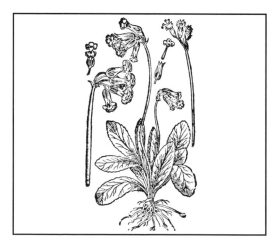

Primula veris, the much-loved cowslip, a true cottage-garden flower.

Candied flower petals, especially violets, are familiar to us: we use them to decorate Easter cakes and violet cream chocolates. But the Elizabethan housewife was much more adventurous and recipe books always included one or more methods for preserving petals or whole flowers.

Candied Flower Petals

To Candy all kinde of Flowers as they grow, with their stalks on.

Take the Flowers, and cut the stalks somewhat short, then take one pound of the whitest and hardest Sugar you can get, put to it eight spoonfulls of Rose water, and boyle it til it will roule between your fingers and your thumb, then take it from the fire, coole it with a stick, and as it waxeth cold, dip in all your flowers, and taking them out againe suddenly, lay them one by one on the bottome of a Sive [a wire cake rack]; then [cover with greaseproof paper and put in a cool oven] and dry your candy presently; then box them up and they will kepp all the year, and look very pleasantly.

From *A Book of Fruit and Flowers*, 1653

Another recipe, from *The Receipt Book of Mrs Mary Eales, Confectioner to Queen Anne* (1719), involves dipping the flowers in a solution of gum arabic, shaking them in a cloth to remove excess moisture, dusting them over with powdered sugar and then drying them suspended from string in front of a warm chimney.

Use 28g (1oz) of gum arabic dissolved in 110ml (4fl oz) of water. Remove the white parts of rose petals.

Ice Cream of Roses

One pint of cream, two handfuls of fresh rose petals, yolks of two eggs, sugar.

Boil a pint of cream and put into it when it boils two handfuls of fresh rose petals, and leave them for two hours, well covered. Then pass this through a sieve, and mix with the cream the well-beaten yolks of two eggs and sugar to taste. Add a little cochineal, and put it on the fire, stirring it all the time, but do not let it boil on any account. Put it on ice.

From *The Gentle Art of Cookery*, Mrs Hilda Leyel, 1947

SALLETINGS

What you will find in the following Sheets, are Directions generally for dressing after the best, most natural and wholesome Manner, such Provisions as are the Product of our own Country; and in such a Manner as is most agreeable to *English* Palates; saving that I have so far temporized, as, since we have, to our Disgrace, so fondly admired the *French* Tongue, *French* Modes, and also *French* Messes, to present you now and then with such receipts of the *French* Cookery as I think may not be disagreeable to *English* Palates.

The Compleat Housewife: or Accomplish'd Gentlewoman's Companion,
E. Smith, 15th edn., 1753 (earliest known: 2nd edn, 1728)

THIS QUOTE FROM a popular eighteenth-century cookery book is evidence of the sense of national pride which English citizens enjoyed during that period. Marlborough's decisive victory against the French ended the War of Spanish Succession and heralded the end of Louis XIV's supremacy in Europe.

It was a time of increased prosperity and steady commercial growth. The decline of Dutch trade monopolies in the Far East and the development of the North American colonies created new sources of raw materials and new export/import markets. Agricultural methods were improving, the population was expanding and a succession of good harvests quelled the unrest previously caused by earlier famines.

Land enclosure had been experienced over the past few hundred years, but after 1750, nearly 15,000,000 acres were enclosed and this more than anything changed the face of Britain, which was still an agricultural nation. The Enclosure Acts permitted owners of large estates to buy out the small owner-occupiers who were suffering from heavy taxes and lack of capital. These dispossessed people, uprooted from the land, became itinerant labourers or else went into trade in the expanding provincial towns which were gaining importance as centres of culture and commerce.

Thus were the medieval strip fields replaced by vast walled or hedged fields whose cultivation was made possible by new methods of improved crop rotation and machine-assisted farming. Jethro Tull led the swing to mechanisation: 'by our Houghing [ploughing with a horse] we can raise as good cabbages and carrots in a field as we used to grow in a garden'. Advances in land drainage contributed to the redundancy of raised beds, which followed flowers under siege from the Landscape movement out of the garden and into memory.

To return to the idea that things French were now definitely *passé*: the offspring of families whose great estates were daily growing greater made the obligatory Grand Tour, a leisurely sojourn through Europe, culminating most usually in a protracted stay in Italy, which was once again the epicentre of cultural activity. But these people were seeing beyond the Renaissance, and paying homage to classical antiquity. They were not in awe of the magnificent villa gardens but found inspiration in the 'view' of Roman ruins, temples and viaducts which were crumbling into the natural terrain. For them, nature was

Above Valerianella olitoria, corn salad or lamb's lettuce.

Opposite Detail from *In the Kitchen* by David de Noter (b. 1825).

a living canvas and it became the preoccupation of architects and landscape designers to construct houses and gardens with a painter's eye for composition. Yet the artists they most admired were the French painters Claude and Poussin, who had worked from Italy in the seventeenth century rather than spend their talents immortalising Louis XIV.

William Kent, a Yorkshireman who trained as a sign writer and later made a name for himself as a painter in Rome, eventually returned to England in 1719 with his patron the Duke of Burlington. He turned his talents to architecture and gardening and was to establish what became known as the 'Landskip' style of garden design. Horace Walpole remarked that Kent 'leaped the fence, and saw that all nature was a garden'.

Kent invented the ha-ha so that grazing flocks could be part of the pretty view without having to be kept from the immediate precincts of the house by unsightly fences or walls. Formal parterres of flowers, hedges and topiary were swept away and replaced by broad vistas of open park and wooded hillsides, dotted with temples, obelisks and sculpture, to give focus to the scheme and to the viewer's thoughts. Kent's designs for Rousham in Oxfordshire epitomised this ideal and set the standards for his followers.

The only walls left standing were those surrounding the kitchen garden, and these once small, intimate enclosures (recalling their monastic origins) became grand edifices. At Holkham Hall in Norfolk the remains of the kitchen garden comprise four separate gardens over 6½ acres, including a hothouse, hotbeds, and an orangery. These gardens, laid out in the 1820s, replaced the original kitchen garden which had been sited nearer the house. In gardens such as these were grown all the startling introductions from England's expanding empire. And to bring these treasures to the peak of their perfection a gardener employed by 'noblemen or gentlemen must take care to make himself well acquainted with cultivation of fruits, flowers, vegetables and in general everything growing in gardens either for pleasure or for use'. Vegetable gardening and fruit growing were becoming a science, and skill with hotbeds, cloches for forcing and glasshouse cultivation was much admired.

But these were the grand gardens, and in the cottager's patch things remained much as they always had been, although even here raised beds were being levelled and fruit was being trained against walls in imitation of the landlord's style. Because it was held to be inappropriate for a member of the lower orders to aspire to be anything 'above his station', and because such a member was inhibited by a smaller purse, the cottager's and small farmer's garden became the repository of traditional English gardening skills. But in both classes of kitchen garden the four-square plan prevailed, with crossing main paths laid according to the compass.

The well-to-do now enjoyed fruit and vegetables at almost every meal, largely because of a new train of medical thought on the properties of food. It was determined by a study of the nature of 'salts' contained within all living tissue, that the relative acidity or alkalinity of the salts could be used to cure illness; scurvy was thought to be caused by too much preserved meat (salt = alkaline) but cured by eating fruit which was acid. At last the lingering taint of Galenic thought was dropping from the vegetable kingdom. In 1750, William Cadogan recommended in his *Essay on the Nursing and Management of Children* that infants be fed as soon as possible on 'meat, bread, butter, raw, baked and stewed fruit and all the produce of the kitchen garden', instead of being nourished solely on milk, bread and spice.

Food presentation underwent a drastic change in the eighteenth century: dining tables

Just over fifty years after this Dutch engraving was published, *c.* 1640, small enclosed gardens with neatly edged and artfully arranged beds were to become a thing of the past, due to the arrival, during the early eighteenth century, of the landscape school of gardening and the rapid development of horticultural 'technology'.

came into use. Previously, since medieval times, food had been displayed on sideboards with the diners seated at a plain linen-covered board, laying out their *nefs*, personal knife, spoon (later a fork was added), napkin and drinking cup. A trencher was placed before them and the food was brought up from the side in procession.

Now tables were much broader. E. Smith's book *The Compleat Housewife* includes 'Schemes . . . for the regular Disposition or Placing of the Dishes of Provision on the Table, according to the best Manner, both for Summer and Winter, first and second Courses, &c.'. Georgian silver eating implements, serving dishes of fine porcelain, damask cloth, and elegantly and elaborately prepared individual dishes now graced the table, which was of highly polished expensive imported wood and itself a fine example of the cabinetmaker's art. What a delicious way to display wealth.

Many of the great traditional British dishes have their origins in this prosperous era and owe their popularity to the redoubtable Hannah Glasse, whose cookery book *The Art of Cooking made Plain and Easy* went through fifty-two editions between 1747 and 1803. She shared E. Smith's distaste for things French and admonished her readers to beware of the 'blind folly of this Age that they would rather be imposed on by a *French* booby, than give encouragement to a good *English* Cook!'.

There is much that we today can borrow from her writings, not least of which should be an increased knowledge of salads and the wide range of leaf and flowers from which they can be made. The English may shudder at the thought of American-style salads that combine fruit, cheese, vegetables and meat in a number of tasty ways, but these are actually quite close to the ideal eighteenth-century sallets, which are far more imaginative than the dreary damp lettuce, unripe tomato and desiccated cucumber so often passed off as salad in English restaurants. And as for salad cream, the less said the better.

Lettuce, Chicory, Endive, Dandelions, Radishes, Cresses, Fenugreek

Lettuce has held its attraction as the finest salad leaf since earliest times, served to Persian royalty in the fifth century BC and adored by the Greeks and Romans, who originally served salads at the end of a meal, but later presented the dish as an appetiser. When John Evelyn compiled his *Acetaria*, serving salad was still a vexed question; he seems to agree with the French who then ate their salads first to 'make way, and prevent Obstruction'. Lettuce has a reputation as a soporific (perhaps this is why it is often served at the end of a meal), and the milky substance exuded from the stem of a bolted lettuce is dangerously high in laudanum.

Pliny noted nine types of lettuce cultivated in Roman gardens, some of which had red-tinted leaves. Evelyn noted seventeen, including the oak-leaf sort and the Genoa which lasted all winter. He further remarks that gardeners worked hard at cultivating this 'Noble Plant' which to his knowledge was in the past the principal salleting served at the best tables, and dressed with vinegar and sugar.

Headed lettuces, similar to our cabbage lettuces, were grown by the ancients and cos-type lettuces were also popular. Similar to today's common practice, these two types were used in preference to the curled, oak leaf, red-tinged and cut-and-come-again loose-leaf sorts. Happily, though, there is more interest being shown today in these unusual varieties, and many mainstream seed merchants list them in their catalogues. It is about time we paid them more attention.

Lettuces require a rich, moist soil to make the best, i.e. fast, growth. They will grow in full sun or dappled shade and so are excellent for intercropping with taller growing vegetables which also require a good deal of moisture. It is advisable to grow lettuces in partial shade if the summer is very hot. They prefer cool conditions for growing and germinating, so it is best to sow the seed in cool weather and during the early evening when the soil will soon be cooled and moistened by nightfall. Lettuce also does well grown through a polythene or organic mulch which helps to keep the roots cool.

Lettuce can be sown outdoors almost all the year round in temperate regions using appropriate varieties. In cold climates an early start can be made by sowing it under cloches, in the greenhouse in prepared beds under the staging, or else by raising individual seedlings in peat blocks or pots for transplanting outdoors once the weather warms.

Heading lettuces are best started in this manner, since it removes the need for thinning. To form good heads, the lettuces should be grown about 12.5cm (5in) apart for small varieties and 30cm (12in) for the larger sorts. Most lettuces, though, will do nicely at 15–22cm (6–9in). But if you sow directly into the beds, begin thinning early on so that the plants are never overcrowded; the thinnings can be used in salads. Otherwise, station-sow the lettuces at the appropriate distance.

Loose-leaf lettuces are not so dependent on thinning, since you are constantly reducing the size of the plants by repeated cutting. They can be sown in rows or broadcast in wide rows.

Lettuce is a good companion for strawberries, carrots and onions.

Wild **chicory** was a prized salad herb among ancient peoples, but the first mention of its garden cultivation occurs in 1616, when Dodoens remarked in his *Pemptades* that it was grown in gardens throughout Germany.

There are many types of chicory, but they are grown either for their slightly bitter leaves that can be eaten raw or cooked, or for their edible root. The Italians make the greatest use of this vegetable and the ball-headed, red-leaved *radicchio* is probably the one most familiar outside that country, along with the blanched shoots or 'chicons' of the 'Witloof', produced by forcing the roots in darkness.

Most chicories are perennials and of easy cultivation. There are basically two sorts: red leaf and green leaf, each having variations of leaf shape from broad and rather twisted to narrow and tapering, sometimes deeply serrated.

Sow the seed from early spring to midsummer in single or wide rows. You can harvest the young leaves – which in red-leaved varieties will first appear green, only turning red as they mature – or allow heads to form, which happens as the summer nears its end. Plants for heading should not be overcrowded; this and damp muggy weather causes them to rot, so space them about 12.5–15cm (5–6in) apart.

On the whole, young leaves are better suited to salads, as they are less bitter. I find that the older plants are best if plunged into boiling water to remove some of the bitterness, and then sautéed lightly in olive oil or butter with a touch of garlic.

In the open garden, **endive** takes over where lettuce leaves off. It is a cool-weather plant and can withstand some

Above left chicory 'Rossa di Treviso', *above right* curly-leaved endive and butterhead lettuce.

pretty sharp frosts. Endive is a species of chicory and another favourite salad plant of ancient cultivation. Pliny mentions it and it was growing in English gardens by the middle of the sixteenth century. It has a bitter flavour, although not as pronounced as chicory.

Sow the seed in late summer in rich, moist soil; it is useful as a follow-on crop where beans and potatoes have been previously grown. Alternatively, sow it among crops like spring cabbage and Japanese onions. Thin the plants to 12.5–15cm (5–6in) and use the seedlings in salads.

The bitterness of endive and chicory leaves can be reduced by blanching. Gather up the leaves around the heart, tie loosely with raffia and slip a tube of cardboard around each one; bottomless cardboard milk cartons are useful for this.

Chicons can be made by lifting the roots of 'Witloof' chicory and planting them into a large pot filled with equal parts of peat and sand. Cut off the leaves and trim the roots to equal lengths of about 15cm (6in). Put the pot into a black plastic rubbish bag, tie the top and put in a cool place.

Don't curse **dandelions**; cultivate the plants, blanch the leaves to use in salads and gather the flowers to make dandelion wine. The wild dandelion has long been used as a salad and pot herb, but it is only since the mid–1800s that it has been cultivated in gardens to improve the flavour and texture of the leaves. John Evelyn described how the French ate the roots; this was apparently their common practice as the French settlers in eighteenth-century New York also used the roots and not the leaves.

As we know, the dandelion is a vigorous perennial, easily raised from seed. The best leaves come from plants grown in cool rich soil that is moist but well drained. Wild and garden-grown plants should be harvested in the early spring before the flowers appear. As the plants age, the leaves become coarser. But their quality can be improved by simple blanching: just tie the leaves together loosely above the crown of the plant.

Many children have their first gardening lesson by sowing a row of **radishes**. They are ruthlessly reliable and so heedless of poor cultivation that few gardeners take much time over them; with the result that the radishes are deformed, woody, riddled with maggots or fly. But they do repay careful cultivation with sweet, succulent, clean roots whose peppery hotness is perfectly complemented by plain bread and butter.

The Pharaohs enjoyed radishes and the Greeks so revered them that gold radish effigies were offered to Apollo at Delphi. Gerard mentions that radishes were eaten raw with bread but mostly used to flavour meat sauces 'to procure appetite'. Every part of the plant is edible: the roots, which today are usually eaten fresh with salt, can be boiled and served with a butter sauce, the leaves can be used raw in salads or boiled and served like spinach and the seed pods of the larger varieties make a nice pickle.

Evelyn preferred the seedling leaves and roots for salad-making and said that they could be had the year round if raised on a hotbed. Today we have summer radishes, either round or tapering, and white, red, black or yellow, and winter radishes, which are mostly of Chinese or Japanese origin and the same shape and colour range as summer varieties, but much larger; 'Sakurajima Mammoth' makes up to 32kg (70lb). Not surprisingly, the big winter radishes are best cooked, although the 'Diakon' radish can be shredded and eaten raw.

Summer radishes grow so quickly that it makes sense to grow them among other vegetables; sown with spinach and slower-growing root crops, the radish seedlings help to mark the row. Radishes are good companions for tomatoes, lettuce and members of the *Cucurbitaceae* family.

The **cresses** provide another peppery taste for the salad bowl, and American, Land or Belle Isle cress is probably the most pungent; a few raw leaves go a long way and it can also be cooked with other greens. This cress is a hardy biennial which can be used throughout the year; spring sowings provide summer crops, a midsummer sowing later summer and winter crops. It appreciates a rich moist soil and partial shade, so grow it among taller vegetables. Use the outer leaves first, but as the plants age, harvest the new growth from the centre of the plant. Remove any flowerheads to promote leaf growth.

Garden or pepper cress grows quickly and is the sort used in combination with mustard for the salad sprout mix. However, it can be grown in the garden as a cut-and-come-again salad, broadcast sowing the seed in wide rows. It likes a light, cool, moist soil.

Rocket, also known as Italian cress or arugula, should definitely be grown, for the spiciness and heat of the leaves is less aggressive then the other cresses. It was a popular salad herb in England until the nineteenth century, but retained its popularity in America and southern Europe – perhaps because historically it is a very macho herb: Pliny said that the seed taken by a man before he was whipped enabled him to bear the pain, and Gerard determined that the leaves provoked lust and increased virility.

Rocket is a cool weather plant, so summer sowings should be made in a partially shaded place. Begin sowing in early spring and make successional sowings every two or three weeks in order to have a

steady supply of young leaves. It grows quickly and is harvested young, so it can be interplanted with tomatoes, beans and slow-growing root crops.

For winter cutting, make a late autumn sowing and cover the row with cloches.

Fenugreek is a common East Indian spice; the seeds are ground and used in curry mixtures. But the strongly flavoured leaves can be used, with discretion, for salads.

The Egyptians mixed fenugreek sprouts with honey and a conserve of fenugreek was once a valuable commodity, imported to England and also used by Arab slave-traders along the African coast.

It is fairly hardy and can be raised under cloches from autumn sowings. Otherwise begin making small, frequent successional sowings in the early spring. It will grow in any type of soil, but requires plenty of moisture in order to germinate and grow well, so pay attention to watering. Harvest the leaves when they are about 7.5–10cm (3–4in) high.

This engraving from John Parkinson's *Paradisus in Sole* illustrates the enormous variety of salad greens cultivated by our gardening ancestors.

1 *Malva crispa*. French Mallowes [hollyhock]
2 *Endiva*. Endive
3 *Cichorium*. Succory [chicory]
4 *Spinachia*. Spinach
5 *Lactuca crispa*. Curl'd Lettice
6 *Lactuca patula*. An open Lettice
7 *Lactuca capitata vulgaris*. Ordinary cabbage Lettice
8 *Lactuca capitata Romana*. The great Romane cabbage Lettice
9 *Lactuca agueno*. Corne Sallet or Lambes Lettice.

Corn Salad, Purslane, Sorrel, Orach

Corn salad or **lamb's lettuce** is one of the joys of the kitchen garden even into early winter. It is an extremely hardy annual, but equally slow growing, so sowings should be made regularly and frequently throughout the summer to have a steady supply of young plants during winter. Some people like to cut-and-come-again but I think it is preferable to uproot the young plants and then pluck them clean under running water; grit seems to cling to corn salad and the leaves bruise easily, so the less handling the better.

Gerard recognised corn salad growing in the gardens of French and Dutch immigrants, so it was probably a popular European salad herb before it caught on in England and America. Certainly now it is more widely grown in France and is one of that country's culinary pleasures – *salade de mâche* with fresh walnut oil and coarsely ground salt and pepper is salad heaven.

Now, as then, there are several varieties, distinguished by the shape of their leaves, from long and tapering to short and oval. It grows best in a light, sandy soil but will grow happily in any reasonably fertile soil. Because of its lateness, it is useful for follow-on sowing, taking the place of tomatoes, spring cabbages, onions and so on. But it does like sun.

Thin the plants to 15cm (6in) if you wish to have sizeable rosettes to supply leaves for plucking.

Purslane was used in Elizabethan times for physic – for, among other things, toothache, loose and sensitive teeth and the treatment of worms – as well as for salad, which seems to have been its main virtue. Purslane was also used to make soup. 'Boil the Purslane in pea soup with a

Plantago coronpus, Buckshorn plantain.

little onion, when your Purslane is boiled enough soak some crusts in the broth, garnish them with Purslane, pour over the broth and serve it up hot', is an eighteenth-century recipe.

Like corn salad, purslane needs a warm, sandy soil and plenty of moisture during dry summer days. Begin successional sowings in early summer or late spring if it is reasonably warm.

Gather the stalks when they are quite young and use the fleshy leaves only (in earlier times the tough stalks were pickled). Remove any flowerheads that form; plants that flower are worthless. There is a golden purslane, but it is even less hardy than the green.

Sorrel, purslane and lettuce were used to make a spring soup, similar to the recipe given above but flavoured with chervil and parsley and thickened with eggs and milk; sorrel is, in the words of Elizabeth David, 'the perfect foil for eggs and fish', and it is most often encountered as a sauce for either of these foods. But the sharp lemony young leaves of sorrel are a pleasing addition to salads.

French sorrel, the type most useful for culinary purposes, is *Rumex scutatus* with broad leaves; common sorrel, *R. acetosa*, is extremely bitter and hardly edible. It is a native of England and was the sort used by the early cooks who, until the introduction of French sorrel, valued it highly. *R. patienta*, or herb patience, is a milder flavoured relative. It was also known as monk's rhubarb, which probably indicates that it was grown in monastic gardens, and it was a popular spinach-like vegetable in the early sixteenth century. It grows to 1.8m (6ft).

All the sorrels are extremely hardy perennials. French sorrel prefers a well-drained, warm soil to the moist, rich soil liked by common sorrel and herb patience. Sorrel grows easily from seed sown in the early spring. It will seed itself, which is an easy means of propagation.

Orach is another spinach-type leaf good to eat raw or cooked with sorrel or spinach. There is a green and a red orach, the latter being the most attractive; there are not many crimson plants that reach 1.8m (6ft).

The Romans and Greeks ate orach boiled like spinach. It was popular in England from the early sixteenth century and was an early introduction to the American colonies. John Evelyn wrote that orach should be cooked in its own juice and that the tender young leaves were useful in cold salads, but 'tis better in Pottage'. In England it lost its prestige after the introduction of spinach.

Orach is an annual to be sown in the spring in rich, moist soil; pick it regularly (pinching out the stem ends to encourage bushiness) and remove all flowerheads to promote leaf production.

Above left Corn salad or lamb's lettuce, *right* sorrel, orach.

Burnet, Hairy Bitter Cress, Ox-eye Daisy, Buckshorn Plantain, Cucumbers

John Parkinson wrote:

The greatest use that Burnet is commonly put onto, is to put a few leaves into a cup with Claret wine, which is presently to be drunke, and giveth a pleasant quicke taste thereunto, very delightfull to the palate, and is accounted to helpe to make the heart merrie. It is sometimes also while it is young, put among other Sallet herbes, to give a finer rellish thereunto.

Burnet is one of the 'weeds' that provide tasty salad greens; the young leaves have a pleasant flavour of cucumber. It is a hardy perennial that revels in sun-baked, dry, impossible soil, especially if it is chalky; add some lime before sowing if your soil is deficient. Otherwise, treat it harshly: Francis Bacon desired burnet, water-mint and wild thyme to be set in alleys 'to perfume the air most delightfully, being trodden upon and crushed'.

Sow fresh seed in the autumn or else propagate by division in the spring. Cut the leaves at 10cm (4in).

Cardamine hirsuta, better known as **hairy bitter cress** or **scurvy grass**, is a dainty little annual weed that most gardeners hoe into oblivion. Yet in the eighteenth and nineteenth centuries, on both sides of the Atlantic, the young leaves were used in salads. So reserve some of the self-sown plants to gather seed for 'controlled' cultivation, or simply eat what you hoe.

The **ox-eye daisy** or **marguerite**, *Chrysanthemum leucanthemum*, provides leaf and petal for salads, and was especially popular in England during the mid-nineteenth century; today it is more often encountered in Italy as one of the leaves of a 'country salad'.

One of the most curious and delicious salad leaves I have encountered is *Plantago coronopus*, the **buckshorn plantain**. When I first saw it, in boxes of salad greens in a Rome market, the vendor called it Herba Stella; later I purchased a packet of seed from a seed merchant in the Cimini hills.

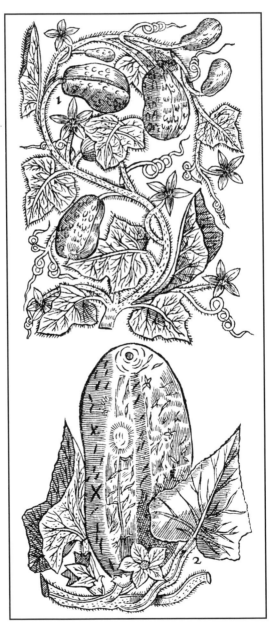

Top Parkinson's 'ordinary Cowcumber', and *above* the 'long yellow Spanish Cowcumber'.

Back home, I discovered that it was a common enough weed – not one that I had ever seen, but then I hadn't been looking – and that Salmon's *Herbal* identifies the Italian salad plant Herba Stella as a well-grown buckshorn plantain. Live and learn, by keeping your eyes open.

The leaves are long, and deeply pennate, with a prickly texture and a mildly bitter but buttery taste. Gerard calls it swine's cress and says that the roots taste like the garden cresses. The young leaves are finer, becoming coarser with age, and these if chopped can still be eaten raw.

It is a perennial that forms large, shaggy rosettes. Sow the seed in the spring and cut the leaves at will; it lasts well into the winter. Once established it will seed itself and makes an unusual edging.

Generations of gardeners have concentrated many hours of effort in the cultivation of **cucumbers**, an exercise which probably began in the gardens of India at least 3,000 years ago. None, though, will have surpassed the herculean efforts of the Emperor Tiberius who so enjoyed this succulent vegetable that he constructed wheeled frames to enable the cucumbers to be moved around the garden, following the sun. For winter supplies, he had other frames glazed with a translucent mineral crystal.

Gerard described how to raise cucumbers on hotbeds and this was the accepted method of achieving the long, straight fruits similar to the ones we can so easily purchase from green markets today.

Formerly the finest cucumbers were raised under glass; outdoor, or ridge, cucumbers were stubby, warty things. But hybridists have been at work and have improved the quality of ridge cucumbers, so that now there are varieties which compare quite favourably to frame cucumbers, but which have the edge since they are happy to grow in the open garden. These varieties are shorter, and have a somewhat bumpy skin, but they are remarkably resistant to disease and will bear fruit in cool temperatures. Also, there are bush varieties which take up less space or can be grown in containers, and sorts which have all or a high proportion of female flowers, and so are more productive.

Seed can be sown *in situ* in early summer when the soil has begun to warm, setting 3–4 seeds at each station. Improvise cloches by cutting clear plastic soft-drink bottles in half, and position over each station. Remove the cloches when the first true leaves appear and then thin the seedlings, leaving only the strongest. Alternatively, sow the seeds indoors in peat blocks or pots during the spring for planting out under cloches. Put 2–3 seeds in each pot and thin as described above. Position the plants at 60cm (24in) intervals.

Cucumbers do well on raised beds, appreciating the deeply dug soil and bottom layer of manure. Trailing varieties can be supported on trellis-work frames, or allowed to travel along the ground. Pinch out the growing tips of trained plants when they reach the limits of the support. Those on the ground should be pinched out at about the sixth leaf. After that, keep the side growths in check by pinching out after the first few fruits have set. By limiting the extension growth you will also help the plant to direct its energy into ripening the fruit it has made.

Make sure that the cucumbers are never short of water; they need a little, often. But when you do water, do it thoroughly. A light sprinkle brings roots to the surface.

Gather the fruit regularly, and be sure to harvest pickling cucumbers while they are still small and sweet.

This kitchen garden from R. Bradley's *The Gentleman and Gardener's Kalendar* (1718) shows trellis shading for wall-trained fruit, glass coldframes and bell jars for forcing and protecting tender crops and fruit trees in Versailles tubs.

Globe Artichokes, Beetroot, Kohl Rabi, Celeraic, Celery, Celtuce

Globe artichoke, unlike its relative the cardoon, got off to a slow beginning in the vegetable garden. It was first grown in Italy during the mid-fifteenth century at Naples and moved north through that country until, near the end of the century, one writer, Emilio Barbaro, described seeing a single showpiece plant in a Venetian garden.

But artichokes soon became a popular food plant in Italy and France, reaching England in the mid-sixteenth century. It grew so well that by the time Parkinson was writing his *Paradisus*, England was exporting part of its crop to Italy and France; 'Wee finde by dayly experience, that our English red Artichoke is in our Countrey the most delicate meate of any of the other . . . so that it seemeth that our soyle and climate hath the preheminence to nourish up this plant to his highest excellence.'

Has the climate and soil changed so radically in the subsequent centuries that England can no longer produce such high-quality artichokes? For they are rarely grown now, except in the flower garden for their stunning foliage and purple thistle flowers. Most of our supplies for the kitchen are from France, and the best from Brittany.

Artichokes require well-dug, light soil and sun, with plenty of well-rotted manure. They do take up a lot of room, so give them a bed to themselves in a sun-baked corner. They also like a moist but well-drained soil.

Obtain fresh offshoots from a nursery, avoiding withered desiccated specimens. Plant in mid-spring about 10cm (4in) deep with at least 60cm (2ft) between each plant. Water well and apply a liquid feed every two weeks during the summer. During the first year remove all the flowering shoots to encourage strong growth which will in turn aid the formation of sizeable flowerheads in the second year.

Harvest the large terminal buds first when they are about 12.5cm (5in) in diameter. Side shoots will then develop, bearing smaller flowers which can also be harvested.

At the end of the season cut the fading foliage to the ground and cover the crowns with a protective mulch of strawy manure or leaf mould.

Plants will continue to produce good quality flowers for at least four years, so after the second year begin propagating from mature plants, selecting offsets that are at least 25cm (10in) tall.

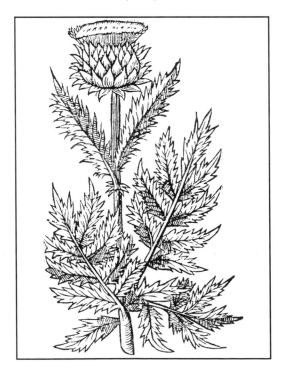

The 'Thistle Artichoke' from John Parkinson's herbal, which is the garden and hedgerow weed.

It may seem odd to place **beetroots** in the salad chapter, but while some of us may enjoy hot buttered beets or the Middle Eastern soup, bortsch, most will agree that beets sliced or diced, pickled or plain, are a fine salad ingredient. Golfball-sized beets dished up whole are perfectly tender with an appetisingly earthy, sweet flavour.

The Greeks and Romans preferred the foliage to the roots, and prepared them with lentils and beans. The red beetroot that we know was uncommon, only commented on in 1556 as a German curiosity. In 1578, Dodoens described the Roman beet (the name may signify an Italian introduction) as a 'strange red beet' that was eaten boiled and dressed with oil and vinegar.

Inevitably, this delicious root gained acceptance as a salad vegetable and John Evelyn remarked that 'The Roots of the Red Beet, pared into thin Slices and Circles, are by the French and Italians contriv'd into curious Figures to adorn their Sallets'.

As well as the familiar purple-red beet, there are yellow or golden-fleshed varieties which have a slightly higher sugar content, and an Italian variety that shows white and pale pink rings when sliced across. The root shapes vary from flat-topped and round, to tapering and cylindrical, the last having the best keeping qualities for winter storage.

Beets prefer a well-drained, light soil which was manured for a previous crop. Keep plants well watered during dry spells.

Begin planting in late spring, and using a bolt-resistant variety, start making

Above left globe artichoke, right *beetroot and kohl rabi.*

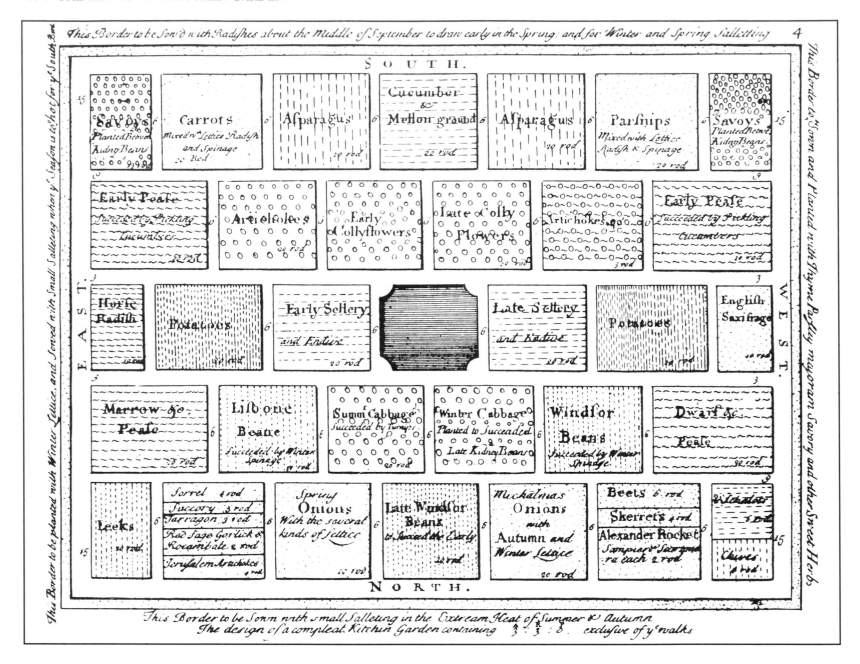

In 1728, Batty Langley published his *New Principles of Gardening* which as he described it was 'illustrated with great Variety of GRAND DESIGNS' including this plan for a 'compleat Kitchin Garden' of over three acres excluding walks. This book he dedicated to King George II. Langley thought of himself as one of the World's Leading Authorities in the areas of fine and applied arts of printmaking, architecture, horticulture and sundry other related areas. Today some assess him as an artful opportunist, but the fact remains that his pattern books for gothic-style architecture and his books on gardening were enormously influential during the changeover days when Renaissance gardens were being replaced by 'the irregular style of gardening' which was to become the Landscape school.

successive sowings through to late summer. Beetroot seed is in fact a cluster of seed, so take care to thin seedlings early on to allow the roots to develop properly; mono-germ varieties are single-seed, so this thinning is not necessary. Beet seed is large enough to sow individually at about 7.5cm (3in) apart in single or wide rows, or interplanted among faster growing vegetables.

Beets make good companions for lettuces, cabbages, onions and the next vegetable, kohl rabi.

Sometimes called the turnip-rooted cabbage, **kohl rabi** has a better reputation in Germany than in most other countries. It tastes like a cross between turnips and cabbages, and is in fact one of the brassicas.

There are two sorts, the red and the white, and the latter is generally considered the finer of the two. The edible part is actually a swollen stem from which the leaves sprout singly, rather than showing at the crown.

It grows easily from seed sown in mid-spring through to the end of summer. It is best to make succession sowings, since small roots are the most flavourful. Like beets and carrots, kohl rabi likes a soil that was manured for a previous crop, following early potatoes for example, and a deeply dug, moist soil. This ensures that the plant grows quickly; slow growth makes kohl rabi tough and woody. Thin the seedlings to about 15cm (6in).

Celeriac is a form of celery that makes an edible tuber. It is enormously popular in France and Germany, where it is served raw in salads or else cooked in soups and stews. It has the warm rich taste of celery, but is slightly more nutty. It is a slow grower and requires good rich moist soil. Start the seed indoors in gentle heat during early spring, sowing the seed in peat pots or blocks. Harden it off thoroughly before planting out in early summer at 30cm (12in) intervals.

Feed the plants regularly, as often as once a week, during the growing season with a weak solution of a high potassium liquid fertiliser. The roots are ready for lifting by the beginning of autumn. In warm gardens they can be left in the ground covered with a straw mulch, but in cold regions it is best to lift them and store them in sand.

Leeks and runner beans are good companions for celeriac.

Celery did not come into common use until the late eighteenth century when it was used chiefly as flavouring for soups and stews, although it had been cultivated in Tuscany during the sixteenth century. Smallage, a cultivated form of wild celery, is of greater culinary antiquity and may have been used to flavour potage and salads.

At one time the hollow-stem celery was preferred to the solid-stem sort which is the type favoured by modern taste.

Celery has a reputation for difficulty, probably because most gardeners attempt to grow the traditional sort which requires elaborate blanching. However, self-blanching celery, although a rough cousin, is somewhat less difficult to grow.

Celery needs a long growing season, and the seed should be started indoors and planted out as for celeriac. The seed is slow to germinate, so an overnight soaking is helpful. Give celery cool moist soil and partial shade, perhaps in the shelter of taller growing subjects. It is shallow rooting so appreciates a top dressing of well-rotted manure which will also serve as a water-retaining mulch.

When transplanting, set the plants, or peat pots or blocks, at least 12mm (½in) below the soil level into the bottom of a trench that is 10–12.5cm (4–5in) deep. Water well and then gradually fill in the trench with fine soil and compost as the plants grow. Keep the plants free from weeds, taking care not to disturb the roots. Water regularly and feed with a high potash fertiliser two or three times during the growing season.

As the plants mature you can begin pulling the larger outer stalks. The centre or heart will keep producing and eventually the entire plant (try not to disturb the roots too much) can be lifted in early autumn and stored in sand.

Use the celery as it grows and the flavour will be much stronger than if it is blanched by occluding light from the stalks for about 10–14 days before harvesting. To do this, use a cardboard tube, stout brown paper tied round with raffia, or simply hill-up the soil around each plant. If the celery is planted in a square, of 1.2m (4ft) or thereabouts, and the plants arranged in a quincunx, the crop will take up less space.

French celery dinant is an easy-to-grow celery, resembling the old smallage, and is invaluable for use as a pot herb. Sow the seed in small pinches in pots or blocks. Do not thin, but harden off as for celery. Plant out at 15cm (6in) intervals and begin cutting after the plants reach 20–25cm (8–10in). Once it is established it will seed itself. In fact, it becomes a bit of pest if you're not careful to remove misplaced seedlings.

Some gardeners recommend putting celery and leeks in the same trench. It also grows well with tomatoes – the shade provided by bush varieties has a blanching effect – and among dwarf French beans.

Celtuce is a mongrel. It is also known as asparagus lettuce and stem lettuce, for it looks like a bolted lettuce with an extraordinarily thick stem. This is the edible part, which has a crunchy celery-like taste, and can be eaten raw or boiled and served with melted butter. It is also good in soup. The mature leaves are too coarse to eat in salads, but young 'thinnings' are acceptable.

Celtuce grows easily from seed sown *in situ* in early summer in any well-drained moist soil. It grows to about 45cm (18in), so thin the plants to about 25cm (10in).

RECIPES

In his book *A Way to Get Wealth* (13th edn., 1676), Gervase Markham included a section devoted to the 'The English Housewife', in which he stipulates that for a woman to be a good cook, 'She must not be butter-fingered, sweet-toothed, nor faint-hearted for the first will let everything fall; the second will consume what it should encrease; and the last will lose time with too much niceness'.

His cookery section is divided into five parts, beginning with sallets and fricasses. The sallets he divides into: simple, compounded, some to furnish out the table, and some 'both for use and adornation'.

A simple sallet consisted of nothing more than a single vegetable: 'Chibols pilled, washed clean, half of the green tops cut away and so served in a fruit dish . . . also chives, scallions, radishes, boiled carrots . . . young lettuce, cabbage leaves, purslane served simply without anything other than Vinegar, sallet oil and sugar. Onions boiled, skinned and served with vinegar, oil and pepper . . . with a world of others too tedious to nominate.'

Compounded sallets were of the 'young buds and knots of all manner of wholesome Herbs at their first springing; as Red sage, Mint, lettuce, Violets, Marigolds, Spinage and many others mixed together and served up to table with Vinegar, oil and sugar'. In this category he gives the ingredients for an 'excellent sallet and which indeed is usual at Great Feasts, and upon Princes tables'. It is not dissimilar to the mixed fruit and vegetable salads which are so typical of modern American compound salads.

An Excellent Salad
Blanched shredded almonds, equal quantity raisins, stoned and washed, same of figs shredded like almonds, capers, twice so many olives, as many currants of all the rest, a good handful of red sage and spinach. Mix with sugar and lay in the bottom of a large dish. Pour over vinegar and oyl and more sugar.

Lay over thinly sliced, peeled oranges and lemons. Cover with the fine leaves of red coleflower [beetroot], layer with olives, and pickled cucumbers together with the heart of a cabbage lettuce shredded. Dress the side and centre of the dish with more orange and lemon slices.

From *A Way to Get Wealth*,
Gervase Markham 13th edn., 1676

Boiled salads also came into this category and his recipe for cooked spinach is quite delicious.

Boiled Spinach Salad
Cook the spinach in its own juice. Drain and return the spinach to the pan with a lump of butter and cook again to absorb the butter. Add a handful of currants, stir and season with sugar and vinegar.

Salads to 'furnish out a table' were made from preserved and pickled vegetables and flowers, with the colours and shapes of the individual ingredients arranged to form emblems or pictures whose theme was pertinent to the occasion.

By the mid-eighteenth century, when Hannah Glasse published her cookery book, *The Art of Cooking Made Plain*, the compound salad had become a salamagundy, in which all the ingredients were arranged decoratively around a central mound of chopped meat, fish and/or vegetables. Often these salads were arranged by colour; all white vegetables and meats, for example or carrots, beetroots and red cabbage to make a red salamagundy. But, as Mrs Glasse said, 'you may always have salamongundy of such things as you have, according to your fancy'.

Hannah Glasse's Salamagundy
Slice two cabbage lettuces as fine as a good thread. Cover a dish one inch thick. Then lay slivers of white chicken on the lettuce round the end to the middle and the other towards the brim. Lay anchovy fillets in between the chicken slices. Dice the dark chicken meat and a lemon; mince four egg yolks, three to four anchovies and parsley. Make a sugar-loaf shaped heap of these in the centre of the dish. Garnish with onions, boiled and very white; one in the centre, the rest round the edge. Pour over oil and vinegar, season with salt and pepper. Garnish with grapes or french beans, blanched.

From *The Art of Cooking Made Plain*,
Hannah Glasse, 1755

This really is a delicious combination of flavours. Arrange the salad on a large serving platter with the chicken slices in an orderly ring around the perimeter. It helps to shape the central mound if you pack the mixture into a lightly oiled basin and then quickly invert onto the centre of the dish. Use small pickling onions and French beans cut to uniform length. The egg whites can be reserved, then chopped and blended with a mild, slightly sweetened mayonnaise to form the centrepiece to another, smaller salamagundy based on bitter red radicchio, peppery watercress and mild blanched celery.

Salads were most often dressed simply with vinegar and honey or finest sugar. Grape verjuice was also acceptable. Oil was used, but not as frequently as today because its quality was unreliable. In 1727, *The Country Housewife or Lady's Director*, written by R. Bradley, advised that when

Clockwise from the top Hannah Glasse's Salamagundy; Salad of radicchio, watercress and celery with chopped egg white and chives; Tomato and Basil Salad; Artichoke Tartlet.

composing salads, 'onions should always be kept in reserve, because it is not everyone who likes their relish, nor is Oil agreeable to everyone; but where Oil is not liked, the Yolks of Hard Eggs, bruis'd and mix'd with Vinegar, may be used. The difficulty of getting good Oil in England is I suppose the reason why everyone does not admire it . . .' Hard-boiled eggs mixed into salad dressings were often used, even when the quality of the oil was assured.

John Evelyn, in his *Acetaria, a Discourse of Sallets* (1699), also used three parts oil to one of sharpest vinegar and hard-boiled eggs (yolks only and mashed with the mustard, oil and vinegar), but suggested substituting lemon or orange juice for the vinegar. He further instructed to 'let steep some Slices of *Horse-Radish* with a little Salt' or a 'pod of *Guinny-Pepper*' in the vinegar, which was the only way these flavourings should be used during the '*Hot Months*'. He also pointed out that 'Some, who are husbands of their *Oyl* [in other words, stingy], pour first the *Oyl* alone, as more apt to communicate and diffuse its Slipperiness, than when it is mingled and beaten with the *Acids*; which they pour on last of all; and 'tis incredible how small a quantity of *Oyl* . . . is sufficient, to imbue a very plentful assembly of *Sallet Herbs*'.

To Dress a Salad

This recipe is not that dissimilar to modern recommendations for salad-making; only the inclusion of eggs and the proportion of oil to vinegar is different. Four parts of oil to one of vinegar is more to contemporary tastes – our ancestors were extremely fond of sourness.

After you have duly proportion'd the Herbs, take two thirds of Oil of Olives, one third of Vinegar, some hard Eggs cut small, both the Whites and Yolks, a little Salt and some Mustard, all which must be well mixed, and poured over the Sallad, having first cut the large Herbs, such as Celery, Endive, Cabbage-Lettuce, but none of the small ones: Then mix all well together, that it may be ready just when you want to use it, for the Oil will make it presently soften, and lose its Briskness.

From *Adam's Luxury and Eve's Cookery*, 1744

The advice to add lettuce and herbs only at the last minute to preserve their crispness is familiar; however there is a tradition, particularly in Germany, of warm, even hot, sweet-sour dressings which, when added to the salad bowl, immediately wilt the leaves and release the flavour of the herbs.

Use the softest textured cabbage lettuces for this salad.

Wilted lettuce

Be sure that the leaves are well drained after washing and place them in the serving bowl. For one head of lettuce make a dressing by softening 1 teaspoon of chives in 1 tablespoon of bacon fat. (Reserve the fried bacon to crumble over the finished salad before serving.) To the hot fat add 2 tablespoons of white wine vinegar and 2 tablespoons of sugar. Stir to dissolve the sugar. Add up to 2 tablespoons of water, or more if the vinegar is strong. Season with salt and pepper to taste. Pour hot over the salad. Toss once and serve.

Try this with spinach thinnings, dandelion, batavian lettuce or finely shredded white cabbage.

Vegetables which are normally served hot as an accompaniment to the main course can do double duty as salads, in which case they should be boiled or preferably steamed only to *al dente*, so that they retain some of the salad 'crunch'.

Kohl Rabi with Soured Cream Dressing

Use 6 small kohl rabi. Peel, dice and blanch in simmering milk until just tender. Put aside to cool. In the salad bowl combine 4 tablespoons of soured cream with 2 tablespoons each of white wine vinegar and lemon juice. Sweeten the dressing to taste with sugar, and season with salt and pepper. Add the kohl rabi to the dressing and toss. Sprinkle some freshly toasted sesame seeds over the dish before serving.

Carrot and Onion Salad

Cut 500g (1lb) carrots into sticks about 2.5cm (1in) long. Blanch them in lightly salted water. Refresh in cold water, drain and cool. Slice a small red onion into thin rounds, or cut up spring onions including some of the green tops. Make a salad dressing using walnut oil and combine all the ingredients. If you haven't any walnut oil, use a mild-flavoured salad oil and substitute orange juice for the vinegar. Season with freshly ground black pepper.

Celeriac and Dill Salad

Peel and cut the root into evenly sized chunks, dropping them into acidulated water as you work to prevent them from turning brown. Drain the pieces and then drop them into a pan of boiling acidulated water. Remove it from the heat as soon as the water returns to a rolling boil, drain and keep the celeriac warm on the back of the stove. Make an oil-and-vinegar dressing, flavoured with Dijon mustard. Add the warm celeriac and sprinkle with chopped fresh dill leaves.

Blanched cauliflower, broken up into bite-sized pieces, seasoned with chopped dill and served with the same dressing or the soured cream dressing, makes good use of this underestimated vegetable.

Spiced Pickled Beetroot

Pickled beetroots are delectable if made correctly; too often the roots are boiled almost to mush and then cut into tiny cubes and bottled up with unadulterated

This engraving from a German manuscript of 1530 shows a busy kitchen and fully employed hearth. Note the shallow braising pot sitting upon a trivet over the open flames.

sour vinegar. The following method is a vast improvement and a perfect accompaniment to cold baked ham.

Prepare a pickle by boiling together 1 cup water, half a cup of vinegar and half a cup of sugar, seasoned with a bay leaf, 4–5 allspice berries and an equal number of black peppercorns and salt to taste. This makes enough pickle for 500–750g (1–1½lb) of boiled beetroot.

Slice the beets into rounds 6mm (¼in) thick. Slice a small onion into paper-thin rounds. Put the beets and onions into a wide-mouthed preserving jar and pour the hot brine over them, straining out the spices. The beets will keep indefinitely in the refrigerator, and the brine or beets can be topped up several times before it becomes necessary to start again.

Cucumber Pickle
Cucumbers were early candidates for the pickle barrel, most frequently preserved in the following fashion, which makes a good sour pickle using whole cucumbers.

To preserve Cowcumbers all the yeere
Take a gallon of faire water, & a pottle of verjuice, and a pint of bay salt, and a handful of greene fennel or Dill; boile it a little, and when it is cold put it into a barrel, and then put your Cowcumbers into that pickle, and you shall keep all the yeere.
From *Delightes for Ladies*, Sir Hugh Platt, 1609

Bread and Butter Pickles
Small ridge or bush cucumbers should be used for this sweet-sour pickle.

Cut 1.20kg (2½lb) of cucumbers into paper-thin rounds. Soak them for at least 3 hours in a brine of 2 litres (4 pints) of water and 150g (15oz) of salt. This helps to preserve their crispness.

Prepare a brine of ¾ litre (1½ pints) each of distilled cider vinegar, water and sugar, 2 tablespoons of mustard seed, 1 tablespoon of celery seed and 1 teaspoon of tumeric. Bring this brine to the boil in a large saucepan, add the cucumber slices and 3 large thinly sliced onions. Reduce the heat and simmer for 10 minutes or until the cucumber slices turn yellow. Bottle while still hot in sterilised jars.

Artichoke Tartlets
When artichokes make their occasional appearance on modern tables they are most frequently plain boiled accompanied by a dipping sauce of melted lemon-flavoured butter or with a vinaigrette. In John Evelyn's day artichokes were an expensive novelty, only recently introduced from Italy, and purchased in England 'for Crowns a piece'. So the recipes for their use were elaborate and there were many means of preserving them for use during winter, including drying, potting in butter and pickling. He wrote that 'The Bottoms are also bak'd in Pies, with Marrow, Dates, and other rich Ingredients'. The following recipe is based on 'How to make Hartichoke pye' from *A Book of Fruit and Flowers* (1653).

Allow one artichoke per person: this recipe is for four artichoke tartlets. Boil the artichokes in acidulated water. Remove the leaves and choke and pull out any tough stings from the bottoms. Season the bottoms lightly with cinnamon and sugar. Place one bottom in each tartlet dish previously lined with *pâté sucré* or short-crust pastry. Put 2 chopped fresh dates on each bottom; dot with butter.

In a saucepan melt 1 tablespoon of butter for each artichoke with the same number of tablespoons of white wine or lemon juice. Remove the pan from the heat and blend in beaten egg yolks – 1 yolk to 2 artichokes. Pour the liquid over the tartlets. Bake the tarts in a medium oven until the pastry is cooked. Sprinkle with more wine or lemon juice if the tartlets appear to be drying out too much while cooking.

CHAPTER FIVE

HOMEGROWN

Unlike vegetables, which took a long time to be accepted into the popular diet as a main ingredient, fruit had always been used, but was acceptable throughout the Middle Ages and much of the Renaissance only if it was well cooked. The idea that fruit was detrimental to health was part of the *Regimen Sanitas*, the medical theories expounded by Galen and the school of Salerno, and rooted in the beliefs of classical antiquity. Fruit was cold and moist and to be avoided by the elderly and not to be fed to young children; thus the most vulnerable sections of the population, had they followed the *Regimen*, would have been deprived of a health-enhancing food group.

However, people must have realised that to follow the *Regimen* strictly would have been to invite starvation, since the 'bad' foods included milk and cheese, salt meat, game, apples and pears: the principal foods of the medieval diet. So people ate fruit, and cooked it well, using it to sweeten dishes and counterbalance the saltiness of preserved meats, a tradition which has the hallmark of Arab and Persian cooking and may have been introduced by returning crusaders (who were also responsible for introducing the *Regimen Sanitas*, which they had encountered in Italy). Or the fruit was eaten stewed with honey, pickled, made into jams or otherwise preserved; murrey was the fruit counterpart to porray or potage, and stews of fruit, thickened with toasted breadcrumbs and highly spiced, followed the medieval predilection for sweet-sour tastes at the table. Cherries were an exception and were popularly eaten fresh when fully ripe; cherry feasts were held in orchards of ripening fruit.

One of the earliest written recipes was for warden pie, wardens being the type of pear grown in medieval orchards. As well as pears, apples for cider, cherries, plums, wild strawberries, quinces, mulberries and medlars were the traditional fruits of the monastic garden; grapes had been introduced by the Romans, and monastic vineyards supplied the raw materials for wine, vinegar and verjuice. Nut trees, especially the walnut, hazel and almond, also had a place in the medieval orchard.

Fruit was undeniably useful in early cookery, providing a contrast to the monotonous blandness of preserved and starchy dishes. Thus a gardener's expertise in the fruit orchard and vineyard was highly valued, and grafting was one of the most highly prized horticultural skills, exercised for a variety of reasons which sometimes cannot have met with success: to get fruit without stones, or to make one type of fruit taste like another. But not all attempts were futile, and the medieval manuscript of Jon Gardener details grafting methods that are practical and accurate: for instance that of raising a healthy stock to accept a scion so that choice varieties could be grown on vigorous roots. In such a way were choice fruit varieties imported from the Continent to grow in English manor-house orchards, which were the jewels of a gentleman's property.

Above Prunus Cerasus, cherry.

Opposite Detail from *Fruit and Flowers* by Isaac Soreau (b. 1604). *Musée du Petit Palais, Paris.*

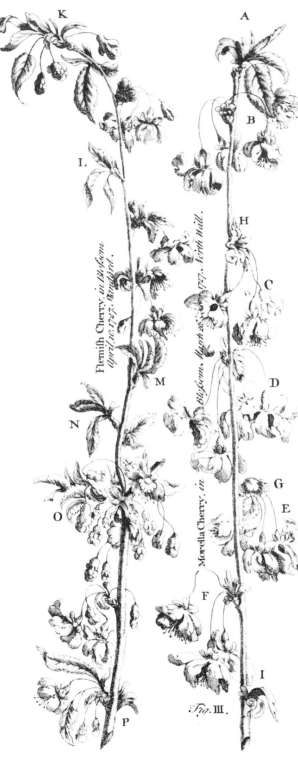

Above The Flemish Cherry and the Morello Cherry and *far right* the Whiteheart Cherry from Batty Langley's *Pomona or the Fruit Garden*, 1729.

During the Tudor period a great many gardening books were published and the best, if not devoted entirely to the planting of a fruit orchard, always included a section on the subject. John Parkinson's *Paradisi in Sole* (1629) devotes the third and final section to 'declare whatsoever Art, striving with Natures, can cause to prosper with us, that whosoever will, may see what can bee effected in our countrie'. He also advised that the orchard should be formally arranged, otherwise 'it can have little grace or forme', and that the trees be planted equidistant from each other in a quincunx for the benefit of the trees and ease in tending them; graceful alleys or 'distances' could also be formed by interlacing the branches of adjacent rows to form an arch. The orchard should also be surrounded with a wall, and while mud walls or quickset hedges were the most popular (because cheaper to erect), a brick wall was to be preferred. This would have been expensive (then as now), but Parkinson points out that 'the gaining of ground, and profit of the fruit trees planted there against, will in short time recompense that charge'.

Pruning was a highly valued skill, and was used to train fruit trees against walls, to shape shady arbours and to make low hedges in the herb garden. In 1600, Sir Hugh Plat wrote that 'Quinces growing against a wall, lying open to the sun and defended from cold winds, eat most deliciously. This secret the Lord Darcey brought out of Italy, *quare* would this suit of all other fruits.' But espalier and fan-trained fruit trees had been around for some time. The Romans doubtless introduced espalier trees to Britain; the evidence of Pompeii, in the position of tree roots and nail holes in walls, shows that their walls were covered in fruit-bearing trees and that they knew that tender fruit trained against a warm wall was more likely to ripen, which was to prove particularly useful in the cold British climate. Also, crops from trees whose natural growth is restricted are larger, although the fruit itself is smaller; otherwise the trees produce small crops of large fruit. (At Pompeii they also underplanted old trees with young ones to replace the losses of time.) Later, in the restricted space of a medieval domestic garden, the use of trained trees was an obvious choice, and the addition of ripe fruit to the verdant picture of a lady's bower would have been welcome. In the Renaissance garden, it would combine beauty with function, an admired trait at the time.

In the eighteenth century, with the growth of the towns and a shift in the population from rural to urban, market gardens mushroomed to supply fresh fruit and vegetables to the city dwellers. Immigrant populations were often responsible for the creation of 'speciality' market gardens, the produce aimed at satisfying their particular needs. Such were the gardens around Liverpool started by the French Canadians, noted for the quality and variety of their produce; as were the Irish-owned potato fields in East London. By the late eighteenth century, London was supplied by the orchards of Middlesex, 'the great fruit garden, north of the Thames'.

The East Anglian counties of Suffolk and Norfolk were famous for pears and cherries, and the Essex towns of Chelmsford and Colchester were the London merchants' best sources of peas and seeds of every description. The south-eastern county of Kent has long been noted as the orchard of England, and in his Encyclopaedia of Gardening, Loudons described the excellence of Kentish gardens and orchards, praising them above all others in the country. Gloucestershire and Worcestershire provided the finest plums and asparagus, and Scotland was noted for its strawberries and raspberries, gooseberries and currants.

These market gardeners made great use of the many refinements in 'horticultural

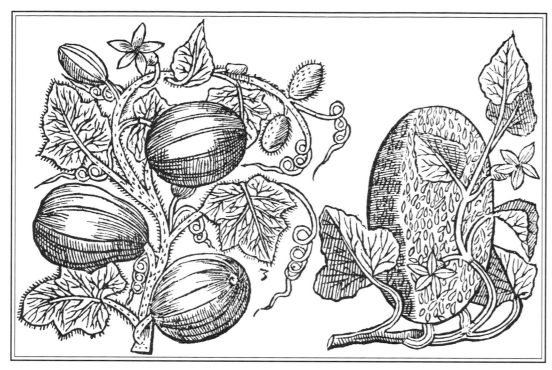

Left The ordinary melon and *right* the Great Muske Melon, according to John Parkinson's *Paradisus in Sole*. For centuries, gardeners spent much time and money raising these prized fruits.

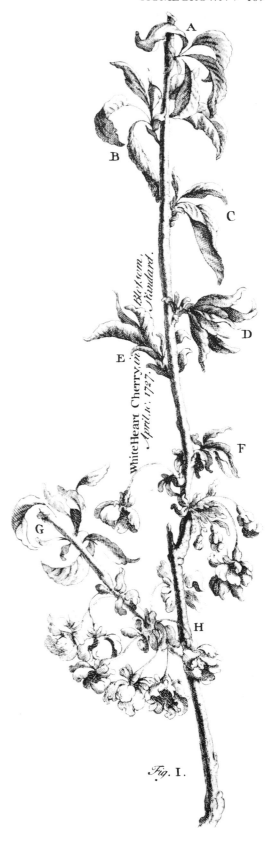

technology'. The earliest glasshouses were glass-fronted orangeries, and in the mid-1700s the Dutch idea of a glass building constructed against a warm wall was gaining in popularity. This led to the invention of free-standing glasshouses, and by the end of the century, as Miles Hadfield points out in his *History of British Gardening*, larger panes of glass were being used in the construction of glasshouses, which were now being heated by warm air passing through brick flues. The idea really took hold in the mid-1800s when the glass tax was abolished, and every advanced gardener could at last afford a greenhouse or conservatory.

The use of glass cloches and hotbeds, to bring in early crops of salad and to cultivate melons and important export crops like cauliflower, greatly extended the growing year and the variety of fruit and vegetables available, as well as expanding the marketplace, and much English fruit was exported to France.

These early advances in the mechanics of growing fruit both coincided with and may have been inspired by the numerous plant introductions from the Americas and the Orient, where the Dutch had usurped the Portuguese and established a trade monopoly. Dutch gardeners were fanatic in their efforts to raise the finest and most exotic fruit gleaned from their new holdings in distant lands. Their success provided the raw materials for a new genre of painting: the Dutch flower piece. These verdant still lifes in which the simple familiar flowers of Europe mingle with the extraordinary fruits of the New World were immensely popular, and the artists went to great pains to achieve a likeness; Jan Davidsz de Heem moved his studio to Antwerp in 1636, since there he would be assured of fresh life models, 'in the finest condition and state of ripeness'.

Apples, Pears, Plums, Greengages, Damsons, Bullaces, Cherries

Cordons, fans and espalier-trained fruit trees have many advantages over trees that are left to assume their natural shape, even on trees which are on dwarfing stock. The chief attribute of a trained tree is that it makes economical use of space; dwarf bush fruit trees can take up to 9m sq (100 sq ft) of space, and in a small garden this would severely restrict the number of varieties which could be grown. But cordon fruit takes a third of the space, and fans and espaliers can make blank walls and fences productive. Regular and careful pruning keeps the trees in good heart, producing better quality fruit.

Cultural tasks are easier to perform on trained trees: pruning, thinning of the setting fruit to improve quality, thorough winter and spring spraying and bird damage control are all easier to do, because access to the trees is not hampered by the size of the tree itself. A formula for happy fruit-fulness.

Pears and **apples** can be cordon- or espalier-trained, while the stone fruits – cherries, plums, nectarines and peaches – are usually made into fans. These shapes are achieved through a regular programme of summer pruning which amounts to cutting back certain shoots to give the tree its structure and to shortening others, which encourages the production of fruiting wood the following season. Pruning should be carried out gradually over several days – there is no need to do the whole collection at once.

Apple trees are available grafted onto dwarfing rootstocks. Even in America they are referred to by number with the letter prefix 'M' to signify East Malling Research Station in Kent. The dwarfest is M27, which is useful in court-yard gardens and for pot-growing. The trees on this stock will fruit in two to three years, but will require excellent cultivation and rich feeding.

The next smallest is M9, again good for small gardens but requiring good fertile soil and permanent staking because of its small root system. M9 is frequently used for cordons and will bear fruit in three years. M106 is semi-dwarfing, also used for cordons, espaliers and fans, and will perform well on most soils. M29 is dwarf, multi-purpose rootstock often used for bush and pyramid trees in small orchards. It is not suited for use on shallow, light soils.

Most apples are diploid, requiring another apple which flowers at the same time for pollination; some are triploid, requiring two pollinators. So when choosing varieties take care that you have sufficient pollinators or you'll have nothing but flowers.

Trees can be purchased which are already trained, but to use these is more expensive than purchasing a one-year-old tree or maiden, and beginning the training yourself. Choose trees which have a good number of laterals and buds well spaced along the length of the main stem.

Cordons can be trained against wires stretched across fences or walls; three parallel wires should be fixed 10–15cm (4–6in) from the wall at 1.8m (6ft), 1.3m (4ft) and 75cm (30in) from soil level. Attach a 3m (10ft) cane at right angles to the wire; the cordon is trained to this and gradually lowered to a 45-degree angle. Cordon rows should incline towards either the north or the east.

Pruning a cordon: in the autumn, plant the trees 75cm (30in) apart and cut back any side shoots longer than 10cm (4in) to 3 buds. Don't prune the leader unless it is a tip bearer, which is pruned back by a quarter of the new growth to an upward turning bud. Remove all blossom the first spring after planting.

In the first summer after planting, keep the leader tied to the cane. Cut back mature laterals growing from the main stem to 3 leaves above the basal cluster. Mature laterals growing from spurs are cut to one leaf.

Repeat this each summer. When the leader reaches the top wire prune it back to half the new growth each year. Begin to lower the cane 5 degrees each year, taking care to keep the cordons parallel.

Espalier trees have a vertical main stem from which branches are trained horizontally in opposite pairs. It is possible to obtain nursery-trained espaliers, but as with cordons, maiden trees are less expensive. Also, M9 stock, which is best for espalier training, is rarely used on nursery subjects.

The wires against which the tree is trained should be stretched parallel at 45cm (18in) intervals, with a 10–15cm (4–6in) gap between wire and wall. Plant the trees 3m (10ft) apart and with the main stem 15–20cm (6–8in) from the wall.

Pruning the espalier: the first winter after planting, cut the leader back to a healthy bud that is 5cm (2in) above the bottom wire and which has a pair of opposite buds close below.

The following summer attach a cane to the wire and train the top shoot from the leader vertically against it. This is the central axis of the espalier.

Left to right Apples and plums.

Train the shoots from the opposite pair of buds horizontally to canes at a 45-degree angle to the leader. These form the first and lowest tier of the espalier, and are lowered to 90 degrees and attached to the lowest wire at the end of the season.

All other shoots should be pinched back to 6 leaves.

Repeat this process in subsequent years until the leader reaches the top wire; subsequently prune the leader back to 12mm (½in) of new growth each spring.

The tiers are pruned each summer as for the cordon.

Low-trained fruit trees bordering the pathways of the orchard were a favourite Jacobean device: 'Cornelian cherry trees plashed low, or gooseberries, currant trees, or the like . . . pippins, Pomewaters or any other sort of apple'.

This practice was carried on at least until the start of this century, with apples and pears being the recommended fruit, trained 'horizontal cordon fashion for the edging of walks, and planted 1 foot from the edging, and trained 1 foot from the ground'. The diagram shown here, taken from George Bunyard's *The Fruit Garden* (1904), demonstrates the use of double and single horizontal cordons for such an edging. To duplicate this in the modern garden, use maidens on M27 rootstock planted 1.5m (5ft) apart. Cut the leader back to a pair of opposite buds, 30cm (12in) above the soil level and train and prune as for the tiers of an espalier. The single horizontals are formed from a single branch and are used to form the ends of the low fruiting fence.

By training the double horizontal cordon to 45 degrees and planting several trees thus trained together, a trellis-work effect can be had as shown in the diagram. Where the branches intersect, tie them loosely together; in time they will grow into one another.

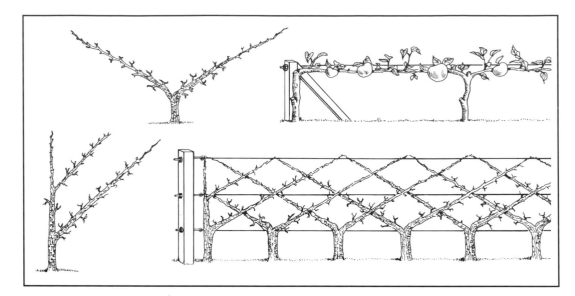

Palmette verrier was an extremely popular form of training for pears and apples, but it is rarely seen today. It is a sort of modified espalier; the side branches were trained horizontally and then turned vertically to run parallel to the main axis. Some variations on this style are shown here.

Pears are usually rooted on quince stock, Type A or Type C. Use C for cordon training and for espaliers of only two or three tiers and A for espaliers of three or more tiers.

To prune a maiden pear for cordon: plant the trees as for apples, but inclined 45 degrees either to the north or the east, and with the scion (point of union between rootstock and graft) uppermost.

After planting, prune any side shoots longer than 10cm (4in) to 3 leaves. Train the leader up a cane attached to the wires, and each summer cut back mature side shoots longer than 22cm (9in) to 3 leaves above the basal cluster. When the cordon reaches the desired length, prune the leader to 12mm (½in) each summer.

Espalier pears are formed in the same manner as apples, with the leader and tiers trained and summer-pruned as previously described.

A fence can be made by planting several trees trained in a double cordon, ending the row with a half-fan. Also shown is a step-over cordon.

To prune a pear for fan: in the first spring after planting, prune the main stem back to a healthy lateral shoot that is approximately 60cm (24in) from the ground and has a pair of opposite buds below that are roughly 30cm (12in) from the ground. If there are laterals rather than buds, prune them back by at least two thirds to an upward facing bud.

Remove all other laterals, pruning close to the main stem.

In the first summer after planting the first fan ribs are formed from the bud shoots or the extension growth of the laterals. When these reach 45cm (18in) tie them on to canes attached to the wires at 45 degree angle to the main stem.

Remove the main stem, cutting it out directly above the topmost shoot. Paint the cut to prevent infection.

Pinch back all the other shoots to one leaf.

Early in the second spring, prune the two ribs back to an upward facing bud 30–45cm (12–18in) from the main stem.

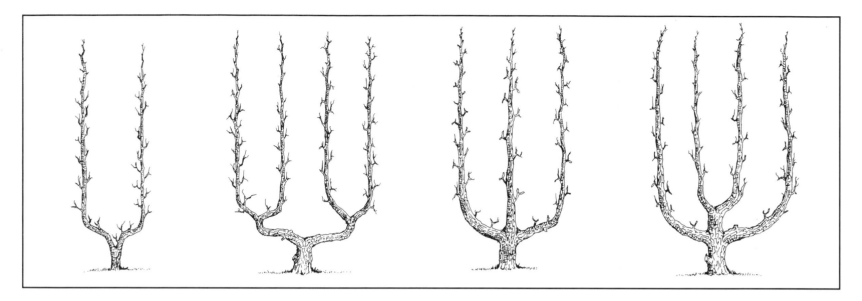

The second summer tie in these rib leaders to canes attached to the wires. Choose two more shoots on the upper side of each rib which are 10–15cm (4–6in) apart, and another shoot on the lower side. Tie these on to canes as they grow to form a fan-like network on each main rib.

The third and each following spring cut back each branch to leave only 60–75cm (24–30in) of the previous season's growth, pruning to an upward facing bud. Tie extension growth from these buds to canes and use to fill in the fan. But don't fill in the vertical section until last, as that growth robs vigour from the horizontal sections.

Rub out any laterals growing towards the wall and pinch any growing out from it to one leaf. Laterals not used to create ribs should be kept to six leaves.

Fan-training against a north- or east-facing wall produces the best quality **plums**, **greengages**, **damsons** and **bullaces**; these fruits are too robust for cordons or espaliers.

Plums are rooted on St Julien 'A', or Pixy, which is a semi-dwarfing stock making trees that are often half the size of those on St Julien; but Pixy trees require

The Palmette verrier was a much used form of training, and as many as eight upright branches could be raised off the central stem.

rich fertile soil and plenty of attention to horticultural details.

The wall or fence must be a minimum of 2m (7ft) high with wires stretched parallel across it at 15cm (6in) intervals beginning 38cm (15in) from the ground.

Plant a maiden tree in the autumn; if more than one tree is being planted, space them 5.4m (15ft) apart. Position the tree at least 20–25cm (8–10in) from the wall with the stem inclining slightly towards the support and the roots fanning out in front of it.

Cherries are also best grown as fans – in this way they can easily be protected from birds, which is reason enough to grow them this way.

Look for trees rooted on Colt stock; plant them the same distance apart and on the same arrangement of wires as for plums.

Start your cherry fan from a maiden tree; these will have plenty of young laterals from which to select four, which

should be well spaced, about 30–45cm (12–18in) from the ground, to be the first ribs.

All pruning of cherries is done during the spring and summer to minimise the risk of developing canker. Summer pruning also limits the amount of vegetative growth, so encouraging fruit buds to form at the base of the previous season's laterals.

To prune a cherry fan: in the first spring after planting, cut back the main stem to the top lateral.

Reduce the length of the laterals to 45–60cm (18–24in), cutting back to an upward-facing bud. Remove all other laterals.

Tie in these first ribs to canes attached to wires at 45-degree angles.

In the first summer select the strongest shoots growing from the pruned laterals, allowing the topmost ones to become the main leader of the rib, and choosing two more, one on the top and the other on the bottom of the rib, to grow on. Remove all the other laterals.

Repeat this process each spring and summer until the wall-space is filled. When the fan is established, pinch out shoots as described for plum fans.

Strawberries, Currants, Gooseberries, Mulberries, Medlars

Henry VIII sent his gardeners out into the countryside around Hampton Court Palace to collect **wild strawberries** for his garden. The large-fruited types with which we are most familiar were unknown in England until the seventeenth century, when the species from which they were hybridised began to arrive from America.

The small-fruited **alpine strawberry**, a sub-species (*alpina*) of the wild *Fragaria vesca*, was also popular. Today we know it as *fraise de bois*. These sorts are especially useful in the kitchen garden where they can be used as edgings around raised beds and beneath fruit trees. I grow my berries on the asparagus bed; whether or not they are mutually beneficial I can't say, although they both do well, but they make a pretty picture – when the plants are in blossom they make a sheet of white flowers.

The fruit is not so juicy as the large-fruited sorts, but the flavour is distinctive, and berries can be picked all summer and into the autumn. They freeze well compared to the large hybrids. There are yellow-fruited varieties that some say taste of pineapple; white-fleshed sorts; and the new variety 'Sweetheart' which has larger juicier fruit than the alpines but is cultivated in the same way.

Raise the plants from seed sown in the early spring under glass. Scatter the seed over the surface of the compost and cover lightly with sand and compost. Put the trays in a shady place and move to the light when the seedlings appear. Prick out the plants into trays when the first true leaves are formed and harden them off carefully. The young plants can be planted out in early summer.

Seed may also be sown in the autumn *in situ* in a shady sheltered place and covered with cloches for winter protection. Alpine strawberries will seed themselves, so keep an eye out for self-sown seedlings to renew stocks, which should be done every 2–3 years, or fill out a border planting.

Red and white currants are not prone to the ailments of blackcurrants and few soft fruits are as versatile in the kitchen: the sharp-tasting, glossy berries can be used on tarts with *crème pâtissière* and to make sorbets and sauces, jellies and glazes.

Currants are easier to pick if the plants are trained as cordons, either single or double. They like a sunny position out of the wind where there is no danger of frosts lingering, since they flower at a time when frosts may still occur. Red and white currants prefer a slightly acid soil that is rich and well drained with a high level of potash.

Plant in the early autumn and cut the leader or main stem back by half. Prune any side-shoots to one bud and tie the leader to a cane fixed to wires. After planting, and then each subsequent winter, apply a thick manure mulch and a dressing of sulphate of potash. Water the plants well during the summer.

Red and white currants fruit on side-shoots growing from the old wood. If at least one quarter of the leader's old wood is removed each autumn, more side-shoots will be produced. Cut back the leader to an upward-facing bud to facilitate cordon training. Cut the side-shoots back to 2–3 buds during the winter. When the cordon reaches the desired height – 1.5–1.8m (5–6ft) is usual – cut the leader back to one bud each winter. The only summer pruning is the necessary cutting-back of all side-shoots to 5 leaves and the pruning of the established leader, also to 5 leaves.

After several years, the fruiting spurs may become overly long and branched. They should then be reduced by simply cutting them back into the old wood.

The **gooseberry** is not native to the British Isles, but it is in Britain that its tart juicy fruit is most appreciated, and bushes have had a place in the English kitchen garden at least since the late thirteenth century, when Edward I imported French plants for his orchards. Although it grows wild throughout southern Europe and western Asia, its worth was overshadowed by the grape, and gooseberries were deemed suitable only for flavouring sauces; the French name is *groseille à maquereau*, the mackerel currant, referring to its use as a sauce for mackerel.

Gooseberries were among the first fruits taken to the New England colonies by the settlers. These early European varieties were not suited to the harsh climate and were chronically prone to mildew, a shortcoming which was later overcome by crossing them with the native American wild gooseberry, which has small, dark, bitter fruit but the necessary stamina. In 1833, Abel Houghton of Massachusetts produced the first seedlings of this cross, but although the fruits were suitably sweet and the plants sturdy, gooseberries in New England never really recovered from their early bad reputation.

Back in England, particularly in the northern counties and in Scotland, goose-berry-growing was fast becoming a national pastime. By the eighteenth century there were well over 300 different varieties, ranging in colour from pale translucent

Left to right Redcurrants and wild strawberries.

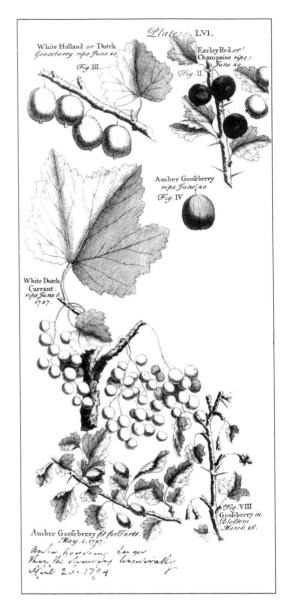

White, red and amber gooseberries and the white Dutch currant from Batty Langley's *Pomona*.

green to darkest purple. There were even varieties with striped berries, and it was the vogue to have bushes grafted with more than one variety, which must have been a spectacularly colourful affair. Today we are left with white, yellow, green and red-berried varieties, the green being generally preferred above the others. Sweet-juiced berries were the most popular until the

abolition of the sugar tax in 1874, when the tart and tangy early varieties we are most familiar with today became acceptable.

Gooseberries do best in a medium-to-light, slightly acid soil, to which has been added quantities of well-rotted manure or compost. The soil must be well drained, but because gooseberries are surface feeders, moisture should be conserved with a heavy mulch. Avoid high-nitrogen feeds, which encourage the disease known as American gooseberry mildew, and soft growth. Dress the plants every other autumn with well-rotted manure.

Normally, gooseberries are grown as bushes, but gathering the fruit from the thorny branches can be tedious and painful. An excellent alternative is to grow them as upright cordons; not only is the fruit easier to gather but it will be of better quality as hard pruning encourages better fruit pro-

duction. The plants will be healthier, since sun and air can easily reach young shoots, and there are no branches on which bud-eating birds can perch; netting is also easier on cordons.

Cordons take up less room in the garden, and can be trained against individual stakes or wire-and-post trellis to section off areas of the kitchen garden, or to form fruiting 'walls' behind flower borders; 1.5–1.8m (5–6ft) is the optimum height for a cordon in the open garden. They can also be trained against a house wall, in which case cordons can be grown up to 3m (10ft) and picked with the aid of a ladder.

Begin cordon-training in the winter, selecting a young bush with one strong-growing upright branch to be the leader. Plant out and cut the leader back by half its length, measured from the uppermost side branch, or lateral. Make the cut above a

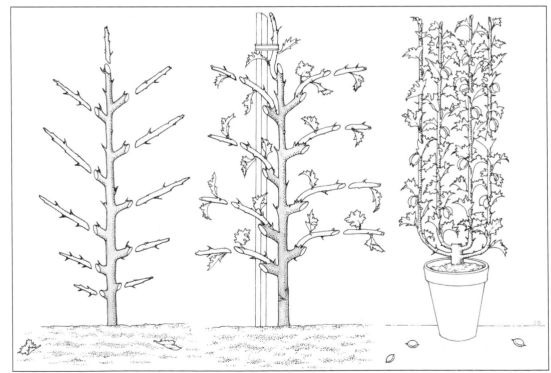

Left Cordon training a gooseberry during the summer; prune laterals but not leader. *Middle* Autumn pruning the laterals and cutting the leader to five buds. *Right* multiple-cordon, pot-grown plant.

side-facing bud. Remove any branches below 10cm (4in) from the ground, and cut back remaining laterals to 2.5cm (1in), making the cut above a bud on the upper side of the branch.

The following summer, cut back the new growth on the laterals to 10cm (4in), but do not prune the leader.

In the autumn, cut back all summer-pruned shoots to 2.5cm (1in) to a bud on the upper side of the branch. Prune the leader to leave five buds.

Repeat the pruning in this order until the cordon has reached the desired height; after this, winter-prune the leader back to one bud. Laterals should be winter- and summer-pruned as described above.

Town gardeners can take advantage of cordon-training, growing a single plant in a container, but making a multiple cordon of up to four upright stems as leaders.

Tansy and wormwood are good companions for gooseberries and most other soft fruits, but should not be grown so close to the fruit bushes as to compete with them for available food.

Mulberries and **medlars** are very much a part of the traditional kitchen garden. Both make handsome trees, the mulberry being the taller, and have been recommended by generations of garden writers since the seventeenth century, although they were grown in European gardens well before then.

Morus nigra, the black mulberry, and *M. alba*, the white mulberry, were both cultivated for the feeding of silk worms, the use of the black variety predating that of the white. It was brought to Rome from Syria and under the Emperor Justinian, who called for an expansion of the silk industry, it was widely propagated until it was replaced by the white mulberry.

M. alba is a native of China and Japan. It was introduced to Italy during the mid-fifteenth century, when it was discovered that silkworms were happier eating its leaves than those of the black mulberry. But its fruit is not as flavoursome, so the black continued in popular cultivation. The deep blue-black juicy berries can only be eaten with pleasure when perfectly ripe and falling from the tree. It was the custom to spread sheets beneath the laden branches so that the falling fruit would not be dirtied, since it would spoil the berries to wash them.

In 1608, James I, following Justinian's example, decreed that mulberries should be grown in order to expand the English silk industry and offered free packets of mulberry seeds to all who would grow them – an offer a fashionable household couldn't refuse. But the scheme never took off, probably because the seeds were of the black rather the white mulberry. But a legacy of that policy is that today mulberry trees are most usually found in the gardens of houses dating back to that period.

Black mulberries were probably introduced to Britain by the Romans and were certainly cultivated in English gardens during the Renaissance period. One of the oldest trees is at Loseley Hall in Surrey, seat of the More-Molyneux family since the reign of Henry VII. Family tradition has it that the great black mulberry tree in the garden was planted by Elizabeth I, the mulberry being the subject of the family's motto: 'The mulberry tree dying slowly, the fruit about to die quickly', and part of its emblem. This particular tree was blown down during the Second World War while the eldest unmarried son was on active service in Europe. This event caused great consternation, since a family legend warned that the More-Molyneuxes would prosper only as long as the tree lived. Happily, the tree survived and the son returned unharmed.

The white mulberry was an early introduction to the American colonies, and in the late eighteenth century William Bartram commented on South Carolina's huge plantations of the species, grafted onto stock of *M. nigra*. However, cultivation of the black mulberry was by comparison infrequent, probably because its lack of hardiness caused it to fail in the early colonial settlements.

Parkinson wrote of the Virginia mulberry, a type which he evidently preferred: 'but wee have had brought us from Virginia another sort, which is of greater respect then eyther of the other two'.

The mulberry requires a warm loamy soil that is well drained, and in cool districts it needs the shelter of a warm wall, where it can be trained espalier-fashion. Specimen trees should be firmly staked until well established.

It eventually grows to 9m (30ft) and is easily propagated by semi-hard cuttings taken in the autumn. These can be rooted under glass with bottom heat, or outdoors in a shady sheltered spot, which is the slower method of the two. Plant the cuttings deep. Also, branches can be layered where they touch the ground. Mulberries benefit greatly from an annual mulch of well-rotted manure, and grass and weeds should be kept from the base of the trunk.

Medlar (*Mespilus germanica*) is perfectly hardy and will grow in almost any type of soil or situation, but it will, of course, do best in a sunny spot in good well-drained soil with plenty of room to show off. Stake it securely after planting and keep it tidy by cutting out dead and overcrowded wood.

Medlar fruits are ready to eat in the autumn, when they are 'bletted', i.e. beginning to rot. This is not as alarming as it sounds. The fruit turns a nutty brown colour and the flesh goes pulpy. Traditionally, medlars are eaten with a glass of port to wash them down, the sweet wine compensating for the lack of any sweetness in the fruit.

Blackberries, Loganberries, Raspberries, Peaches, Nectarines, Apricots

Brambles, or wild blackberries, have been used to create kitchen-garden hedges since the Renaissance, their thorny wands weaving in and out amongst the crab-apples and cobnuts, and providing berries for wine and preserves, and leaves and young shoots for fabric dyes and physic.

Modern cultivars of blackberry with larger fruits, thornless stems and various other attributes are largely hybrids of American origin. Popular varieties of cultivated blackberry include 'Himalaya Giant', which makes thick canes up to 3m (10ft) in length and large berries, but which is really only suited to the very large garden; and 'John Innes', which is somewhat more restrained in habit, and is late-fruiting, from the end of summer into early autumn. 'Oregon Thornless' is not armed with the painful barbs and vigorous habit which make other blackberries so difficult to deal with; it also has attractive, finely cut foliage and produces an abundance of excellent fruit.

Loganberries appeared late in the last century in a garden in Santa Cruz, California, and are a hybrid between a wild blackberry and cultivated raspberry. Since then these large, slightly acid fruits have been improved upon and the 'Thornless Loganberry' is probably the best strain to choose for the quality of its fruit and habit of growth, making thornless canes up to 2.4m (8ft) long.

Other hybrid berries include the **boysenberry, tayberry** and the new **sunberry** and are all the result of crosses between the various species of *Rubus*.

Blackberries and the hybrids require deeply dug and water-retentive soil; light soils should have peat, humus or manure added to help hold water. Be sure that the bed is free from all perennial weeds before planting; this should be done any time between mid-autumn and early spring. Plant so that the roots are about 8cm (3in) below the soil, spacing the plants at 2.4–3m (8–10ft) intervals. The canes require support, so plant them against a wall or trellis; these berries, especially those with decorative foliage, look well trained over an arch at the entrance to the garden.

Immediately after planting cut the canes down to a bud about 23cm (9in) above ground level and mulch with manure. As new canes grow during the first summer, tie them into the wires. The following season, tie new canes together and keep them away from last season's fruit-bearing canes in order to prevent the spread of disease. At the end of cropping, cut the old canes out completely and tie the new ones in their places.

Against a wall, a fan arrangement is the easiest to handle. Splay out the old canes like fan ribs either side of the new canes, which you should tie closely together in the centre.

Water the plants well as the first berries start to ripen and at any time when the ground begins to dry out. During winter mulch with manure after top-dressing the bed with sulphate of potash.

New stocks can be easily raised from layers started in midsummer by bending the shoot tips over to the ground and pegging securely. Cut the new plant from the parent the following spring.

Raspberries are in my opinion the finest fruit summer has to offer. I have the greatest difficulty gathering the berries since the succulence of a sun-warmed raspberry is truly irresistible. Sadly, birds feel the same way, so raspberries must be netted.

Raspis, as the berries were known during the sixteenth century, lacked charisma, and in their early years were considered a very poor second to blackberries. Parkinson allows that raspberry leaves could be used in place of blackberry to make soothing gargles, and questioned, in his pleasantly down-to-earth manner, whether there was any truth in the rumour that red wine was really made from raspberries and not grapes.

By the late seventeenth century improved forms of the wild raspberry were finding their way to England, mostly from the Low Countries. By the early 1800s, raspberries

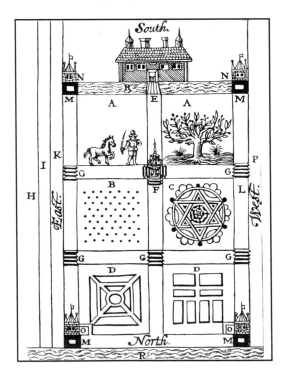

William Lawson's ideal garden set in an orchard from his *New Orchard and Garden* of 1618.

Left Raspberries, *above* blackberries and *right* loganberries.

were being cultivated in America and the wild raspberry was hybridising with native species; I wonder if the 1856 cultivar 'Clarke' is still available?

Raspberries like cool, moist soil that is deeply dug and well drained; they do well in shade, although if heavily mulched and kept well watered, raspberries can be grown in the sun. But remember that hot dry conditions inhibit fruit production.

Always buy certified stock that is guaranteed to be virus-free. Plant in the spring or fall and do not plant too deeply; cover the roots with only 5–7.5cm (2–3in) of soil, spreading them out well to encourage suckers. Cut the stem and mulch as for blackberries.

There are several ways to train raspberries, but the simplest method suitable for an average-sized kitchen garden is as a single row against parallel wires, 45cm (18in) apart, stretched between posts.

Keep newly planted canes weed-free and remove any flowers for the first season to concentrate the plants' energies on cane production. As new canes grow, tie them into the wires; these canes produce next season's fruit.

At the end of cropping cut out all old canes right to ground level and all but 6–8 of the new canes. Be sure that these are securely tied to the wires to prevent wind damage. Mulch well and top-dress in the autumn or early spring with sulphate of potash. Always water the plants at the base, never from overhead, and keep weeds down by mulching, since hoeing will damage surface roots and any newly formed suckers.

Peaches, nectarines and apricots are rather special, requiring more attention than other fruits because of the tenderness and the susceptibility of the flowers to frost.

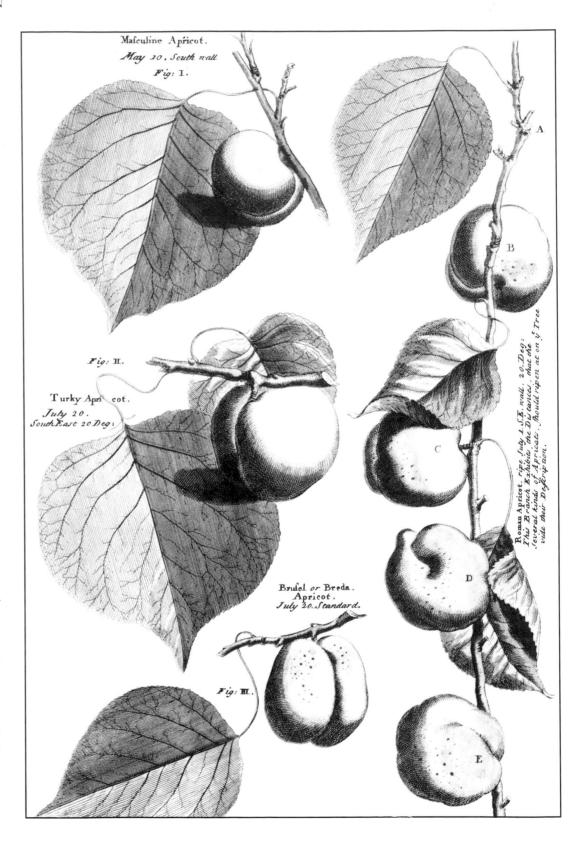

Four varieties of apricot, popular in the eighteenth century, from Batty Langley's *Pomona*.

The first two require pollination by hand; apricots are self-fertile. All will grow well outdoors if trained against a sunny wall and given some protection from frost when in flower. All three enjoy a deeply dug, rich soil that is moisture-retentive, and are best planted during the dormant season. The base of the stem should be at least 23cm (9in) away from the wall, but inclining towards it. Fan-training for all is the same as for a cherry.

The Chinese cultivated a wide variety of peaches and the fruit's presence in Chinese gardens has been traced back to the tenth century BC. Peach fruit and flowers were used as decorative motifs and were the subject of myth and superstition. Pliny states categorically that the peach had recently been introduced to Italy from Persia. By the middle of the sixteenth century it had reached England, probably from France.

The peach grows easily from its tough stone and requests for supplies of peach stones appear on early seventeenth-century lists of seeds to be sent from England to the American colonies. By 1648, the peach was firmly established and grew so abundantly that farmers were feeding their hogs with the surplus fruit. By the mid-1700s the peach was so well naturalised that William Bartram determined it to be a native American plant. Of these three fruits, the peach is the hardiest, which probably accounts for its success.

Nectarines are smooth-skinned peaches with a firmer, more succulent flesh, and were little grown until the sixteenth century, and even then were slow to catch on, perhaps because the nectarine is not as reliably hardy as her sisters.

Apricots also did not begin to appear in gardens until the sixteenth century. It is said that Henry VIII imported apricot trees from Italy and that the fruit was grown as espaliers at Hampton Court Palace. By the end of the seventeenth century, the variety 'Moor Park' was established as the most popular variety and is still in cultivation today.

Throughout history **the grape vine** (*Vitis vinifera*) has ranked above all other fruit as the most economically and culturally important. Its cultivation dates back to at least 4000 BC and the earliest grower's manual is Fourth Dynasty Egyptian (2440 BC). We all know how important wine has been to humanity in the celebration of religious festivals and personal triumphs, as well as providing welcome oblivion for some whose triumphs too often turn to tragedy.

How it arrived in England is open to question; it may have been with the Roman legions or via earlier Phoenician traders who traded with the tin miners along the Cornish coast. But it was an immediate success and vineyards were an established agricultural feature by the time of Domesday, when thirty-eight vineyards were recorded, scattered over a wide area.

As vintners, the French have, of course, always been held in the highest esteem. Some of their skill was transplanted to England with the Norman Conquest and soon the vineyards of Gloucestershire, Herefordshire and Ely were famed for the quality of their wine.

Interest in English wine has waxed and waned over the centuries, probably due to the effects on the vine of the vagaries of the British climate. However, since the seventeenth century, dessert grapes grown under glass have been the subject of much serious endeavour. Even today, the ardent viticulturalist will never be short of professional advice gleaned from the numerous papers and books devoted to the subject.

However, if you will be satisfied with growing a grape vine purely for decorative purposes and happy that they are suitable only for delicious jelly or perhaps some homemade wine, the cultivation and pruning is simple enough. At one time I had a rustic-work pergola, over which I had trained a white grape and red rose. Within five years the grape was well established and producing pounds of fruit, and the pale green bunches with the claret-red rose made a lovely picture.

If you wish to train grapes up a pergola, you must train wires over it; otherwise, wires trained against a wall would be suitable. Grapes will grow in any good soil, but require a site with plenty of sun and good air circulation. Plant in early spring in deeply dug soil to which you have added well-rotted manure. Cut the cane down to leave two or three healthy buds. These will produce the main stems, or rods, which you train up the wires.

After the last frost, select the healthiest shoot to be the leader and train it up the wire. As the vine grows you can allow other strong shoots to grow in order to increase the number of main rods.

When the vine has filled the desired area begin a regular system of pruning to keep the plant in order. A healthy vine makes startling amounts of growth and can easily become jungly. In the autumn, cut the side-shoots to two buds to form fruiting spurs, and tip the main stems by half the length of new growth. In the spring, pinch out all but the strongest two shoots growing from the spur. When these have reached 10cm (4in) remove the weakest and begin training the remaining cane as it grows. Pinch out when it reaches 45cm (18in) long and remove all flowers during the first two years.

Thereafter, each winter cut the new growth on the rods back by half and cut the side-shoots back to two buds. Then in the spring grow on the strongest shoot coming from the spur, tie it in and eventually pinch out the growing tip at two leaves past the third bunch.

Asparagus, Rhubarb

Like the grape, **asparagus** has had just as much attention paid to it, with elaborate instructions about trenching, dressing with salt and seaweed, and how, when and where to cut the spears. It's enough to put you off. Yet in my childhood we would gather asparagus growing wild along the sidings of a derelict railway line; that bed received no fancy treatment, and the spears were tender and succulent.

Raised beds suit asparagus well, as they appreciate the loose soil and rich manure foundation. The thick string-like roots are far-ranging and raised-bed conditions allow the crowns to develop quickly.

Asparagus can be raised from seed, which must be fresh, but a bed is usually started with 1–2-year-old crowns. Select crowns that have masses of thick roots which are not withered or broken. Choose 1-year-olds, since they are less likely to suffer damage by transplanting.

Plant in the spring, setting the crowns 45cm (18in) apart, spreading the roots out around each crown, and 15–20cm (6–8in) below the soil surface. If your soil is at all heavy, mix some sand into it before covering the crowns; asparagus demands good drainage.

Don't cut any crowns until the third season. Then begin harvesting in early summer by cutting below soil level or snapping off when the spears are roughly 15–20cm (6–8in) tall. Finish cutting about six weeks later. Thereafter, let the spears grow to their full height and support the fronds, which feed the crowns, with twiggy branches or string and cane grids to prevent the crowns from being disturbed by rocking. Cut out female fronds – those bearing berries. (There is an all-male variety of asparagus available.) In the autumn, cut down all foliage as it turns yellow. Mulch the bed with well-rotted manure and in the spring feed it with a general purpose fertiliser.

Tomatoes grown on the bed after the

A neatly ordered orchard with every inch of wall covered in vines or trained fruit, from John Lawrence's *Gentlemen's Recreation*, 1716.

asparagus has finished are supposed to protect the asparagus fronds from attacks of asparagus beetle. Basil and parsley are also good companions with asparagus.

Cooks did not become interested in **rhubarb** until some time in the eighteenth century. Before then the apothecaries and herbalists were the main users; they valued the roots as a cure for a variety of ailments but chiefly for bowel disorders. The leaves and flowers have for a long time been regarded as poisonous, although over the years there have been reports of their use as a food.

Rhubarb is generally raised from root divisions planted at any time of year, although the spring or autumn are the most suitable times. It takes up a lot of room, so give it a corner to itself, sunny but sheltered. It likes acid soil, so, if necessary, add some peat as well as plenty of well-rotted manure to the soil before returning it to the planting hole. Be sure that the bed is free of perennial weeds.

Plant the crowns so that the buds are just above the level of the soil and about 1m (3ft) apart. Firm them in well and water if necessary. Cover the crown with a mulch of manure or leaf litter.

Many gardeners force rhubarb for an early crop by covering the crowns with overturned buckets, barrels, or specially designed earthenware pots to exclude the daylight.

Rhubarb leaves are a good addition to the compost pile, and a spray made from a strong infusion of rhubarb leaves is said to protect brassicas and other roots from club root and white fly.

Above Asparagus and *below* rhubarb.

Figs, Quinces, Walnuts, Butternuts, Cobnuts, Filberts, Hazelnuts

Figs are wonderfully ornamental trees for the kitchen garden, but it is something of an achievement to get them to ripen in the open in cool climates. However, if they are trained as fans against a warm sunny wall, with the young fruit formed at the end of summer protected during the winter, the chances are that they will ripen in time for summer picnics.

First of all, figs must have their roots restricted, otherwise they will be all leaf. Do this by planting during spring in a narrow border against the wall into a planting well 60cm deep and 60cm square (24 x 24 x 24in). Make the walls of the planting well from paving slabs with the top edges protruding about 5cm (2in) above the soil level. Although the bottom of the well is open, you can restrict the roots' downward growth by filling the bottom half with well-packed brick or limy rubble (figs prefer an alkaline soil). Fill up the well with planting compost to which you have added limy rubble.

Position the fig tree at least 23cm (9in) from the wall and spread out the roots well before covering with soil.

Wires should be fixed to the wall as for plum fans.

To prune a fig fan: select a plant that has two or more ribs already formed (most figs are supplied as 2–3 year-old container-grown plants). Choose two healthy shoots, one either side of the main stem, to form the ribs. Prune out other laterals close to the main stem.

Tie the selected laterals to canes attached to wires at angles of 20 degrees and cut each one back to an upward-facing bud, 45–60cm (18–24in) from the main stem. The following summer prune and tie in extension growths and select new shoots to be ribs, as for cherries. But in order to have plenty of tiny figlets by the end of summer it is necessary to cut out the terminal bud of each shoot after at least 4–5 leaves have appeared on the shoot. Then, from the axil of each leaf, new shoots will appear and bear young figs. Do this pinching-out early enough to allow the new shoots and fruit to develop before autumn.

Any other pruning and tidying should be done in the spring after all danger of frost has passed.

Although there is no reason why a **quince** shouldn't be trained against a wall or along a fence, it is such a beautiful tree that it makes quite a feature grown as a standard, its papery pink-and-white flowers decking the bent branches. But its greatest pleasure is the aroma of the ripening fruit, a bag of ripe gathered fruit is one of the joys of autumn, having a fragrance more like a bouquet of flowers, some say primroses, than fruit. It is unique.

In Gerard's day, the quince was grown as a protective hedge around vineyards, but it had been in cultivation for centuries throughout Europe and the Middle East before he wrote of its virtues; Jewish tradition suggests that Eve's snake was coiled in a quince rather than an apple tree.

Quinces grow slowly and on their own rootstocks. They can be bushes or half-standards. Plant in the autumn in moist fertile soil. The only pruning necessary is the removal of overcrowded or crossing branches, dead or diseased wood or any that is not producing. Any long side shoots can be pinched back as for pears.

Quinces really prefer the banks of ponds or streams to ordinary garden conditions, but as long as a quince is given plenty of moisture and mulched well during the spring, it will be productive enough.

All the fruit thus far discussed will benefit from an annual spring mulch and a dressing of general-purpose garden fertiliser. Also, keep fruit trees well watered during the summer when the fruit is forming.

Juglans regia, the English **walnut**, has always played an important role in the design of the orchard and kitchen garden, and it was frequently planted along with other productive trees to make protective belts around the kitchen garden. Parkinson wrote in his description of 'The ordering of the Orchard',

The best way to avoide and amend the inconveniences of high, boisterous, and cold windes, is to plant Walnut trees, Elmes, Oakes or Ashes, a good distance without the compasse of your Orchard, which after they are growne great, will bee a great safeguard thereunto, by breaking the violence of the windes from it.

But walnut trees grow to quite a formidable size, and most modern gardens would have room for only one tree. That tree, though, would be the garden's showpiece, for the walnut is one of the most graceful trees, with its broad, spreading head and fragrant, pinnate leaves.

Walnuts are slow-growing trees which live to a great age; usually a tree will not begin cropping until it is more than five years old.

Pliny said that the walnut was introduced to Italy from Persia; and the ancient Romans believed that during the Golden Age when men lived on acorns, the gods consumed walnuts – hence its genus name, *Juglans* = *Jovis glans* = Jupiter's nuts. Botanical etymology is a strange and wondrous thing!

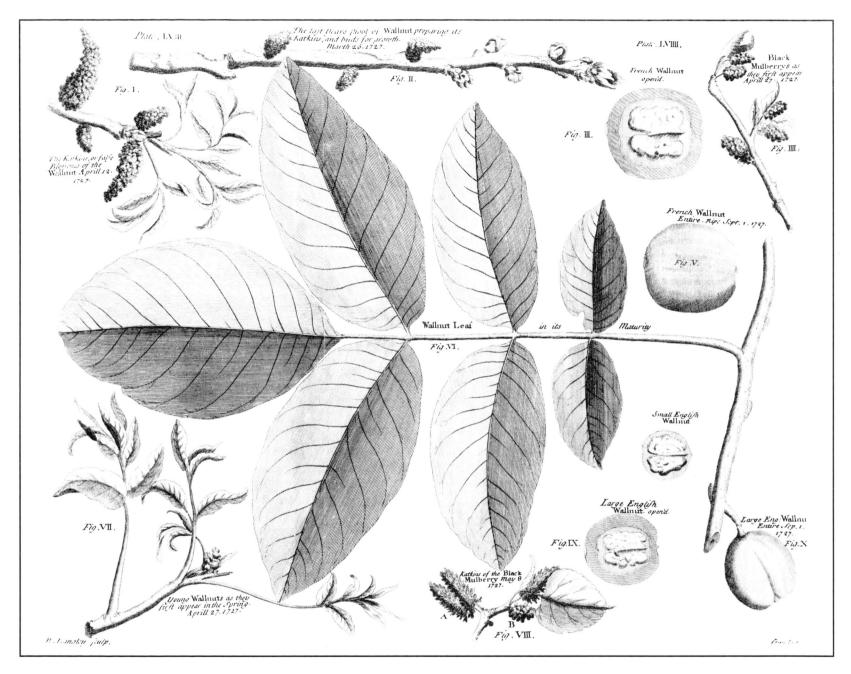

Generations of herbalists have valued the bark and leaves of the walnut for the treatment of skin diseases; and the young green fruit, made into a pickle, was used to prevent scurvy as well as being served with cold meats and as a sauce for fish. Walnut oil was widely used as a frying oil, and Parkinson recommended that it should be

From Langley's *Pomona*, a Black Walnut, and in the corner *top right*, a Black Mulberry.

used like almond oil for cosmetic purposes to soothe rough skin and heal scars; today we reserve it for salad dressing. Walnut wood was used to veneer furniture, being too brittle to use for the main structure.

The walnut flowers in mid-spring after the leaves are fully out, and by the end of summer the nuts are ready to gather. Walnut trees do well in any soil and situation except, as Parkinson wrote, 'They loveth not to grow in waterie places'.

The **butternut**, *J. cinerea*, is an American native, and was introduced to the early settlers by the Indians who used the nuts in potage; the mature nut has a strong flavour, but the young fruit is often pickled like that of the English walnut.

Cobnuts and **filberts** stand next to the walnut in kitchen-garden worthiness. The cob is a cultivated form of hazel, *Corylus avellana*, and the filbert of *C. maxima*, but they are frequently referred to collectively as cobnuts.

Kent has for centuries been the heart of cobnut cultivation in England: a tradition which may have begun with the Romans, who introduced improved forms of the hazel, which grew wild throughout Europe and the Near East. Filbert seeds were among the list of Old World plants requested to be sent to the colonies by the Massachusetts Company in 1629.

The **hazel** is one of the few trees to have been credited with magical properties. The hazel was one of Thor's trees and so the Saxons chose hazel groves as holy places. But as Hilderic Friend argued in his book *Flowers and Flower Lore*, the association probably arose from the Anglo-Saxon word *wic-en*, meaning 'to bend', which referred to the hazel's pliant wands. This evolved into 'witch' and the hazel came into use as a divining rod. To confuse matters, in America, a branch of the winter-flowering tree *Hamamelis mollis* was commonly used for divining, and this too became known as 'witch hazel'.

Cobnuts, filberts and hazels are all grown in a similar way. Cobnuts are not at all fussy about soil or situation, but perform best on a not too rich, sandy, slightly alkaline, loam. In the seventeenth and eighteenth centuries, cobnuts were espalier-trained against north-facing walls. Today cobnuts are most usually grown as small, goblet-shaped trees about 1.8m (6ft) tall, with a short main trunk about 30cm (12in) high and 8–12 main branches. A single tree will eventually have a spread of 4.5m (15ft) and can yield up to 4.5kg (10lb) of nuts in a good year, but it is advisable to have at least two trees of different cultivars. The 'Purple-Leaved Filbert' is an especially attractive garden feature with nicely coloured foliage in the spring and long, wine-red catkins. The flowers appear in late winter or early spring.

Plant new trees in the autumn and prune a single-stem young tree back to about 45cm (18in) from the ground. Laterals will form the next summer and some of these can be selected for training as the main branches.

Keep the stem clear of branches below 30cm (12in) to form the trunk; a 2–3 year-old tree will have at least 3–4 main branches and these should be pruned back to 23cm (9in) to encourage the growth of lower-placed branches. In following winters, prune out all new growth so that the tree never has more than 12 upright-growing leaders. Keep the centre free of branches. When the tree reaches the desired height, cut the leader branches back to a weak lateral. Hazels sucker freely and these should be cut cleanly away from the base, cutting underground.

Once the tree is established, prune it in the summer and winter, when the catkins are mature and able to pollinate the flowers. In the winter, also cut back vigorous laterals formed during the summer to 3–4 buds. In late summer you should 'brut' these strong laterals, i.e. break in half. Leave the broken ends dangling, to be pruned away in the winter. This seemingly brutal act encourages the formation of female flowers. Feed and manure-mulch the trees in the winter and keep a broad band of earth around the base of the tree free of grass and weeds.

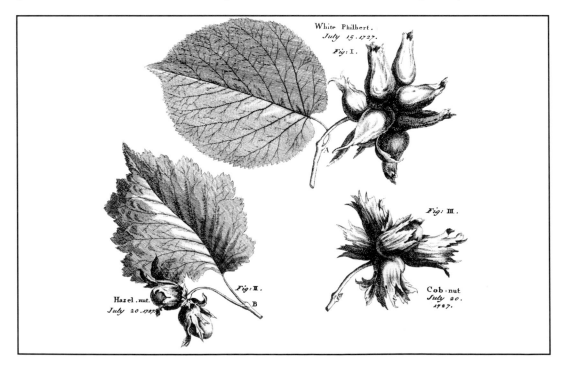

Hazel, cob and filbert nuts from Batty Langley's *Pomona*.

Opposite September from a catalogue of fruits by nurserymen Robert Furber, 1732. *Victoria and Albert Museum, London.*

Apples			Black Cluster			Montauban		
	S|D|E|W	7. Black Cluster		S|D|E|W	13. Montauban		S|D|E|W
1. Windsor Pearmain	S	D	E	W	8. White Cassolette	E	W	14. Admirable	E	S
2. Scarlet Pearmain	S	D	E	Nectarines		15. Chanceller	S
3. Silver Pepin	S	D	E	9. Brinion red at stone	S	D	E	W	16. Teton de venus	E
Grapes		10. Brinion w. at stone	S	D	E	W	17. Golden Pavie	S
4. Brown Cluster	E	E	Peaches		18. Incomparable	S
5. Cromwell black	E	W	11. Italian	E	19. Parpere	S
6. White muscadine	E	E	12. Pavie Blanch	S	20. Pavie rouge	S

Pears			Vermilion		
21. Bellguard		E	28. Vermilion		E
22. Red Magdalen	E	W	29. Green Musk	W
23. Purple Albarge	S	30. Gross Rousselett	D	E
Plumbs		31. Tillvert	D	E	E
24. Scarlet Prince	S	D	E	32. Wr. S. Catherine	D	E
25. Musk Robart	D	E	33. Queen Mother	S	D	E
26. Ambrosia	S|D|E	34. Yellow Perdrigon	D|E|E
27. Poir du Prince	S	D	E		

35. Damascus		D|E|E
36. Pomgranate	S|D|E
37. Yellow Albeen	D|E|W
38. Imparrick	D|E|W
A. Dwarf Medlar	D|E|E
B. Red berried Honysuckle	
C. Passion Fruit	

RECIPES

Apples for cooking and crab-apples for cider-making and verjuice featured in the earliest English gardens. Centuries of cultivation and the ease with which apples can be cross-bred led to the several hundred different varieties which were available to gardeners during the early 1800s. Since then the lists have shrunk and varieties like 'Bramley' and 'Cox' predominate, but there is a growing interest in the collection of old-fashioned apples and a number of nurseries now hold stocks of truly antique varieties like 'Court Pendu Plat' which with 'Golden Pippin' predates most of the other apples we grow.

'Bramley', 'Cox' and 'Golden Delicious' can be bought from the greengrocer, and while some may argue that the flavour of a freshly picked 'Cox' is superior to one taken from a shelf (and I'm sure it is), I would rather devote my orchard space to varieties that can't be picked off the supermarket shelf and savour a just-ripe 'Cornish Gillyflower' or 'Pitmaston Pineapple'. One of the most memorable gardens I know is my neighbour's orchard. Planted by his father well over 50 years ago it contains 138 different varieties of apple. The pleasure of sampling in his orchard is the 'pomaphile's' equivalent to that of a wine-lover wandering at will through the finest *caves* in France.

To return to crab-apples: this fruit is now a hedgerow feature which started out in the fruiting fence that surrounded early kitchen gardens. When these were replaced by bricks, and lemons supplanted verjuice in cookery, crab-apples were moved further away from the kitchen and the garden. However, crab-apples make a superior jelly, which can be flavoured with herbs or scented geraniums (rose is the nicest); and the following is Gervase Markham's recipe for making verjuice, prettily flavoured with rose petals.

Verjuice

To make Verjuyce, you shall gather your Crabs as soon as the Kernals turn black, and having laid them for a while in a heap to sweat together, take them and pick them from the stalks, blacks and rotteness; then in long Troughs with Beetles for the purpose, crush and break them all to mash, then make a bag of course Hair-cloth as square as the press, and fill it with the crusht Crabs, then put it into the press, and press it, while any moisture will dropt forth, having a clean vessel underneath to receive the liquor; this done, turn it up in sweet Hogsheads, and to every Hogshead put half a dozen handfuls of Damask rose-leaves, and then bung it up, and spend it as you shall have occasion.

From *The English Houswife*,
Gervase Markham, 1676

Apple Cream

Take twelve pippins, pare and slice or quarter them, put them into a skillet with some claret wine, and a race of ginger sliced thin, a little lemon peel cut small, and some sugar. Let these stew together till they be soft, then take them off the fire and put them in a dish, and when they be cold take a quart of cream boil'd with a little nutmeg, and put in one of the apple stuff to make it of what thickness you please, and so serve it up.

From *The Accomplish't Cook*, Robert May, 1685

During the seventeenth century it was realised that apples grew particularly well in the New England and Virginia colonies and the old familiar sorts imported by the settlers were rapidly hybridising to produce delicious new varieties. These were soon propagated by grafting for export to England and France. One of the earliest was 'Yellow Sweeting', developed in 1635.

Virginia Apple Cake

Butter a shallow, medium-sized baking pan. Make a bread dough by sifting together 150g (5oz) of flour with ½ teaspoon of salt, 1½ teaspoons of baking powder and 2 tablespoons of sugar. Work in 55g (2oz) of butter with a form until the mixture resembles breadcrumbs. Beat together 125ml (4fl oz) of milk and 1 egg and stir well into the flour. Spread the dough in the baking pan.

Peel, core and slice 500–750g (1–1½ lb) apples and arrange them in neat rows over the dough. Combine 85g (3oz) each of super-fine and brown sugar with ½ teaspoon of cinnamon and a pinch of powdered cloves. Sprinkle over the apples and dot with butter. Bake at 180°C (350°F) for 40 minutes.

Also during the seventeenth century, the sweet heavy wines of France were especially popular in England, and home wine-makers set out to replicate these beverages with home-grown fruits and flowers. In the last quarter of that century, John Worlidge wrote that the gooseberry 'yeilds so delicate a wine that you cannot solace yourself with a finer Summer Repast,' and that the fruit could be used to make brandy 'very near as good as the best French Brandy'. Elder-flowers were found to impart the necessary musky flavour to make an ersatz Frontignac, the much-prized muscatel wine of Frontignan.

Green Gooseberry Wine

This recipe, which combines elderflowers and gooseberries, dates from the years of the Second World War, when the cookery columns of daily newspapers encouraged the beleaguered British to self-sufficiency. It has been adapted to allow for modern methods of home wine-making.

Put 1.5kg (5lb) crushed gooseberries in

a large earthenware crock. Pour over 4.5 litres (1 gallon) boiling water and leave to infuse for six hours.

Strain the gooseberries through a jelly bag, pressing and squeezing to get out all the juice. Reserve the juice in a covered bowl.

Put the pulp back into the crock and pour over another 4.5 litres (1 gallon) of water. Stir, cover and leave overnight.

Early the next morning, gather a large handful of elderflowers and put them to one side in a cool dark place. Strain the pulp again through a clean, warm jelly bag, pressing and squeezing to extract all the juice. Discard the pulp and combine the two lots of juice. Measure the liquid and for every 4.5 litres (1 gallon) of liquor add 1.3kg (3lb) sugar. Add the elderflowers, stir gently and cover with a clean cloth. Put in a warm place and leave to ferment for four days. Strain the wine into demi-johns and fit air-locks. Bottle when clear and leave to mature for at least three months.

Quince and Apple Preserve

This recipe combines three favourite fruits – apples, pears and quinces – although the latter are not as widely used as they once were.

Peel and core 2kg (4 lb) quinces and 500g (1 lb) sweet dessert apples and cut them into rounds 6mm (¼in) thick. Peel 1kg (2 lb) cooking pears and cut them into quarters. Toss the fruit in lemon juice to prevent it from browning.

Put the peels and cores into a large pan, just cover them with water and boil until the cores begin to disintegrate. Strain the liquid into a bowl. Boil the quince rounds until they are just tender, then lift them from the water with a slotted spoon, taking care to keep the slices intact.

Weigh all the fruit. Make a clear syrup by boiling 340g (12oz) of sugar for every 500g (1 lb) of fruit in the juice from the peels and cores. Add the fruit and then simmer slowly until the mixture takes on a soft red colour; this may take several hours. Pour into sterile jars and seal.

Quinces appeared in many forms, baked whole in pastry cases or made into wine and into the delicious preserve that took its name from the Portuguese word for quince, *marmelo*. The passage of time altered the word to marmalade and the fruit to oranges.

Quince Marmalade

Weigh the quinces. Peel and chop half the weight into chunks.

Put the chunks into a large pan and just cover them with water. Bring to the boil and cook them to a pulp. Pass them through a sieve. Peel, core and cut the remaining whole quinces into uniformly small pieces. Add them to the purée, return all the fruit to the pan and bring to a gentle simmer. Cook until the small pieces are tender and the purée has thickened. Stir frequently or else the fruit will scorch.

Measure the purée and to 1 litre (2 pints) of fruit, add 1.35kg (3 lb) of sugar. Heat slowly until the sugar has melted and then bring to a rapid boil and cook until setting point is reached.

The finished texture of this marmalade is similar to that of a fruit butter; thick and spoonable and well-flavoured with single or mixed spice.
Based on a recipe from *Food in England*, Dorothy Hartley, 1954

Apple and Ginger Butter

My German grandmother made the following apple butter to serve with roast pork, but quinces can be substituted. Also, any of the stone fruits can be used instead and the spice adjusted accordingly.

Wash 1kg (2 lb) of sound cooking apples. Cut them into quarters and put into a preserving pan with 300ml (½ pint) of natural apple juice, or water and the juice of one lemon. Add 2.5cm (1 in) of fresh root ginger cut into thin slices. Cook the apples until soft, then pass the fruit through a sieve. Measure the purée and add between ½ to ¾ of this amount in sugar, depending on the sweetness required. Return the purée to the pan and cook slowly, stirring all the time to prevent it from sticking and burning. As it thickens, the hot purée bubbles and spits like molten lava, so beware of the spatters.

To Pickle Quinces

Boyle your Quinces that you intend to keep, whole and unpared, in faire water, till they be soft, but not too violently for feare you break them, when they are soft take them out, and boyle some Quinces pared, quarter'd, and coar'd. and the parings of the Quinces with them in the same liquor, to make it strong, and when they have boyled a good time, enough to make the liquor of sufficient strength, take out the quartered Quinces and parings, and put the liquor into a pot big enough to receive all the Quinces, both the whole and quartered, and put them into it, when the liquor is thorow cold, and so keep them for your use close covered.
From *A Book of Fruit and Flowers*, 1653

Plum Pickle

In a large earthenware bowl, combine 1kg (2 lb) each of good plums, greengages and damsons; leave the damsons whole but cut the large fruit into halves and quarters. Do not remove the stones.

Boil together 1kg (2lb) of sugar, 900ml (1½ pints) of distilled cider vinegar, 1 stick of cinnamon and 5–10 whole cloves (depending on taste) until the sugar is dissolved. Pour the liquid over the fruit and leave overnight. Strain off the liquid into a pan, bring it to the boil and pour it over the fruit and leave overnight again. The next and final day, bring the fruit and liquid gently to the boil, then reduce the heat and simmer slowly for 15 minutes. Stir occasionally but don't pulverise the fruit; the finished pickle should contain whole pieces of plum. Bottle the pickle and seal it while hot.

This is delicious with roast goose at Christmas. When serving this pickle it is a kindness to warn guests about the stones.

To Pickle Currants for Present Use

Your currants may be either red or white as you like, but don't let them be quite ripe. Give tham a Warm in white Wine Vinegar, with as much Sugar as you like; and keep them well covered with Liquor. Clove-July-Flowers may be done so.

From *Adam's Luxury and Eve's Cookery*, 1744

Pickled Apricots

Make a syrup by boiling together for 20 minutes 500ml (1 pint) distilled cider vinegar, 1kg (2lb) brown sugar and a stick of cinnamon. While the syrup is boiling peel 1–1.5kg (2–3½lb) apricots by plunging them into boiling water for a minute or two and then draining them under cold water: the skins should then rub off easily. Cut the fruit in half and remove the stones. Stick a clove in one half of each apricot.

Put the fruit into the gently boiling syrup, a few at a time, and cook them until soft. Put the fruit into sterile bottles and then pour over the syrup. Seal while hot.

Sauces have always been extremely important to the English menu, and cullis, a much reduced and hence highly concentrated meat stock, was the basis for sauces from the fourteenth century until well into the eighteenth. But it was strictly for the wealthy, requiring numerous meat and poultry bones and carcasses, as well as knuckles of veal and calves' feet. Ordinary folk prepared their sauces with butter, eggs or breadcrumbs as the binding agent, and by the nineteenth century this became the prevalent practice.

Fruit sauces are not so much used today; the service of red currant or cranberry jelly

and the ubiquitous apple sauce only hints at the marvellous flavour contrasts which gave traditional fruit sauces their popularity.

Fruit clusters are easily thinned on trained trees which improve the quality of mature fruit.

Gooseberry and Fennel Sauce

In the eighteenth century, this was the sauce to serve with mackerel.

Gently cook 500g (1lb) of gooseberries with just enough water to prevent them from sticking. When they are soft, pass them through a sieve to remove the skin and seeds. Put the purée into a pan with chopped fresh fennel leaves to taste, and cook it for several minutes. Add sugar (the sauce should remain tart), a knob of butter, salt and pepper. Serve hot with grilled mackerel.

As an alternative the sauce can be flavoured with powdered ginger.

Strawberries Preserved in Wine

Pick over the berries, removing hulls and stalks, and discarding any damaged or over-ripe fruit. Fill a wide-mouthed preserving jar with alternate layers of strawberries and caster sugar. When the jar is completely full, pour in enough medium-sweet sherry, or brandy if you feel extravagant, to cover. Seal the jar well and allow the strawberries to mature for several days before straining off the liqueur.

Serve the fruit with home-made vanilla ice cream or simply with the liqueur.

Apricot Brandy

Make a thin syrup by boiling ½ a teacup of sugar in one of water. Add to the liquid several bay leaves, fresh if possible, and a blade or two of mace. Allow the syrup to cool. Cut 500g (1lb) of apricots into halves. Remove and crack the stones and extract the kernels. Put the apricots and kernels into the syrup and leave to marinate for at least 24 hours.

Using a slotted spoon, remove the apricots, bay leaves and mace and put them into a wide-mouthed preserving jar. Pour several tablespoons of the syrup over the apricots and then fill the bottle with brandy.

Vodka can be used instead of the brandy, but with a few peppercorns added to the flavouring.

Raspberry Wine

Pick and bruise your Raspberries, and add to them the same Quantity of white Wine, and let it stand two or three Days close covered, stirring it once a Day; then strain the Liquor, put it into a steen with a Faucet, with some sugar, and in four or five Days you may bottle it.

From *Adam's Luxury and Eve's Cookery*, 1744

Left to right In the jars, Strawberries preserved in Wine, Plum Pickle and Apple Butter. The recipe for the lattice-top pie is Italian Pears.

A 'steen' was a large earthenware container with a close-fitting lid in which liquids were stored; in this case it was obviously fitted with a tap to help in draining off the liquid after it had steeped. Measure the raspberries and wine by volume and use one third that quantity of sugar; don't add sugar at all if you are using a sweet dessert wine.

Conserve of Damsons

Conserve of prunes or Damsons made another way. Take a pottle of damsons, pricke them and put them into a pot, putting thereto a pinte of Rosewater or wine, and cover your pot, let them boile well, then incorporate them by stirring, and when they be tender let them coole, and straine them with the liquor also, then take the pulpe and set it over the fire, and put thereto a sufficient quantitie of Sugar, and boile them to their height or consistencie, and put it up in gally pots, or iarre glasses.

From *Delightes for Ladies*, Sir Hugh Plat, 1st edn., 1602

In making conserves, jams and other preserves the usual proportion of sugar to fruit is from three-quarters to the full weight of the fruit; in making jellies the same proportion of sugar to juice is used, measured in volume. In the recipe above a pottle is a volume measure, equivalent to roughly 2 litres (4 pints). The liqueur may be made into a jelly, and the pulp used to make the conserve.

Jelly to Serve with Game

This recipe makes good use of grapes that don't achieve full ripeness during a cool summer.

Into a large preserving pan put 2.75kg (6lbs) of grapes, 250ml (10fl oz) of distilled cider or white wine vinegar, 10–15 whole cloves and one stick of cinnamon. Bring to the boil and cook until the grapes are soft. Pour boiling water through the jelly bag and then strain the grapes; don't squeeze the bag. Return the juice to the pan and boil it rapidly for 15 minutes. Add warmed sugar and boil until setting point is reached. Pour the jelly into sterile jelly jars and seal.

The quantity of sugar in jams and conserves can be reduced by substituting half a teaspoon of salt for every 500g (lb) of sugar. Thus, 4lb of fruit would use 2lb of sugar and 1 teaspoon of salt. It doesn't give the jam a pronounced saltiness and any trace of salt soon disappears. The appearance of the jam is somewhat cloudy, but otherwise the jam will set and taste just as well as pure sugar jam.

Honey may also be substituted for half the sugar quantity, but unless you keep bees, or are making just a small quantity of special jam, this could prove to be an expensive exercise.

Mulberries and medlars would provide the raw materials for just such epicurean preserves.

Medlar Jelly

Cover some nearly ripe medlars with water and simmer slowly until the fruit is reduced to pulp. Pour boiling water through a jelly bag and then pour in the medlar purée. Leave the bag to drip overnight, resisting the urge to squeeze the bag.

The next day, boil the juice with 500g (1lb) of sugar to every 600ml (1 pint) of juice. Pour into small, sterilised jars, seal and leave for several weeks to mature before use.

Mulberry Jam

In a preserving pan, combine in alternate layers 1kg (2lb) ripe mulberries with 1kg (2lb) of sugar. Allow fruit and sugar to stand overnight. The next day, make a purée of 500g (1lb) of peeled and chopped apples cooked in a tablespoon of water and the juice of half a lemon. Add the purée to the mulberries and then boil rapidly until setting point is reached. Pour the jam into sterilised jars and seal.

To Preserve Mulberries Whole

Set some mulberries over the fire in a skillet, and draw from them a pint of juice, when it is strained; then take three pounds of sugar beaten very fine, wet the sugar with the pint of juice; boil up your sugar and skim it, and put in two pounds of ripe mulberries, letting them stand in the syrup till they are thoroughly warm; then set them on the fire, and let them boil very gently; do them but half enough, so put them by in the syrup till next day; then boil them gently again, and when the syrup is pretty thick, and will stand in a round drip when it is cold, they are enough; put all together in a gallip[ot] for use.

From *The Compleat Housewife or, Accomplish'd Gentlewoman's Companion*, E. Smith, 1728

Mulberry gin, according to Douglas Bartram in his informative and inspiring book, *The Gourmet's Garden* (1964), is 'the connoisseur's liqueur'. It is made in the same way as sloe gin, but without the sugar: fill a bottle half-full with mulberries 'picked on a dry morning' and then pour in enough gin to fill the bottle.

In her book *Food in England*, Dorothy Hartley includes an eleventh-century recipe for 'Peris in Syrippe' in which 'wardens' (the name by which for centuries cooking pears were known) are stewed in red wine and sugar with cinnamon and ginger. This is a familiar recipe today, and possibly one of the finest ways to serve this fruit. What is intriguing is the use of saffron – to provide the richness of colour and taste so desired by the medieval gourmet.

Elaborate fruit pies, made in deep pastry cases or 'coffyns' and filled with all manner of fresh and dried fruit, spices and nutmeats, with the juices thickened by the addition of egg yolks and cream, put our humble pies to shame. Recipes for these pies are also a good example of the ostentatious school of cookery in which the lavish use of expensive ingredients, to prepare what would have been one incidental dish among many of greater consequence, served as a guide to the host's

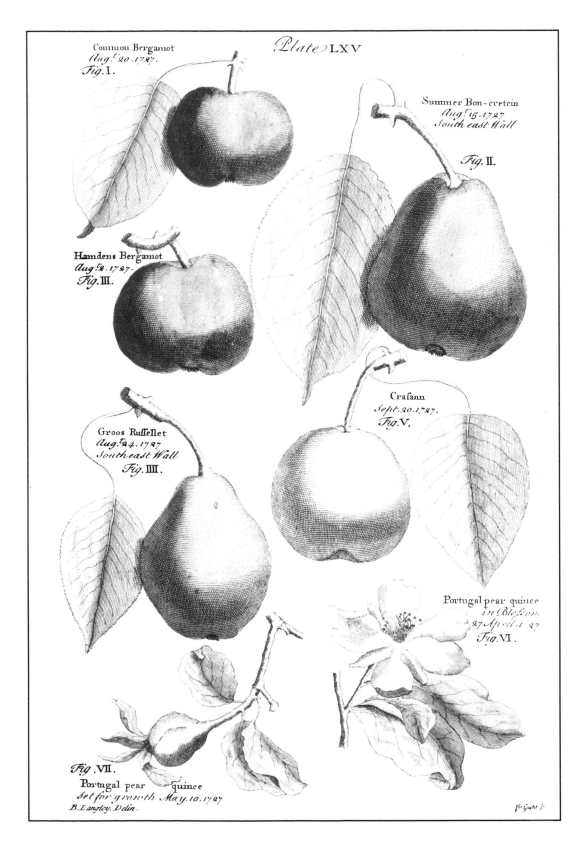

Common Bergamot
Aug.ᵗ 20. 1727.
Fig. I.

Summer Bon - cretein
Aug.ᵗ 15. 1727.
South east Wall
Fig. II.

Hamdens Bergamot
Aug.ᵗ. 1727.
Fig. III.

Plate LXV

Crafann
Sept. 20. 1727.
Fig. V.

Groos Ruffellet
Aug.ᵗ 24. 1727.
South east Wall
Fig. IIII.

Portugal pear quince
in Bloffom.
27 April. 1727
Fig. VI.

Fig. VII.
Portugal pear quince
Set for growth May. 10. 1727
B. Langley. Delin.

Jac Gucht Sc

wealth. The following recipe is typical of the genre and could be made equally well with quinces or pippins, in which case dates and orange slices were included.

Warden Pye

Take fairest and best Wardens, and pare them and take out the hard cores at the top, and cut the sharp ends at the bottom flat; then boyl them in White-wine and Sugar, untill the Syrup grow thick: then take the Wardens from the Syrup in a clean dish, and let them cool, and set them in the coffin, and prick Cloves in the tops, with whole sticks of Cinnamon, and great store of Sugar . . . ; then cover it and only reserve a Vent-hole, so set it in the oven and bake it; when it is bak'd, draw it forth, and take the first syrup in which the wardens were boyl'd and taste it, and if it be not sweet enough, then put in more sugar and some Rose-water, and boyl it again a little: then pour it in the Vent-hole and shake the Pye well: then take sweet Butter and Rose-water melted, and with it anoint the Pye-lid all over, and then strew on it store of Sugar, and so set it into the Oven again a little space and then serve it up.

From *The English Housewife*,
Gervase Markham, 1676

Italian Pears

To make a dish in the Italian fashion
Take pleasant pears, slice them into thin slices, and put to them half as much sugar as they weigh. Then mince some candied citron and candied orange small, mix it with the pears, and lay them on a bottom of cold butter paste in a patty-pan with some fine beaten cinnamon, lay on the sugar and close it up, bake it, being baked, ice it with rose-water, fine sugar and butter.

From *The Accomplish't Cook*, Robert May, 1685

The above recipe is a slightly more modest version of Warden Pye. Don't cut the pears too thinly; the modesty of the ingredients can be compensated for by the finished appearance, if the fruit shape retains some of its definition and can be recognised as pears through a lattice top. The fact that you can recognise the principal ingredient is, I think, what 'Italian fashion' refers to. Use puff or shortcrust pastry.

Pear varieties from Batty Langley's *Pomona*.

CHAPTER SIX

JOY OF THE NEW

Above Capsicum annum.

Opposite Detail from *Vegetable Market* by Lucas Van Valkenborch (*c.* 1530–97). *Kunsthistorisches Museum, Vienna.*

T HE CRUSADES of the Middle Ages introduced the wealth of the Orient to Europeans. Their desire for the fabulous spices and exotic fruits and vegetables of China, India and Persia led to the development of overland trade routes. Servicing the marketplace by caravan was slow and costly, but medieval consumers were demanding more goods, whatever the price. The quest for a sea route from Europe to India became the dream of every entrepreneur.

In 1270, the Portuguese made initial explorations of Africa's west coast; twenty-one years later, two Genoese adventurers, Vivaldo and Doria, vanished without a trace while trying to find India.

The search for the route continued for another two centuries; valiant missions from many countries set out, only to return in failure (if they returned at all). Finally, in the spring of 1498, the Portuguese explorer Vasco da Gama reached Calicut. He would have got there sooner but for squabbles between Spain and Portugal, arising from a notable mistake on the part of a Genoese explorer working for Spain: Christopher Columbus thought, when he landed in the Bahamas in 1492, that he had reached the Indies, and held this belief to his dying day in 1506, although most of his contemporaries were convinced it was a New World.

The Great Age of Discovery began, and its impact on the European horticultural scene was profound and immediate. From the first Spanish outpost of Santo Domingo, established by 1500, new crops were being introduced to Spain. By 1574, a Spanish book entitled *Joyful Newes Out of the Newe Founde Worlde* appeared in English translation. It was written by Dr Nicolas Monardes of Seville, and was originally published by him in two volumes in 1569 and 1571. He had never actually been to the New World, but relied upon first-hand experiences of others who had; such was the excitement generated by the influx of unknown plants that his work, containing descriptions of tobacco, capsicums and many other curiosities, was an immediate best-seller.

The colonisation of North America began in earnest during the reign of Elizabeth I, 1558–1603. This was a period of relative peace and greater prosperity, when time and resources could be lavished on improving the domestic scene. One could afford to replace hedges with brick walls, and decorate the garden with fountains, topiary and trelliswork arbours. Refugees from Holland and northern France came to England, many of them skilled horticulturalists who passed on improved knowledge of gardening techniques that were to prove invaluable in the founding of New World colonies, and in the eventual development and adoption of unfamiliar food plants introduced from the New England settlements.

The founding of the Pilgrim settlement at Plymouth in 1620 coincided with a period of

great advance in the field of botany. Men of means exercised their intellect by sponsoring plant hunters in their quest for new plant curiosities. While the collectors were initially concerned with finding plants of medicinal or economic value, their brief was eventually extended to include decorative flowers for the pleasure garden and vegetables, fruits and herbs for the kitchen.

American-Indian crops, like corn, potatoes and pumpkins, began to appear in European gardens. Some introductions were immediately successful, like capsicums, while others, like the tomato, were treated with the greatest suspicion; and still others, like the scarlet runner bean, were initially grown only for their flowers.

The native inhabitants of the New World taught the settlers a thing or two about cookery, and if there is a national style of American cuisine it might well have evolved from the Indian cookery described by Robert Beverley in his book *History and Present State of Virginia*. Published in 1705, this book documents the development of the Virginia colonies and was prepared as a sort of early advertising campaign to encourage further development of the new territories.

'They have two ways of Broyling, viz. one by laying the Meat itself upon the Coals, the other by laying it upon Stocks raised upon Forks at some distance above the live Coals; which heats more gently and dries up the Gravy: this they, and we also from them, call Barbacueing.' On the whole, Beverley had little time for Indian cookery, complaining that 'They have no other sauce but a good stomach' and remarking that its only attribute was that it was 'performed with little trouble' – something that is true today of the best American home cooking.

The big selling point of Virginia was the fertility and abundance of the land. Beverley eulogised the kitchen gardens of Virginia, writing that they

don't thrive better or faster in any part of the Universe than here. They have all the Culinary plants that grow in England, and in far greater perfection, than in England. Besides these, they have several Roots, Herbs, Vine-fruits and Salate-flowers peculiar to themselves. These they dish up in various ways, and find them very delicious as Sauce to their Meats, both Roast and Boil'd, Fresh and Salt; such are Red-Buds, Sassafras flowers, Cymnels, Melons and Potatoes . . .

While gardeners on both sides of the Atlantic were busy experimenting with the multitude of introductions, the colonists had to investigate the best means of growing familiar food plants in a wholly unfamiliar climate. In the northern settlements the growing season was short and the winters bitterly cold; in the south, the growing season never ended. So, while one gardener was avid for early maturing vegetables and fruit, looking for crops that would store well, another was experimenting with autumn sowing and rotational cropping for prolonged seasons. Perhaps this explains why in the north, vegetable gardens were organised in single broad plots bordered by paths and fruit bushes; crops went in and out quickly. In the south the four-square plan with individual beds for each crop was most popular, to permit a longer period of cultivation in each area. Nevertheless, the plan of an early American garden would have been similar in every respect to a sixteenth-century European garden, with box-edged knots and orchards of fine fruit.

Back in the Old World, cooks were keeping up with gardeners, adapting to new equipment and new methods. The cooking range made its first appearance in the seventeenth century. Built into the old hearth or free-standing, it had a separate oven and

This engraving is from Olivier de Serres' *L'Théâtre d'Agriculture* (1663 edn). He wrote that the garden should have four separate areas: Potager, Bouquetier, Medicinal, Fruictier – vegetables, flowers, physic and fruit.

flat heated surface for pots and kettles. This made it possible to cook different types of food in a variety of ways and caused the invention of individual cooking utensils – pots and pans replaced the cauldron and spit over an open hearth, so that meat, vegetables and fruit could be cooked separately. Prepared dishes of meat and fish served with separate sauces and garnished with New World vegetables became increasingly common. Nonetheless, these innovations were only for the rich, and among the countryfolk vegetable potages continued in favour throughout the sixteenth and seventeenth centuries.

A favourite way of serving new food plants was in boiled salads – cooked vegetables served cold with a dressing of vinegar and sugar (oil was not much used until the end of the seventeenth century). This is not surprising: salads had been popular for centuries; any of the new vegetables, such as beetroot from Italy and kidney beans, had to be cooked to be edible; and most foods were thought to be safe only when well and truly cooked, which could explain why some imports were slow to seize the European palate.

Innovations at table were dramatic. Trenchers of stale bread were replaced by plates first of pewter, then porcelain, which furthered the cause of separate courses; around this time, the sweet or dessert course became part of the menu, and the introduction of arrowroot from the West Indies made blancmange and similar decorative moulded dishes easier to prepare.

Until the seventeenth century, forks were used only by the wealthy, chiefly to eat fruit and sweetmeats. Knives for slicing off chunks of spit-roasted meat, spoons for scooping up porray, and fingers had been the only utensils required. But the general acceptance of forks meant that difficult foods such as fish and small cuts of meat could be eaten individually.

Doubtless these refinements in the art of cooking and dining enhanced the use of rare and often expensive new fruits and vegetables in the menu. After all, who would want simply to toss into the potage produce that had taken much skill to grow, or else large sums to buy?

Eggplants, Tomatoes, Potatoes

The three weird sisters of the Renaissance kitchen garden were the **aubergine** or eggplant, **tomato** and **potato**. The first two were known respectively as the mad apple and the love apple, and the latter was regarded with great suspicion because it so resembled its relative, *Solanum nigrum*, the deadly nightshade.

The aubergine, *S. melongena*, did not appear in European gardens until the sixteenth century, but had been grown long before then in the East; fifth-century Chinese courtesans coloured their teeth with a black aubergine-based dye to obtain a polished effect which must have looked alarmingly like pewter.

Gerard called them 'madde or raging apples' and remarked that although in Egypt and Barbary they were roasted under ashes and that 'the people of Tolledo do eat them with great devotion', he would prefer to eat the familiar foods of England, rather than perilous foreign delicacies – a sentiment shared by many Englishmen today. Nevertheless, the aubergine was grown in gardens, but chiefly for decoration. It was not much eaten until the nineteenth century, and has always had its greatest following in the Mediterranean regions.

Aubergines require warmth to do their best, and in the cool north should really be grown in greenhouses or else under cloches. Don't attempt to grow them outdoors without cloche protection unless you are confident of at least 10–15 weeks of a minimum daily temperature of 20°C (70°F).

Sow the seed indoors during early spring; bottom heat will help to ensure even germination. Prick out the plants into individual peat pots and gradually harden them off. Plant them out when all danger of frost is past, giving the plants a place in the sunniest part of the garden.

When a plant is about 15cm (6in) tall, pinch out the terminal bud to encourage the formation of lateral stems which will bear the self-pollinating flowers. Water well throughout the growing season. A manure mulch will feed as well as keep the plants moist.

The tomato suffered from the same prejudices as the potato and aubergine until some time in the mid-sixteenth century, when a brave Italian chef decided to see what the tomato could do for his country's cuisine. It wasn't long before tomato sauce followed all the other marvellous Italian innovations into French and English kitchens.

Glasshouses built against sunny walls, as shown here, (from *The City Gardener*, 1721) allowed gardeners to raise the New World's exotica.

Love apples are aptly named, since the tomato is one vegetable that deserves to be in every kitchen garden – nothing compares with the flavour of a freshly picked tomato, warmed by the sun: pure bliss. And, like apples, there are more varieties to choose between than 'Moneymaker' and 'Alicante'. There are yellow toms, striped toms, cherry or cocktail-tiny toms and the large-fruited 'Beefeater' types so popular in America. The latter will grow just as well in England, and it is a silly idea to think, as some people do, that because of their size there isn't as much flavour; supermarket imports may be a bit weak on taste, but not the homegrown ones. The same is true of the 'Marmande' types, mostly grown on the Continent. 'Roma', the pear-shaped Italian cooking tomato is terrific in salads and is the sort I now grow exclusively. It crops heavily, even in a bad summer, it is delicious raw or cooked and, best of all, it doesn't need staking or pinching out since it is a determinate or bush form.

Start the seed indoors as for aubergine and plant out after all danger of frost is past. Tomatoes really do repay the effort spent in covering a bed with black plastic mulch and planting through it. Tomatoes like steady adequate moisture throughout the growing season, and a mulch ensures this, dramatically lessening the risk of blossom-end rot developing.

When planting the tomatoes out, be sure to plant them deeply, up to the first set of leaves. If the plant is leggy after its spell indoors, lay it on its side, burying the stem up to the first leaves. Roots will form on the stem. Be sure to plant tomatoes in the sunniest part of the garden.

Left to right Aubergines, or eggplants, and tomatoes.

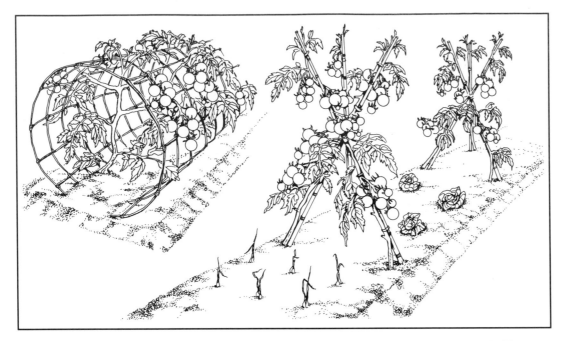

Left A wire cage support for bush tomatoes helps to lift fruit trusses off the ground. *Right* Training indeterminate varieties of tomato up tall canes in the Italian fashion.

As the plants grow they require training. Bush plants can be lifted off the ground by growing them through a cylinder of wire mesh laid along the bed before the plants are put out. Indeterminate varieties do best if staked. Italian gardeners make a tepee of three or four canes and train one plant up each cane. This is more secure than staking individuals. Otherwise they can be raised inside upright wire cylinders. Pinch out the lateral shoots on these varieties and then remove the terminal bud when the height of the support is reached.

Tomatoes grow well with carrots, onions and parsley and will also help protect gooseberries and asparagus foliage. It is best not to mix them with brassicas, and supposedly with potatoes (although I have done so on numerous occasions without any bad effects at all). Marigolds are extremely beneficial to tomatoes.

It may sound extravagant that the **potato** should be described as an 'instrument of destiny', causing nations to rise to pre-eminence or sink into a slough of despair, but such seems to be the case. Its cultivation by the indigenous peoples of the Andes helped to make the Incas the masters of the South American continent; Frederick the Great commanded that Prussia and Pomerania should be planted with it and thereby laid the foundations of a mighty European state. The Irish nation more than trebled its population on the strength of the potato, and was then brought to its knees by a terrible famine following the total failure of the potato harvest in the mid-nineteenth century. The ensuing migration of starving Irish to the United States provided that country with the labour force to support its growing industrial economy, helping it to become a world power.

How the potato reached Europe has been the subject of much speculation, but what is certain is that in 1537, a Spanish scouting party entered an Andean village and discovered, in homes left empty by fleeing Indians, beans, maize and 'truffles', which were in fact potatoes. Their nutritional value was soon recognised, and Spanish ships regularly included potatoes in their stores. By 1576 it was in cultivation in Spain, and from there it was introduced to Italy, where it was seen by Clusius, who later described it in his *Historia Plantarum* of 1601 as a popular garden plant used as a food and also as pig fodder.

A more questionable claim regarding the potato's introduction was made four years earlier, in England. When John Gerard published his *Grete Herball*, he included a description of the 'Potatoes of Virginia' which he was growing successfully in his Holborn garden (he was so proud of this achievement that the picture of him on the book's frontispiece shows him holding a spray of potato flowers). But his assertion that it was first discovered in America in the Virginia colonies is unlikely – it was introduced there only after it had become established in Europe.

Equally spurious is the credit given to Sir Walter Raleigh for the potato's introduction from the colonies. What may have happened is that Sir Francis Drake, sailing to rescue the beleaguered Roanake settlers, raided Spanish ships and helped himself to stores from the Spanish settlement of Cartagena on the Colombian coast, acquiring potatoes in the process. He then carried out his mission, and may have given some tubers to Thomas Hariot, one of the evacuees, who then presented them to his patron Raleigh, who gave them to Gerard, who was cultivating many plant arrivals from the New World. But this, of course, is speculation.

Unless you have a large garden, it is hardly worth growing main-crop potatoes, as they are easily bought and comparatively cheap. It is far better to use the space you have to grow earlies, or varieties that can't easily be purchased, such as the delicious 'Pink Fir Apple'. This potato was introduced at the end of the nineteenth century, and is a main-crop that keeps its new potato flavour well in storage. It is a waxy potato with a sweet flavour, ideal for salads. Other varieties worth growing are 'Arran Comet', 'Dunluce' and 'Ulster Sceptre', both of which are earlies, high-yielding and with the creamy-white flesh desirable in an early potato. 'Wilja' with pale yellow flesh, and 'Romano' with firm white, are second earlies; they rarely disintegrate during cooking. The main-crop 'Drayton' is an improved 'King Edward' with the same cooking qualities but higher yields. 'Bintje' and 'Jaune de Hollande' are excellent for salads; and for novelty (one of the pleasures of 'grow-your-own') try 'Orkney Black'. As you might expect from its name, it has purple black flesh, and although its appearance at the dinner table may cause some to wrinkle their noses – the darkness fades to a dirty white – it has a curious, sweet, nutty flavour.

When potatoes finally did achieve recognition, it became the goal of most gardeners to raise the earliest crops possible, so methods of cultivation were as elaborate as the recipes. In *The Manse Garden* by the Rev. N. Paterson (1822) the method entails laying the seed potatoes on a board in a warm bright place in January, and covering them 5cm (2in) deep with moist sand or sawdust. By March, the young plants can be lifted from the board with their roots enmeshed in the mulch and planted out in a warm border to mature. There is no reason why this method should not be used today for raising an early crop in a greenhouse under the staging. It can also be adapted for growing potatoes above ground in a thick mulch resting on the soil surface.

During autumn, work well-rotted compost or manure into the soil (fresh manure should never be used near potatoes as it encourages a range of diseases), then spread a thick layer of leaves over the top. Potatoes like a slightly acid soil. Scatter a few spadefuls of soil over the leaves, and the following spring plant the sprouted tubers on top of the leaves, which will have rotted down. Cover the tubers with a generous 30cm (1ft) deep blanket of straw or hay.

The potatoes will grow into the straw mulch; when you want some for the table, simply push aside the mulch and take what you need, and later harvest in the usual manner. Be sure to maintain the thickness of the mulch throughout the growing season. Besides taking the digging out of potato growing, the mulch keeps down weeds and after harvest can be left in place to rot down and improve the soil.

Potatoes are particularly good subjects for raised-bed growing, as the well-manured deeply dug soil fits their requirements exactly. Work in some leaf compost the autumn before planting.

The tubers should be planted in trowel holes 15cm (6in) deep; space earlies 23cm (9in) apart and main-crop up to 30cm (12in). This is considerably closer than conventional planting, and although the yield will be slightly smaller, the potatoes will be of better quality. There is no need to earth up the plants as the dense foliage keeps light out and moisture in; early shoots can be protected from frost with leaf or straw mulch, or with sheets of newspaper. Otherwise, follow conventional methods of cultivation.

Marigolds seem to encourage potatoes to do their best, and can be planted to make a golden collar around the edges of the beds; sweet corn, beans and cabbages are good neighbours to potatoes, but don't plant pumpkins, raspberries, cucumber or sunflowers near by.

Leonard Meager's *New Art of Gardening* was published in 1697. This plan for a small garden shows the garden areas divided by low fences, with some beds given cloche and what appears to be net protection.

Peppers, Jerusalem Artichokes, Runner Beans, Sweet Corn

Of all the imports from the New World that altered the flavours of Old World cuisine, none had a greater and more immediate impact than the colourful and spicy fruit of the genus *Capsicum*. Until the introduction of **capsicum** in the early years of the sixteenth century, mustard was the common hot seasoning; although black-pepper berries were known and used, they were a rare commodity and used only occasionally by the well-to-do. So it is not surprising that the new arrival, which could be brought to bear its colourful fruit in the cool climate of northern Europe, should have found immediate stardom.

Capsicum was a standard crop of the Indian tribes of South and Central America and the West Indies, where it was first encountered by Spanish explorers who introduced the different varieties to Spain. In 1593 Charles d'Ecluse described its cultivation in the Spanish province of Castilia and in Moravia; it quickly became a common crop in southern Europe; and it was introduced to Hungary during the Turkish occupation, becoming the emblem of Hungarian cuisine.

Hot chilli varieties of capsicum had already reached India by the seventeenth century, and were so well established in the sub-continent's menu that early European traders mistakenly thought that the plants were indigenous: John Evelyn described it in his *Acetaria* (1699) as 'Indian Capsicum . . . superbly hot and burning', and the 1633 edition of Gerard's *Herball* says that the plants 'are brought from forrein countries, as Ginnie, India and those parts into Spaine'.

In addition to sweet or bell peppers, there are dozens of other chillies in cultivation, as a trip through a Mexican marketplace will reveal. All are classed as *Capsicum annuum*, but each has its own name, shape, colour and temperature – from pungently warm to tongue-blistering. Travelling gardeners should experiment with these, as packets of seed purchased on holiday can be raised in a warm greenhouse or under cloches in the open garden.

But for timid palates and outdoor growing in cool climates, the greatest success is had from sweet peppers like 'Big Bertha' and 'Canape', the pungently flavoured 'Yellow Hungarian Wax', and the hotter variety 'Long Red Cayenne', which has long slender fruits, deep red when mature: good for drying, bottling, and prepared hot sauces.

Start the plants off indoors in warmth. Prick out seedlings individually into peat pots and plant them out when all danger of frost is past. Set the plants 25–30cm (10–12in) apart on a quincunx, and plant deeply to the first set of true leaves. Although they are natives of hot, sunny countries, capsicums do best in temperatures of 20.5–24°C (65–75°F), and will do well in the dappled shadow of a taller growing crop.

Planting through a black plastic mulch will also help to retain moisture, which is vital since the flowers will drop if the plants are allowed to dry out. Organic mulches may also be used, but they should be put in place only after the first flowers have formed. If the weather is excessively dry, syringe the plants with water, but only in the morning – overnight dampness encourages disease.

Bushy capsicum plants will be sturdier and more productive, so pinch out the growing tips at 45cm (18in). Don't use high-nitrogen fertilisers, but aim for slow, steady growth; peppers are part of the tomato/potato family, so use a tomato fertiliser. Peppers also appreciate an acid soil, so if necessary work a small amount of aluminium sulphate into the soil before planting.

When harvesting, always cut the fruit; never tear it from the plant. To ripen any fruit left at the end of the growing season, take up the entire plant and hang it upside down in a cool dry place.

Good companions for peppers are sweet basil and aubergine (eggplant). Because the plants do not like bathing in full, hot sun, but it must be well watered, they do well with sweet corn; they also must have plenty of water and the tall stalks will provide dappled shade for the peppers.

Capsicums are an invaluable aid to the organic gardener. Caterpillars and rabbits will avoid crops sprinkled with cayenne powder and a spray made from a handful of chillies, a sweet pepper and several cloves of crushed garlic infused in a gallon of water can be used to control aphids and other common garden pests in the flower and vegetable garden.

The **Jerusalem artichoke** has nothing whatever to do with the Holy City, but came from North America, possibly from the Mississippi River valley, some time in the early sixteenth century. It was better received than the potato, and spread like wild fire, until in 1833 William Cobbett complained that it, 'to the great misfortune of the human race, is everywhere but too well known'.

It is a relative of the sunflower and the name is probably a corruption of the Italian

Left Sweet bell peppers, *right* jalapeno pepper and long Hungarian wax peppers.

girasole or sunflower, for it was recognised as being a *helianthus*. *Jane Grigson's Vegetable Book* gives the best account of its early history that I have read – she records a Mr Goodyer's complaint about the windiness of this vegetable, one which is frequently aired today.

In spite of this social drawback, the roots make a soothingly mellow winter soup and can be served simply sautéed to accompany roasts. But give the plants a space all on their own in the garden, for they spread rapidly and are impossible to eradicate once they take hold.

The Jerusalem artichoke grows up to 2.5m (8ft) tall or more in any kind of soil with the modicum of attention. Drop the tubers into 10cm-(4in-) deep holes, about 30cm (12in) apart. As the plants begin to show through, draw the soil up around the stems. Stake them with twiggy branches or cane and string grids.

To harvest, cut the stems down as they fade and gently lift the tubers. Store in a cool dry shed or else in sand.

The **scarlet runner bean**, a native of South America, was a late New World export, apparently first introduced in the early part of the seventeenth century by the great English plantsman and collector, John Tradescant. But it was grown solely as a garden flower, the climbing vines used to garland arbours and garden walls with long-lasting sprays of cheerful red flowers. This use remained popular even after Phillip Miller recommended the seed pods as a food in the mid-1700s.

Modern gardeners still recognise the runner bean's decorative value. Well-grown plants provide a beautiful green screen, as I saw in a London mews off St James's Street: half-a-dozen half-barrels had been planted with tepees of runner beans stationed outside a row of office windows, cheering up an otherwise bleak prospect and brightening the street image

of a shady cul-de-sac. In the kitchen garden the beans are grown either in rows and trained up a vertical framework of poles and twine or else in groups around a tepee of tall canes. Either method is adequate, and other crops can be interplanted around and within the frame.

Oddly, considering their New World origins, runner beans are not as widely grown in the United States as they are in Europe; few English gardens are without them. The international seed merchants, Thompson and Morgan, are including a number of varieties in their American catalogue, including 'Butler', a long-lasting stringless variety. In the meantime, the favourite American pole bean is appearing

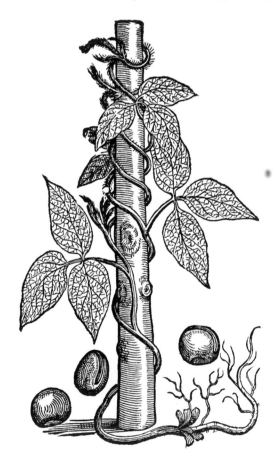

The runner bean, called *Phaseolus Brasilianus*, from Matthias l'Obel's *Icones Plantarum* of 1581.

on the lists of UK seed merchants, so the exchange goes on.

The runner bean is a perennial, but only in hot, humid climates. In Mexico it is raised as such to shelter balconies and patios. Northerners must grow it as an annual.

Sow the seed outdoors in late spring or early summer. If cloches are put over the bed several weeks in advance, the soil will have warmed, which greatly aids germination. The deeply dug, well-drained soil and manure foundation of a raised bed provide ideal soil conditions for runner beans. They like a sunny spot, but with some shelter from strong winds which may topple a fully laden support.

Put the seed in pairs, 5cm (2in) deep and about 25–30cm (10–12in) apart, in rows. As they grow, remove the weakest plants. If you calculate on 8–10 plants per family member, you will have adequate fresh supplies and some left for freezing, for which the beans are ideal.

Runner beans like humidity and moisture, so never let the bed dry out. A plastic or organic mulch is a great help, also keeping weeds at bay. It is traditional among gardeners to begin spraying the plants daily as the first flowers appear, to assist the setting of the pods. But the most important factor for good cropping is plenty of moisture at the roots. Pick the beans regularly to keep the plants cropping.

Carrots, beets, brassicas and summer savory, the bean herb, grow well with beans. Some people grow beans with sweetcorn so that the corn stalks support the beans. Onions are said to be detrimental to beans.

To the native inhabitants of pre-Columbian Mexico, **corn** was the very fabric of mankind, used by their gods in the act of creation. In fact, throughout the Americas, this vegetable was venerated and cultivated on a vast scale, and with the bean formed a major part of the daily diet.

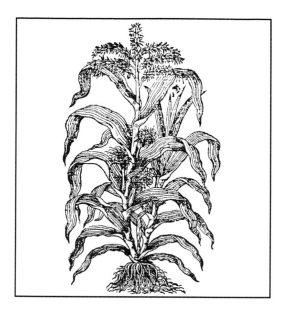

Zea mays, maize or sweetcorn.

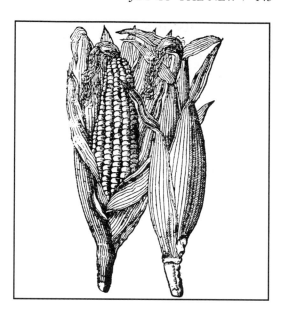

Ripe ears of corn showing kernels and silk.

Columbus included corn amongst his New World souvenirs, and its cultivation rapidly spread throughout the warmer regions of Europe and Asia, reaching China and India by the mid-sixteenth century. This rapid assimilation later led to the confusion of travelling Europeans, who thought corn a native of Asia and started calling it 'Turkey corn'.

Meanwhile, back in the New World, the Jamestown settlers were discovering the secrets of corn-growing from the local natives. Today, in our kitchen gardens we still follow their methods, hilling the plants and interplanting with beans, although we no longer drop a fish into the planting hole.

There are basically two types of corn: non-sweet dent, and sweet corn, the type we grow to eat boiled, with lashings of butter and a sprinkle of salt. Within the last category there is an enormous number of varieties with varying degrees of sweetness (contributed by the ability of the kernels to retain their sugar content after gathering before it is coverted to starch), size of cob, degree of earliness and the colour, from ivory white to deep golden yellow, as well as the bronzy red, deep purple and multi-coloured 'Indian' corn beloved of dried flower arrangers.

Not surprisingly, the widest choice is to be found in America; as a vegetable, sweet corn has been slow to achieve popularity in Britain, although this is now changing, probably as a result of the shrinking of the Atlantic Ocean divide. Sweet corn is now offered as a starter in many 'American-style' British restaurants; it comes to supermarkets, shrink-wrapped, from Spain; and British seed merchants are offering some of the best early varieties that America has to offer. 'Early Extra Sweet' and the white-kernelled 'How Sweet It Is' are both All-America winners, have high sugar content and make good early crops in cool regions.

Sweet corn is really a warm weather lover, so unless you are sure of long hot summers it is best to start the seed off in warmth under glass. Sow two seeds in 7.5cm (3in) peat pots in loose sandy compost when the weather is just beginning to warm. This is especially useful for early extra sweet varieties that have shrivelled seeds; the warm moist peat ensures even germination which can be difficult to achieve when sown in the open. When the seedlings are about 7.5cm (3in) tall, remove the weakest. Otherwise, station-sow the seed outdoors when the soil is truly warm.

Sweet corn is wind pollinated so must be sown in blocks; a single raised bed given over to their use is ideal. Also, if you are growing more than one variety, space the beds well apart to avoid cross-pollination.

Plant out the seedlings in rows about 45cm (18in) apart, spacing the plants at 30–38cm (12–15in) intervals. Drop a teaspoonful of blood, fish and bone meal into the bottom of each hole before you put in the plant or sow the seed. Shades of the fish-in-the-hole trick. Corn loves nitrogen.

Water is vital to successful growth and I find that by drawing up the soil around the base of growing plants every second week not only gives added support to the stalks but creates irrigation channels. When you need to water, simply pour the water into the channels. Be sure to water thoroughly – the soil should be moistened to a depth of at least 12.5cm (5in). Hoe gently to keep down weeds as the plants grow; corn is shallow rooting and resents disturbance. Don't be tempted to remove the suckering sideshoots; they have no adverse effect on the plant, but their removal does.

Corn is ready to harvest when the kernels fill the ear to the very end of the cob – if you pinch the end and feel it pointed rather than rounded, the ear is not ready.

Pick the corn when you mean to use it. Although some varieties are bred to retain their sugar for several days, corn is normally at its sweetest the day it is harvested. Otherwise, keep it refrigerated.

Peans and beans are beneficial to corn and can actually be grown up the stalks. Squash, pumpkins and cucumbers are also good neighbours and their broad leaves act as a living mulch.

Melons, Marrows, Pumpkins, Squash, Gourds

Melons in a cool climate are hothouse babies. They are probably native to Africa, which explains why, in any garden except those in hot, humid climates, they must be cloistered in the greenhouse or protected by cloches or coldframes.

In Europe, the Italians first brought melons to perfection, but they had no far-reaching popularity until the advent of hothouse science in the late seventeenth century. Then the growing of melons became an exacting discipline and any garden writer worth his ink devoted pages on how best to cultivate this delicious fruit. The hotbed was a prerequisite of successful melon-growing; a deep pit of fresh dung, layers of earth and a handful of melon seeds. The heat generated by the decomposing manure provided the essential warmth.

However, cantaloup melons are more tolerant of cool weather and I have managed to raise a few plants in a cold-frame. But the summer was too short and the position not sunny enough to ripen the three little fruits. Perhaps a more concentrated effort next time and a primitive hotbed under the frame will produce results. Melons do provide gardeners with the sort of challenge they like.

If you decide to pick up the gauntlet, you must definitely start the seed indoors so that the young plants can get on quickly. Plant on a mound and water frequently. In a row the melons can be trained along under glass-barn cloches or medium-sized plastic tunnel cloches. In a coldframe, plant two melons at opposite corners and keep the fuzzy stem ends picked off in each case.

Because insects can't reach the melon flowers you will have to hand-pollinate regularly. Male flowers grow in clusters, females singly. Take off all the petals from the male and shake the pollen on to the fully open female flower. Do all the flowers at the same time and early in the morning if possible.

As the fruit forms, gently lift it on to an inverted flowerpot to lift it from the shade of the leaves. Any small fruit that sets late in the season should be removed.

Melon leaves are a good addition for the compost pile.

It has been thought that **marrows, pumpkins, squashes and gourds** were Old World natives. Some members of the Cucurbit tribe, like cucumbers and melons, have been grown in Asia and Europe for centuries. However, the plants we are considering are almost certainly American in origin, cultivated there for at least 10,000 years and perhaps longer.

The early colonists first discovered the pleasure of eating summer and winter squash, and the usefulness of pumpkins and gourds, from the native inhabitants. They found that the Indians baked the squashes whole in smouldering ashes, ate the long-stemmed male flowers filled with a variety of stuffings and used them to add flavour to potage. Pumpkins were grown among the corn rows and hollowed-out gourds provided kitchen utensils, storage jars and bowls. After their European introduction early in the sixteenth century, they became enormously popular and were considered superior to cucumbers, as the flesh was far more versatile and the seeds could also be eaten in a variety of ways.

But this popularity has waned, and although pumpkins, marrows, and zucchini are still widely grown, the wide range of summer and winter squash is only just beginning to recover some of its former status. One has only to compare the seed catalogues of American and British merchants to wonder at the difference.

Summer squash includes the soft-skinned types that ripen early; winter squash have hard shells – they are ready for eating in the autumn and generally keep well throughout winter. Pumpkins come in many shapes and shades of orange and, if not used to make lanterns for Halloween, can be used for pies and soups, breads and stews. Gourds are also hard-shelled, but the flesh is inedible since it dries out as the fruit ripens. And there are varieties which cross over the categories.

Summer squash varieties include the familiar courgette or zucchini, pattypan and summer crookneck. Winter squash include butternut and acorn, buttercup, banana and hubbard. The spaghetti marrow is more of a summer squash, but the fruit will keep. It is especially delicious; just steam it for twenty minutes and then use a fork to scrape out the pasta-like strands to serve with a tomato and mushroom sauce.

All the squashes have similar growing requirements. They like a well-drained soil, and are not fussy about whether it is clay, loam or sand. They are not hardy, so if you plan to sow *in situ* be sure that there is no danger of frost. Otherwise start the seed indoors in individual peat pots, sowing two seeds to each pot. Keep the seedlings moist and then harden them off gradually as the first true leaves appear.

A mélange of vegetables, including peppers, sweet-corn, marrow, runner beans, potatoes and tomatoes.

These crops take up a lot of space; the leaves are generally quite large and the vines do best if left to sprawl along the rows. There are bush varieties, and these of course are best if space is at a premium. Many people grow the plants in 'hills' which are in fact holes. Several seeds are sown at 7.5cm (3in) intervals around the hole's perimeter of 20–25cm (8–10in). The hole is filled with well-rotted manure and covered over with soil. The plants are then thinned to leave only four or five of the healthiest. Alternatively, you can raise a mound of manure, cover it with soil and set one plant on the top of each. This method ensures good drainage. Water the crops regularly and thoroughly.

Female flowers will sometimes appear before the long-stemmed male flowers are there to pollinate them, in which case they will simply wither and drop off. But this is only temporary and the plant soon catches up.

Decorative gourds can be trained up a trellis around a patio where their bright colours can be appreciated. After harvesting gourds, polish the shells with good wax or apply a protective coat of polyurethane varnish.

Summer squashes should be picked regularly to keep the plant producing. The skin should be tender and the flesh seedless. A winter squash is ready when the skin will not break under pressure from your thumbnail. But don't go around regularly poking and prodding as damaged skins inhibit keeping qualities. When you do pick a winter squash, leave a length of stem on the fruit.

Usually, I let a vine make only 4–5 fruits before pinching out the terminal bud to encourage the development of laterals.

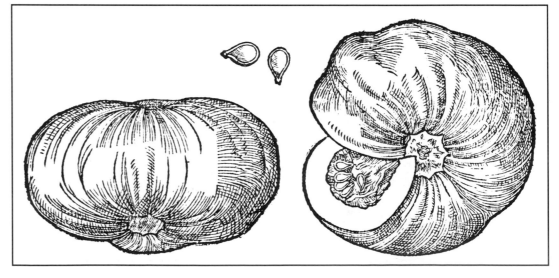

Top left and right Two melon varieties and *bottom* pumpkin from l'Obel's *Icones Plantarum.*

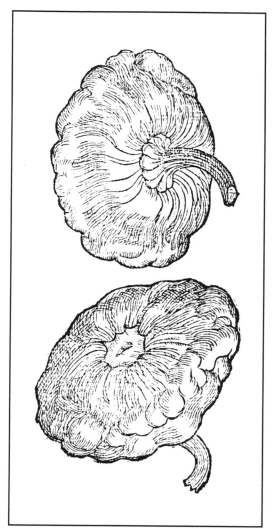

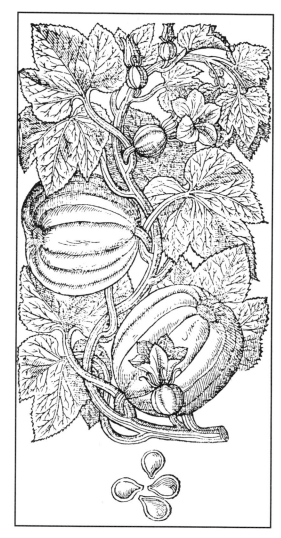

Top left A melon and *middle* patty pan squash; *top right and bottom* pumpkin, from l'Obel's Icones Plantarum.

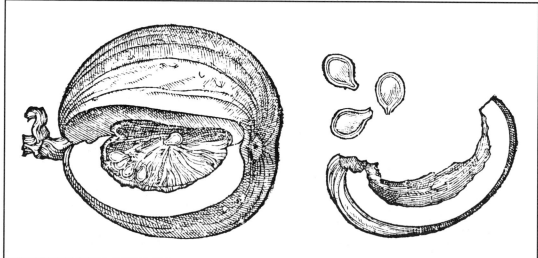

Nasturtiums, Sunflowers

Nasturtiums and **sunflowers** are now so much a part of the European horticultural scene that their New World roots are easily forgotten. Sunflowers in particular are a vital part of the economy of France and Belgium where huge crops are raised for the lovely oil crushed from the seeds. There is nothing quite like the sight of a huge field of sunflowers, slowly turning their blossoms to follow the sun. The foliage is used as cattle fodder and the stalks used to be used to make paper. An entirely useful plant.

Sunflowers are native to Mexico and Peru, in which country the ancient Inca civilisation revered the flower as an emblem of their sun god. Several North American Indian tribes valued the sunflower as a food: they grew it along with corn and mixed the seeds in corn-based potages. When it arrived in England, some time in the sixteenth century, it was much enjoyed. Gerard wrote that the immature flower buds could be eaten boiled and dressed with salt and vinegar, or butter and salt, rather like the artichoke.

In her book *Annuals and Biennials* Gertrude Jekyll wrote of the sunflower that it is 'not very easy to use in careful gardening, the whole appearance being coarse and out of scale with most garden flowers'. Of course, she was a designer of great subtlety and there is nothing restrained about sunflowers. The best use I have seen was in a garden in Hampshire where the plants were used to provide a cheerful show above a white picket fence in front of half-timbered thatched cottage: nothing could have been more appropriate.

I think that it is probably best to treat the sunflower as a half-hardy annual, starting the seed indoors in the spring and planting it out after the last frost. Sunflowers will grow in any well-dug garden soil and like plenty of nourishment.

This illustration from *Jardinier François* clearly shows the nature of the raised beds and also a forcing ground fenced by simple wooden palisades.

In the garden sunflowers can be made into a concealing screen for unsightly garden features like tool sheds or compost heaps, or they can be used to provide shade for plants like cucumbers.

Another good companion is sweet corn, but potatoes and runner beans are said to be detrimental (although my beans fared not too badly).

Indian cress is the other name for nasturtium, and the earliest use in Europe of this South American native was as both a decorative garden flower and a vegetable, the leaves and flowers being used in salads much as cress was used. The immature seeds were pickled as a caper substitute and recipes for this use appear in many cookery books after its introduction in the late sixteenth century.

Once you sow nasturtiums, you have them for life. They are among the easiest of hardy annuals; just scatter the seed and watch them grow. One of the nicest ways I have seen them used was in rural Sweden where they had been trained up twine around a porch, providing a colourful orange, yellow and red screen that set off the blue paintwork brilliantly.

Don't, however, give them too rich a soil: all you will get is foliage with the flowers hidden under masses of leaves. They like a bit of a struggle. Use nasturtiums for screens and the bushy sorts in the vegetable patch against black fly: they don't so much prevent black fly as attract the insects away from more valuable crops onto their stems. Nasturtiums in greenhouses are said to repel white fly; and grown up apple trees they prevent attack by woolly aphids.

At Barnsley House, the marrows and squashes find their way up the arbour to ripen amid the sweet peas.

RECIPES

When the Spaniards first encountered cayenne, they noted that the pods were dried and ground, then blended with flour and made into small loaves without leavening. The loaves were slice into wafers which were then dried and pulverised for use as required. This method was described by John Evelyn, the end result being preferred by him as a 'very proper Seasoning, instead of vulgar Peper'.

Peperonata

Like so many New World introductions, sweet peppers were highly esteemed as an ingredient for 'sallets', lightly cooked and dressed with oil and vinegar. Peperonata, the salad of sliced sweet peppers served with Italian antipasti, doubtless has its origins in this tradition. This salad looks most attractive if made with green, yellow and red sweet peppers, and although it is not necessary to peel the peppers, the toasting process softens the flesh and enriches the flavour.

Using a kitchen fork, hold each pepper over a gas flame until the skin blisters. Then hold it under cold running water and peel off the papery skin. Alternatively, cut the peppers in half, remove seeds and membranes and toast them skin-side up under a hot grill.

Slice the peppers into long thin strips and lay them in a shallow dish. Pour good olive oil over them, grind on black pepper, sprinkle with coarse salt and leave to marinate for several hours, before serving with plain grilled meat or with hot crusty bread and fat black olives.

In Bulgaria olive oil is replaced by mustard sauce; and the salad may be further dressed with some finely chopped sweet onions.

Scarlet runner beans were first grown in the ornamental garden for their bright flowers.

Salsa Cruda

This recipe is for the hot, piquant sauce which is a standard Mexican condiment, served in a bowl for spooning over main dishes like *tamales* or *tacos*, or simply as a dip for *tostaditos*, fried corn tortilla chips.

Jalapenos are short, stubby, smooth-skinned green chillies, and exceedingly hot – one is adequate for untrained palates. If you are not able to grow them, they are available fresh from Asian and West Indian shops, or tinned as part of Mexican food ranges from delicatessen shops.

To make 500ml (1 pint) of sauce, peel, de-seed and chop 6–8 ripe, meaty tomatoes. Grill, peel and chop 1 large sweet green pepper. Finely chop 1 large onion. Shred 1 jalapeno (more if you like playing with fire). Take care not to touch your eyes after dealing with the chilli, and wash your hands and the chopping board thoroughly afterwards (some cooks even wear rubber gloves). Combine all the ingredients in a small bowl with the juice of a lime and a pinch of salt.

The Basques have a similar recipe, traditionally served with poached eggs, but the heat comes from cooking rather than chillies. Soften one finely chopped onion in 2 tablespoons of bacon fat. Add several cloves of chopped garlic, 6 peeled and chopped tomatoes and 2 peeled and chopped red sweet peppers. Cook slowly to make a purée.

Pastry cases filled with sweet or savoury mixes of meat and fruit had long been a favourite method of food presentation. Once the potential of New World vegetables to replace the pastry was recognised, sweet peppers, tomatoes, marrows and pumpkins (fruit and flower) all found a place on the table as 'dainty parcels'.

Today, mixtures of onion, finely minced or ground meat and rice are common fillings for stuffed peppers. But the flavours of the sixteenth century can be recalled by the addition of nutmeats (pine kernels and almonds were particular favourites) and dried fruit.

Although in was popular in Spain and Italy, it took some time for the potato to catch on in the rest of Europe, possibly because as a member of the solanum family it was identified with more poisonous relatives; and people would try to eat the green tops as well, which are particularly hot and bitter. Gerard noted that the Burgundians thought that the potato induced leprosy, and also that the vegetable was likely to cause wind – a widely held belief! But he noted too that this shortcoming could be alleviated by 'rosting in embers', the most commonly recommended preparation for the new vegetable, along with 'boyled and eaten with oyle, vinegar, and pepper'.

It was not until at least the mid-1800s that the potato was widely cultivated in England, although in Wales and Scotland it was already established, probably due to the Enclosure Acts, which kept grazing cattle off crop fields. The Irish love affair with the potato was more immediate (Raleigh may have been the first to grow them in the Emerald Isle, since he had acquired an estate at Youghal about the time the potato made its first appearance in England). In any case, one of the most delicious recipes is an Irish one.

(For culinary purposes potatoes are divided into floury, waxy, old and new; the following recipes make use of each type, and describe the correct method for boiling each, as this is the most popular method of preparation.)

Colcannon Serves 2–4

Colcannon is simplicity itself, and an excellent example of the one-pot tradition of cookery.

Put 500g (1lb) of peeled potatoes into a large saucepan. Cover with 500g (1lb) of cabbage cut into manageable pieces. Pour over boiling water to cover. Add ½ teaspoon of salt, cover the pan and boil steadily until the potatoes are cooked. Take care not to overcook.

Drain well and mash the cabbage and potato together with 125ml (4fl oz) of double cream, pepper and more salt to taste. Serve in a hot dish with lashings of butter.

Punch-nep

This Welsh dish is similar to Colcannon: use white turnips instead of cabbage, and pour the cream into holes poked into the mash after it has been put into the serving dish.

Pewter plates are proudly displayed on the dresser in this kitchen scene of the seventeenth century. There are also numerous sizes of cauldron for open-hearth cooking.

It is worth noting that when floury potatoes are being cooked on their own, it is best to boil them in their skins, and peel (or not, as desired,) after cooking.

German Potato Salad

This old German recipe for a hot salad dresses the potatoes with a sweet-sour sauce; use waxy potatoes if possible ('Pink Fir Apple' is excellent) as they will not break up and spoil the look of the dish.

Scrub but do not peel 900g (2lbs) of waxy potatoes. Cover with cold water, add a pinch of salt and boil in a covered pan until the potatoes are tender. Drain them well and leave to cool in the saucepan. Peel and cut into thin slices.

Meanwhile, in a large frying pan render the fat from 125g (4oz) of fatty bacon; there should be roughly 2 tablespoons. Soften but do not fry 1 finely chopped onion in the bacon fat.

Add 1 tablespoonful of flour to the fat and onion and cook for several seconds. Add 250ml (8fl oz) of water and 125ml (4fl oz) of distilled malt or cider vinegar and blend well into the flour until smooth. Add 125g (4oz) sugar, and salt and pepper to taste. Taste and adjust the sweet-sourness. If the dressing is too thick, add more water. Cook for several minutes; it should have a sheen and not be lumpy or sticky.

Add the potatoes, then pour the mixture into a bowl and mix gently, taking care not to break the slices. Sprinkle with parsley and crumbled bacon. Reheat in a low oven or double boiler when required.

Many of the earliest recipes combine potatoes with sugar, spices and sweet wine in pastry shells; potatoes were a novelty and deserving of special treatment.

Excellent Plain Potato Pudding

In 1806, Mrs M. E. Rundell published *A New System of Cookery*, intended for the instruction of her daughters rather than for the general public: it was immensely popular and remained in print for several decades. From it comes this recipe which makes good use of old main-crop potatoes. These should first be peeled, soaked in water for 15 minutes or so and then put into boiling water to cover and cooked until tender.

Take 8 ounces of boiled potatoes, 2 ounces of butter, the yolks and whites of two eggs, a ¼ pint of cream, 1 spoon of white wine, morsel of salt, juice and rind of 1 lemon; beat all to a froth; sugar to taste. A crust or not as you like. Bake it. If you want richer, put in more butter, sweetmeats and almonds.

From *A New System of Cookery*,
Mrs M. E. Rundell, 1806

A shortcrust pastry and the addition of slivered almonds make a nice contrast in texture. Bake at 180°C (350°F) until set and the pastry is golden.

Polpettone di Fagiolini alla Genovese

Since the day Catherine de Medici and her native Italian cooks set foot in France, few have done more for Italian cooking than Marcella Hazan with her exceptional two-volume work *Classic Italian Cookbook*. This recipe is from the second volume and is for the Genoese (and vegetarian) version of *polpettone*, which 'anywhere else in Italy is a meat loaf'. It bears similarity to the previous recipe and to the bean tansy on page 41.

Boil, unpeeled, 250g (8oz) of potatoes. Meanwhile, top and tail 500g (1lb) of French beans and refresh them in cold water, then cook them in 3 litres (4½ pints) of salted water until they are tender but still firm. Drain them immediately and then cut into long pieces. Put the pieces into a large bowl.

Peel the cooked potatoes and pass them through a sieve or food mill into the bowl with the beans. Add 2 eggs, 100g (3½ oz) grated Parmesan cheese, 1 teaspoonful of marjoram, salt and pepper to taste. Blend together well.

Grease a shallow baking dish with olive oil and then dust with dry breadcrumbs. Pour the potato and bean mixture into the dish and bake at 180°C (350°F) for 1 hour.

New potatoes, freshly dug, are among the most exquisite of vegetables, and best eaten unadorned except perhaps for a sprinkle of chopped herbs – parsley or young chives for preference. Use new potatoes when they are no larger than a golfball. Rub them over lightly in cold water to remove soil and drop them into rapidly boiling water. Add a pinch of salt and reduce the heat to simmer. When the potatoes are cooked, drain them and return them to the pan; then add seasoning and plenty of butter.

Another excellent method of enhancing the flavour of small fresh potatoes is simply to put them, whole, in a heavy saucepan over very low heat with a large chunk of butter. Cover them and cook slowly until tender. Season with salt, pepper and herbs.

Pumpkin is an underrated vegetable in Britain, yet enormously popular in Italy and France as well as its native North America. I've always thought that the saying should be 'as American as pumpkin pie' since there is nothing ethnic about apple pie, but spicy pumpkin pie always recalls the smell of autumn bonfires, apple ducking and the maple leaves' fiery tints during a Midwest-American fall.

Pumpkin Purée

Many people use tinned pumpkin-pie filling for ease, but, inevitably, it's well worth starting from scratch.

Cut the pumpkin in half and scrape out the seeds and stringy fibres in the centre. With the shell side facing, bake the pump-

Clockwise from the left Pumpkin Soup, Cucumber and Nasturtium Salad, Sweet Corn Fritters and Peperonata.

Centrepieces such as the stuffed swan in this seventeenth-century kitchen scene had been popular since medieval times.

kin in a large dish in a moderate oven 180°C (350°F) until you notice it beginning to cave in (20–30 mins); test it for tenderness with a skewer. When the pumpkin is cooked through, scrape the pulp from the shell. For a 23cm (9in) pie you will need 250g (8oz) of prepared pumpkin. Freeze the remainder for use in soups, pumpkin bread, etc.

Pumpkin Pie
Line a 23cm (9in) pie dish with 250g (8oz) of shortcrust pastry; flute and raise the edge of the crust.

Combine 3 lightly beaten eggs with 250g (8oz) of sugar, 1 teaspoonful each of salt and mixed spice. Stir in 250ml (8fl oz) scalded milk and 125ml (4fl oz) of heavy cream. Then add the pumpkin, blending well. Pour the mixture into the pie dish and bake the pie in a hot oven 200°C (400°F) for 10 minutes, then reduce the heat and bake it in a moderate oven 160°C (325°F) for 20–25 minutes or until a knife stuck into the centre of the filling comes out clean.

Robert May gave a recipe for pumpkin pie in *The Accomplish't Cook* (1685) in which chopped pumpkin and eggs are flavoured with thyme, rosemary, marjoram, cinnamon, nutmeg and cloves, blended with eggs, fried and then layered with sliced apple rounds and raisins in a pie dish and baked with a custard of egg yolks and verjuice or white wine.

Judging by the relative complexity of this recipe with its spices and numerous culinary procedures, pumpkin did at one time enjoy a certain popularity, but this has been sustained primarily in south-western France. Pumpkin soup is a regional dish of the Orleanais and is simplicity to make.

Potage au Poitron

Soften a finely chopped large onion in butter. Add a tablespoon of white wine just as the onions begin to turn translucent. Pour in 500ml (1 pint) of strong chicken stock, simmer for 15 minutes and then pass the mixture through a sieve to break up the onions. Add 1 litre (2 pints) of pumpkin purée, season with salt and pepper, and simmer for 30 minutes.

Just before serving stir in 125ml (4fl oz) double cream, and sprinkle over a generous teaspoonful of toasted cumin seeds.

Sweet corn, fresh from roadside farm stalls, is an American summer fixture, just as the following fritters are *the* side dish with fried chicken. Boiled sweet corn is increasingly popular in Britain, yet when I first arrived from America seventeen years ago this vegetable was 'as scarce as hen's teeth' in the shops. So my aunt sent me a packet of seed for an early variety, and I grew my own in my London allotment. The lengths to which an immigrant will go! Of course seed was available, but not in the wide variety I was used to. Now seed merchants in Britain offer nearly as wide a choice as their American counterparts.

Corn Fritters Serves 4–6

Cut the kernels from 6 ears of fresh corn. In a large bowl, beat 2 egg yolks (reserve the whites) with 2 tablespoons of flour and 1 tablespoon of milk. Add the corn and season with salt and pepper. Beat the whites until they are stiff and fold them into the corn mixture. Fry the batter in hot oil, dropping it by the tablespoonful into the pan, or else on a well-greased very hot frying pan. The oil must be very hot otherwise the batter will soak it up like a sponge.

Sweet Corn Chowder Serves 4

Slowly fry 250g (½lb) bacon and in the fat sauté until tender 1 finely chopped onion and 125g (4oz) celery. Drain off all but 2 tablespoons of the bacon fat and blend in 2 tablespoons of flour. Cook the flour for a minute or two, then add 500ml (1 pint) of warm milk and 250g (8oz) each of sweet corn kernels and cold cooked potatoes cut into small cubes. Season with salt and pepper and a leaf or two of fresh coriander (in other words, use it sparingly).

Bring the chowder to the boil adding more milk if it is too stiff. Sprinkle a dash of cayenne on each bowlful before serving.

Brinjal Masala

Cut 1kg (2lb) of aubergines in half lengthwise. Salt them on both sides and leave them on a plate for 1 hour in order to extract the bitter juices. Drain, rinse and chop them coarsely.

Cut 1–2 green chillies in half and remove the seeds. Mix together in a small bowl ½ teaspoon each of chilli powder, powdered cumin and coriander. Heat 2 tablespoons of sunflower oil in a heavy saucepan and just as it begins to smoke add 1 teaspoon of mustard seed. When the seed begins to pop, add the mixed spices and fry them quickly for several minutes. Add the chopped aubergines and fry quickly for 10 minutes or until tender. Add the green chillies, 125ml (4fl oz) of natural yoghurt and 2–3 tablespoons of water. Stir and then add 1 teaspoon of sugar and a pinch of salt. Sprinkle toasted cumin seeds over the top before serving.

Melanzanine con la Mozzarella
Serves 4

Home-grown aubergines don't always reach maturity and this recipe from volume two of Marcella Hazan's *Classic Italian Cookbook* makes good use of infant fruit.

Cut 8–10 baby aubergines in half lengthwise. Sprinkle with salt and leave for 30 minutes to extract bitterness. Drain and pat dry. Deeply score the flesh, taking care not to cut through the skin. Arrange the aubergines in a single layer, flesh-side facing, in a heavy-bottomed frying pan.

In a small bowl combine 2 large, chopped cloves of garlic, 30g (1oz) of chopped parsley, a generous teaspoon of salt and a liberal grind of fresh black pepper, 30g (1oz) fresh breadcrumbs and 1 tablespoon of olive oil. Spoon the mixture evenly over the aubergines, forcing it gently into the cuts. Dribble 85ml (3fl oz) of olive oil over the aubergines, pouring some of it into the pan.

Cover the pan and cook the aubergines slowly over a medium-low heat until the flesh is tender and creamy. Put a slice of best mozzarella on top of each aubergine, replace the pan, cover it and increase the heat. Cook until the cheese melts. Serve warm.

Stuffed Patty-pan Squash

Cook a whole squash in boiling salted water until it is just tender. Drain, then cut away the stem end and scoop out the seeds from the centre. The squash will resemble a small bowl which can be filled with stuffing mixtures, such as meat and rice flavoured with herbs or green peppers, or peas and mushrooms in a cheese sauce. Put the stuffed squash into the oven to heat through.

Baked Acorn Squash

Cut the squash in half lengthwise and scoop out the seeds. Fill the cavity with a mixture of butter and brown sugar. Put the squash into a baking dish, flesh-side facing, and grind black pepper over the top. Pour in just enough boiling water to cover the bottom of the dish and bake at 180°C (350°F) until tender.

Serve this dish with ham, turkey, game or roast pork.

BIBLIOGRAPHY

Above Viola tricolor, 'Heart's Ease'.

AMHERST, Alicia *A History of Gardening in England*, Bernard Quaritch, London, 1895.

AUSTIN, T. (ed.) *Two Fifteenth Century Cookery Books*, 1888.

AYRTON, Elisabeth *The Cookery of England*, André Deutsch, London, 1974.

BARTRAM, Douglas *The Gourmet's Garden*, Faber and Faber, London, 1964.

BONNEFONS, Nicolas de *Le Jardinier François*, trans. John Evelyn, 1672.

Book of Fruit and Flowers, A, 1653 (facs. edn Prospect Books, London, 1984).

BRADLEY, R. *The Country Housewife and Lady's Director*, 1727.

BUNYARD, E. A. *Old Garden Roses*, Country Life, London, 1936.
and Lorna Bunyard *Epicure's Companion*, J. M. Dent, London, 1937.

BUNYARD, George and O. Thomas, *The Fruit Garden*, Country Life, London, 1904.

CANDOLLE, Alphonse, L.L.P. de *Origine des Plantes Cultivées*, 1883.

CHAN, Peter *Better Vegetable Gardens the Chinese Way*, Gardenway Publications, Pownell, Vermont, 1985.

COBBETT, William *The American Gardener*, 1821.
The English Gardener, 1833.

COPELY, E. *Cottage Cookery*, 1849.

CRISP, Sir Frank, ed. Catherine Childs Paterson *Medieval Gardens*, 1924.

DAVID, Elizabeth, *Italian Food*, Penguin Books, London, 1969.
Spices, Salts and Aromatics in the English Kitchen, Penguin Books, London, 1970.

DODOENS, Rembert, trans. Henry Lyte *A Niewe Herball or Historie of Plantes*, 1578.

DRUMMOND, Jack C. and Anne Wilbraham, *The Englishman's Food*, Jonathan Cape, London, 1939.

ESTIENNE, C. and J. Liebault, trans. Richard Surflet *Maison Rustique or the Countrie Farm*, 1600.

EVELYN, John *Acetaria: A Discourse of Sallets*, 1699 (facs. edn. Prospect Books, London, 1982).

FAIRBROTHER, Nan *Men and Gardens*, Hogarth Press, London, 1956.

FENTON, Alexander and Eszter Kisban *Food in Change*, John Donald, Edinburgh, 1986.

FRANCK, Gertrude *Gesunder Garten Durch Mischkulturen*, Sudwest Verlag, Munich, 1980.

FRIEND, Rev. Hilderic *Flowers and Flower Lore*, Sonnenschein, London, 1884.

GARDENER, Jon *The Feate of Gardening*, 1440.

GERARD, John *The Herbal*, revised edn. Thos Johnson, 1633.

GLASSE, Hannah *Art of Cooking Made Plain and Easy*, 1755 (7th edn.).

Right The Tudor period saw the beginning of the division of the garden into separate areas for flowers, fruit and vegetables including herbs. William Lawson, writing in *The Country Housewifes Garden*, said that while it was advantageous to grow most flowers in a separate garden, since 'they will suffer some disgrace' if mingled with onions and parsnips, there were exceptions. Roses and lavender, which 'yield much profit and comfort to the senses', hyssop, sage, thyme, pinks and southernwood were all suitable for making 'comely borders' in the kitchen garden. However, we today have taken the divisions a step further and create herb gardens – enclaves of fragrance and soft colour from the subtle foliage. It has become our custom to dispose the areas of the garden around the house, placing them near the rooms they serve: the flower garden next the main living room and the vegetable garden near the kitchen entrance and reached via the herb garden, be it a spacious walled enclosure such as this, or a narrow stretch of border along a path leading to the vegetable beds.

GORDON, Lesley *A Country Herbal*, Webb and Bower, Exeter, 1980.

GRAY, Thomas *MS. Notes from William Verral's Cookery Book*, first publ. 1759; facs. edn. 1948.

GRIEVE, Mrs M. *Culinary Herbs and Condiments*, Harcourt, Brace, New York, 1934.
A Modern Herbal, Jonathan Cape, London, 1931.

GRIGSON, Jane *Jane Grigson's Vegetable Book*, Michael Joseph, London, 1978.
Jane Grigson's Fruit Book, Michael Joseph, London, 1982.

HADFIELD, Miles *A History of British Gardening*, John Murray, London, 1979.

HARTLEY, Dorothy, *Food in England*, Macdonald, London, 1954.

HARVEY, Prof. John *Medieval Gardens*, B. T. Batsford, London, 1981.

HAZAN, Marcella *Classic Italian Cookbook*, Knopf, New York, 1976
More Classic Italian Cooking, Knopf, New York, 1978.

HAZLITT, W. *Old Cookery Books and Ancient Cuisine*, 1902.

HEDRICK, Ulysses Prentice *A History of Horticulture in America*, Oxford University Press, Oxford, 1950.

HEMPHILL, Rosemary *Fragrance and Flavour*, Angus and Robertson, London, 1959.
Spice and Savour, Angus and Robertson, London 1964.

HENISCH, B. A. *Fast and Feast: Food in Medieval Society*, Pennsylvania State University Press, Pennsylvania, 1976.

HENSLOW, Rev. Prof. G. H. *Origin and History of our Garden Vegetables*, Journal of the Royal Horticultural Society, vols xxxvi, xxxvii. London, 1910, 1911.

HILL, Thomas *A Most Brief and Pleasaunt Treatise. . .* , 1558.

HOWARD, Mario *Mischkulturen für Flach und Hugelbeete*, BLV, Munich, 1985.

Jardinier Français, Le, or *Rapin's French Gardener*, trans. John Evelyn, 1672.

JASHEMSKI, W. F. *The Gardens of Pompeii*, Caratzas Brothers, New Rochelle, N.Y. 1979.

JEKYLL, Gertrude *Annuals and Biennials*, Country Life, London, 1916.

KEEBLE, Sir Frederick and A. N. Rawes *Hardy Fruit Growing*, Macmillan, London, 1946 (2nd edn.).

LAWSON, William *The Countrie Housewifes Garden*, 1617.

LEIGHTON, Ann *American Gardens in the 18th Century*, Houghton Mifflin, New York, 1976.

LEYEL, Mrs C. F. *Green Salads and Fruit Salads*, George Routledge and Sons, London, n.d.

LEYEL, Mrs C. F. and Olga Hartley *The Gentle Art of Cookery*, Chatto and Windus, London, 1925.

LOUDON, Mrs Jane *Gardening for Ladies*, 1841.

LOUDONS, *Encyclopaedia of Gardening*, 1822.

MARKHAM, Gervase *The English Housewife*, 1637.

MAY, Robert *The Accomplish't Cook or the Art and Mystery of Cookery*, 1685.

MCLEAN, Theresa *The Medieval Garden*, Collins, London, 1981.

MEYER, J. E. *The Herbalist Almanac, 50 Year Anthology*, Meyerbooks, Glenwood, Illinois 1977.

MONARDES, Nicolas *Joyfull Newes Out of the New Found World*, English trans. 1925, reprint Tudor Translation Series.

NEILL, Patrick *Fruit, Flower and Kitchen Garden*, 1838.

NORTHCOTE, Lady Rosalind *The Book of Herbs*, John Lane, The Bodley Head, London, 1912.

ORGAN, John *Gourds* Faber and Faber, London, 1963.

PARKINSON, John *Paradisi in Sole, Paradisus Terrestris,* 1629.

PECKHAM, A. *Complete English Cook*, 1767.

PLAT, Sir Hugh *Delightes for Ladies*, 1618.
Queen's Closet Opened, 1683.

Practical Guide No. 5, National Vegetable Research Station, Wellesbourne, 1979.

ROBINSON, W. *Gleanings from French Gardens*, 1877.

ROHDE, Eleanour Sinclair *Culinary and Salad Herbs*, Country Life, London, 1940.
Herbs and Herb Gardening, Medici Society, London, 1936.
Rose Recipes, Routledge, London, 1939.
The Story of the Garden, Medici Society, London, 1932.
Uncommon Vegetables, Country Life, London, 1943.
Vegetable Cultivation and Cookery, Medici Society, London, 1938.

ROYAL HORTICULTURAL SOCIETY, *The Fruit Garden Displayed*, Cassell, London, 1986.

de SERRES, Olivier *L'Théâtre d'Agriculture*, 1633.

SMITH, E. *The Compleat Housewife or Accomplish'd Gentlewoman's Companion*, facs. edn., Literary Services and Productions Ltd, London, 1968.

STOBART, Tom *Herbs, Spices and Flavouring*, Penguin Books, London, 1970.

STUART, D. C. *The Kitchen Garden*, Robert Hale, London, 1984.

STURTEVANT, Dr. E. Lewis *Sturtevant's Notes on Edible Plants*, J. B. Lyon, Albany, New York, 1919 (facs. edn. publ. Dover Books, New York, 1972).

SWITZER, Stephan *Compendious Method for Raising Italian Broccoli*, 1729.

TANNAHILL, Reay *Food in History*, Eyre Methuen, London, 1973.

THOMAS, Graham Stuart *The Old Shrub Roses*, J. M. Dent, London, revised edn. 1979.

WHEATON, Barbara Ketchum *Savouring the Past*, Chatto and Windus, London, 1983.

WHITE, Florence *Flowers as Food*, Jonathan Cape, London, 1934.
Good Things in England, Jonathan Cape, London, 1932.

WHITEHEAD, G. E. *Garden Herbs*, A. & C. Black, London, 1944.

WILSON, C. Anne *Food and Drink in Britain*, Penguin Books, London, 1976.

WORLIDGE, John *Systema Horti-Culturae*, 1677.

INDEX

Numbers in italics refer to captions of illustrations

Above A string of autumn onions.

USEFUL ADDRESSES

Samuel Dobie & Sons Ltd.
Upper Dee Mills
Llangollen
Clwyd LL20 8SD

S. E. Marshall & Co Ltd
Wisbech
Cambs. PE12 2RF

Suttons Seeds Ltd
Hele Rd
Torquay
Devon TH2 7QJ

Thompson & Morgan
London Rd
Ipswich
IP2 0BA

Unwins Seeds Ltd,
Histon
Cambs. CB4 47E

Suffolk Herbs
Sawyers Farm
Little Cornard
Sudbury
Suffolk

John Chambers
15 Westleigh Rd
Barton Seagrave
Kettering
Northants NN15 5AJ

Chiltern Seeds,
Bortree Stile
Ulverston
Cumbria LA12 7PB

Henry Doubleday Research Assoc.
Ryton Gardens
Ryton-on-Dunsmore
Coventry CV8 3LG
(Membership of in the HDRA is necessary to
purchase from their Heritage Seeds List)

Hollington Herb Nurseries
Woolton Hill
Newbury
Berks RG15 9XT

Donald MacLean Potato Museum
Dornock Farm
Crieff
Perthshire PR7 3QN

Country Gardens
69/71 Main St
Easte Leake
Leics. LE12 6PF

Right Posthumously published in 1594, the
Gardener's Labyrinth by Didymus Mountain
(Thomas Hyll's pen-name) gives us, through its
instructions on the making of gardens for profit and
pleasure and the engravings which accompany the
text, a fairly clear idea of what gardens looked like
during the late Tudor period. The section regarding
'the forme of the disposing the quarters into beddes,
and apt borders about' is especially interesting to
those of us who wish to make a vegetable garden
with raised beds: 'The quarters well turned in, and
fatned with good dung a time before, and the earth
raised through the dunging, that in handsome
maner by a line set downe in the earth, be troden out
into beddes and seemely borders, which beds raised
newly afore with dung, and finely raked over, with
the clods dissolved and stones purged forth, shall be
artely troden out, into three foote of breadth, and
into what length the owner or gardener will: but to
such a breadth especially troden forth, that the
weeders hands may well reach into the middell of
the same, least they thus going to the beddes, and
weeding forth the unprofitable hearbes and grasse,
may in the meane time treade downe both the
seedes shooting up, and plantes above the earth. To
the helpe of which, let the pathes between the
beddes be of such a reasonable breadth (as a man's
foote) that they passing along may freely weede the
one halfe first, and next the other halfe left to
weede.'

Family Trees
Botley
Hampshire
SO3 2EA

Reads Nurseries
Hales Hall
Lodden
Norfolk
(figs a speciality)

Ken Muir
Honeypot Farm
Weeley Heath
Clacton-on-Sea
Essex CO16 9BJ

USA

J. W. Jung Sed Co.
Randolph
Wisconsin 53957

Earl May Seed & Nursery Co.
Shenandoah
Iowa 51603

Thompson & Morgan
P.O. Box 1308
Jackson
New Jersey 08527

W. Atlee Burpee Co
Warminster
Pennslyvania 18974

Park Seed Co
Cokesbury Rd
Greenwood
South Carolina 29647–0001

Vermont Bean Seed Co
Garden Lane
Fair Haven
Vermont 05743

The Cook's Garden
Box 65
Londonderry
Vermont 05148

Stark Brothers Nurseries
Louisiana
Missouri 63353–0010

ACKNOWLEDGEMENTS

ACKNOWLEDGEMENTS

I should like to thank Dot and Ormond Knight, Frank and Joan Burton, and Mr and Mrs O. J. Plummer for the use of their gardens in which to grow and photograph the subjects of this book; also Judith Hopkinson of Hollington Nurseries who allowed us to photograph in their wonderful herb garden at Woolton Hill, Newbury, Berkshire – the Hopkinsons are past gold-medal winners at the Chelsea Flower Show, and the gardens are open for prearranged tours, while the nursery offers a mail order service from the extensive herb-plant list; and Jessica Houdret of Farnham Royal Herbs, Farnham Royal, Buckinghamshire, who offers a number of educational courses on things herbal.

Thank you also to Di Lewis and Kirstie Owen for their magnificent contribution; also to Melvin Sumray, of Sumray Lithographics, Norwich; Derek Fell; George Wright; John Last; Eileen Tweedy and the Lindley Library librarians; John Manners and the instructors at the Norfolk College of Horticulture for putting me right; Sir Michael and Lady Hanham of Dean's Court, Dorset; Sue Holt and the Dereham Public Library for her helpful response to my numerous short-notice requests; and to Inés Stalder for providing the German translations.

Grateful thanks, too, to Chapel Antiques and Hungerford Arcade, both of Hungerford, Berkshire, for their assistance in the preparation of the cookery photographs.

I am profoundly grateful to Jean Parrish for providing me with so much inspiration, culinary and otherwise, over so many formative years, and especially so to Will Allen who first gave me the idea for this book; and to Anne Askwith, the editor, and Penny Mills, the designer, for putting it all together so efficiently and beautifully.

ILLUSTRATIONS CREDITS

The Bridgeman Art Library *pages* 23, 43, 71, 107, 127, 135
Derek Fell 10, 11, 15, 19 above left and below
Jessica Houdret 66
John Last 7, 82
Andrew Lawson 151
Di Lewis 18, 19 above right, 29, 63, 67, 81, 103, 131, 155, 159
Fine Art Photographic Library Limited 87
George Wright 7, 10, 14, 18, 130, 163
Mansell Collection 40, 105, 153, 156
The black and white diagrams on pages 12, 56, 112, 113, 120, 140 are by Dianne Breeze